1st Deep Machine Translation Workshop (DMTW 2015)

Prague, Czech Republic
3 – 4 September 2015

ISBN: 978-1-5108-3155-1

Preface

This volume contains the papers presented at DMTW-2015: Deep Machine Translation Workshop held on September 3-4, 2015 in Prague.

Each submission was reviewed by at least 2, most by three, and on the average 2.8, program committee members. The committee decided to accept 13 papers. The program also includes 1 invited talk. The submission and proceedings creation has been handled by the EasyChair system.

We thank the QTLeap EU project for providing local funding for the workshop organization, and to Rudolf Rosa for handling local arrangements and for his technical help with submissions, web page and proceedings.

August 28, 2015

Prague, Czech Republic

Jan Hajič

António Branco

Program Committee

Eneko Agirre	University of the Basque Country
António Branco	University of Lisbon
Aljoscha Burchardt	Deutsches Forschungszentrum für Künstliche Intelligenz GmbH
Rosa Del Gaudio	Higher Functions LDA
Jan Hajič	Charles University in Prague
Eva Hajičová	Charles University in Prague
Petya Osenova	Sofia University and Bulgarian Academy of Sciences
Martin Popel	Charles University in Prague
Khalil Sima'An	University of Amsterdam
Kiril Simov	Bulgarian Academy of Sciences
Gertjan van Noord	University of Groningen
Deyi Xiong	Soochow University

Table of Contents

Linguistic Linked Open Data: What's in for Machine Translation?

Christian Chiarcos
Angewandte Computerlinguistik
Fachbereich für Informatik und Mathematik
Goethe-Universität Frankfurt am Main
Robert-Mayer-Str. 10
D-60325 Frankfurt am Main
`chiarcos@informatik.uni-frankfurt.de`

During the past years, the notion of Linked (Open) Data has gained considerable reception in different communities working with language resources, ranging from academic and applied linguistics over lexicography to natural language processing and information technology. In this context, the Open Linguistics Working Group of the Open Knowledge Foundation (OWLG, `http://linguistics.okfn.org/`), founded in 2010 in Berlin, Germany, is playing an important integrative role, by reaching out to a broad band-width of disciplines, by facilitating interdisciplinary information exchange through meetings, workshops, datathons and joint publications, but most notably by introducing and maintaining the Linguistic Linked Open Data (LLOD) cloud diagram. Being deeply involved in this emerging community at the intersection between the different disciplines mentioned above, I will introduce the basic concepts of Linked Open Data for linguistics/NLP, summarize motivations and history of Linguistic Linked Open Data so far. Since creating the first instantiation of the LLOD cloud diagram in 2012, LLOD has attracted a lot of activity, we have reached an agreement on vocabularies for many aspects of language resources and the number of resources included is continuously on the rise. This growth is documented, for example, by declaring LLOD "the new hot topic in our (= language resource) community" (Nicoletta Calzolari, LREC-2014 closing session). But with substantial amounts of data being available, the focus of activity in the LLOD community is slowly shifting from resource creation to applications of Linguistic Linked Open Data. The primary promise of providing open, but heterogeneously structured and scattered language resources in a more interoperable way has been fulfilled, and it facilitates using and re-using existing language resources in novel contexts. Beyond this, innovative LLOD-based applications for common problems in Natural Language Processing, Digital Humanities and linguistics are on the horizon. The second part of the talk will give a glimpse on these prospects by discussing use cases and potential applications of LLOD for (Deep) Machine Translation.

Proceedings of the 1st Deep Machine Translation Workshop (DMTW 2015), page 1,
Praha, Czech Republic, 3–4 September 2015.

Modelling the Adjunct/Argument Distinction in Hierarchical Phrase-Based SMT

Sophie Arnoult
ILLC
University of Amsterdam
s.i.arnoult@uva.nl

Khalil Sima'an
ILLC
University of Amsterdam
k.simaan@uva.nl

Abstract

We present the first application of the adjunct/argument distinction to Hierarchical Phrase-Based SMT. We use rule labelling to characterize synchronous recursion with adjuncts and arguments. Our labels are bilingual obtained from dependency annotations and extended to cover non-syntactic phrases. The label set we derive in this manner is extremely small, as it contains only thirty-six labels, and yet we find it useful to cluster these labels even further. We present a clustering method that uses label similarity based on left-hand-side/right-hand-side joint trained-model estimates. The results of initial experiments show that our model performs similarly to Hiero on in-domain French-English data.

1 Introduction

Labelling Hierarchical Phrase-Based models (Hiero) (Chiang, 2005) allows to disambiguate Hiero, while benefitting from its broad coverage. Using syntactic labels for labelling as Zollmann and Venugopal (2006) do with Syntax-Augmented Machine Translation (SAMT) or, e.g., Li et al. (2012) in an inspired approach, yields however unwieldy models with large non-terminal vocabularies. We propose to approach the labelling problem from the other end, using the adjunct-argument distinction to minimally label Hiero.

We interpret adjuncts in the general sense of modifiers, and not only of adjuncts in semantic frames. Generally speaking, the adjunct-argument distinction accounts for a difference in selectional preferences: arguments are selected by their heads, while adjuncts select their heads. This distinction is modelled in Tree-Adjoining Grammar (Joshi et al., 1975; Joshi and Schabes, 1997), through substitution and adjunction. Shieber and Schabes (1990) and Shieber (2007) have proposed Synchronous Tree-Adjoining Grammar (STAG) by for SMT, and the adjunct/argument distinction has been applied to Syntax-Based models notably by DeNeefe and Knight (2009) and Liu et al. (2011).

We do not attempt here to model adjunction in Hiero, rather we reduce the adjunct-argument distinction to one of type. The semantic aspect of this distinction–adjuncts modify the meaning of a phrase, while arguments complete it–makes it appealing for Machine Translation, as one may expect that it can be preserved across a bitext. To circumvent mismatches, we label both sides of the data to derive bilingual labels. The label set that we derive is minimal as we start from two labels for adjuncts and arguments on both sides of the data, and derive only four new labels for non-syntactic phrases; after combining source and target labels into bilingual labels, the label set contains thirty-six labels only.

We conduct experiments on French-English data, and show that while direct application of this small adjunct/argument label set leads to sub-optimal results, promising results can be obtained by clustering bilingual labels. While further tests are required, our model is currently limited by Hiero's phrase-length limit; to fully apply adjunct/argument labelling, one needs to extend this model, with reordering rules for instance, or by exchanging the phrase-length constraint for a constraint on recursion.

Proceedings of the 1st Deep Machine Translation Workshop (DMTW 2015), pages 2–11,
Praha, Czech Republic, 3–4 September 2015.

2   Labelling Adjuncts and Arguments for Hiero

Our labelling procedure follows that of SAMT (Zollmann and Venugopal, 2006) to some extent. We start from sentence pairs that have been parsed on both sides of the data into dependencies, and we map dependency labels to either adjuncts or arguments, as is Figure 1[1].

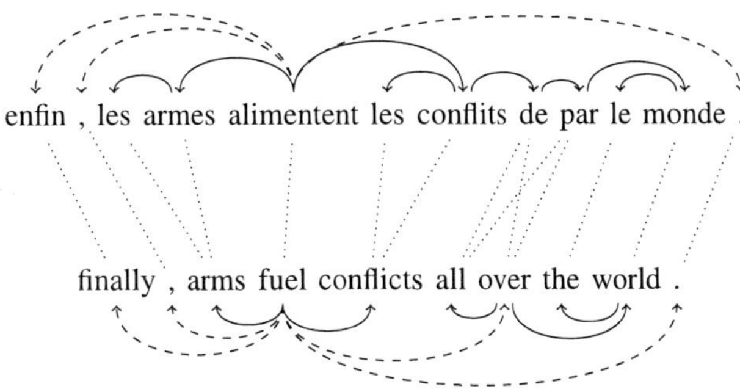

Figure 1: Example sentence pair. Adjunct dependencies are indicated with dashes.

Dependency labels vary per parser, but we broadly map modifier and punctuation labels to adjuncts, and remaining labels to arguments. Table 1 presents the mapping from the dependency converters of Candito et al. (2010) for French and of Johansson and Nugues (2007) for English.

Table 1: Adjunct-mapping criteria for English and French

	head-governor relation	other constraints on head h, governor g, etc.
English	ADV, APPO, PRN	
	AMOD	relation(g, governor(g)) ! = ADV
	PMOD	h precedes g
	NMOD	POS(h) $\notin$ {*CC, DT, EX, POS, MD, PRP, PRP\$, RP, SYM, WDT, WP, WP\$, WRB*}
	P	h has no dependents
French	mod, mod_rel	
	ponct	h has no dependents

2.1   Phrase-Labelling scheme

Next, we define phrase labels to allow for recursion over non-syntactic phrases. Our phrase labelling procedure is summarized as Algorithm 1. This scheme follows SAMT and beyond that Combinatorial Categorial Grammar (CCG) (Steedman, 2000), but it is coarser on the one hand, and it is adapted to syntactic differences between adjunct and arguments, on the other.

It is coarser in that the added phrasal labels, while corresponding to incomplete constituents or constituent sequences, are in fact kept to a minimum, that do not reflect the combination logic of CCG: we distinguish incomplete adjuncts, incomplete arguments, sequences of arguments, and default all remaining phrases to a single type.

To reflect specific adjunct/argument behaviour, we let constituents that miss adjuncts keep their type, thus reflecting the fact that adjuncts do not alter the syntactic type of the phrases they modify; for the same reason, we label sequences of arguments and adjuncts as a sequence of arguments; finally, we label

---

[1]Word alignments are tentative, but the adjunct/argument labels are factual; the labelling of *"de par le monde"* is the result of a parsing error.

sequences of adjuncts as a single adjunct, reflecting the absence of linguistic restriction on the number of adjuncts for a given phrase (although we do not actually test whether adjuncts have the same governor).

Algorithm 1: Labelling procedure for extracted phrases.

---

input : A phrase ϕ and a dependency tree with adjunct (A) and argument (C) labels.
output: A phrase label for ϕ
if ϕ *matches a dependent* D **then** Label(ϕ) $\leftarrow$ Label(D)
else if ϕ *matches a sequence of dependents* D_i **then**
    if *all* D_i *are adjuncts* **then** Label(ϕ) $\leftarrow$ A **else** Label(ϕ) $\leftarrow$ C$_S$
else if ϕ *matches a dependent* D *less some left and/or right sub-dependents* SD_i **then**
    if *all* SD_i *are adjuncts* **then** Label(ϕ) $\leftarrow$ Label(D)
    else
        if D *is an adjunct* **then** Label(ϕ) $\leftarrow$ A$_I$ **else** Label(ϕ) $\leftarrow$ C$_I$
else Label(ϕ) $\leftarrow$ P

2.2   Bilingual labelling

The adjunct/argument label set presented thus far can be equally applied on the source and target sides of the data. To account for parsing differences and linguistic divergence (Dorr, 1994; Hwa et al., 2002; Arnoult and Sima'an, 2014), we combine source and target labels into composite, bilingual labels. The resulting label set consists of 36 labels.

Table 2 shows some phrase pairs for the example of Figure 1.

Table 2: Adjunct/argument-based phrasal labels

label	French phrase	English phrase	label	French phrase	English phrase
AA	enfin ,	finally ,	$C_I C_I$	alimentent	fuel
CC	les armes	arms	$C_I C_I$	monde	world
CA	de par le monde	all over the world	$C_S C_S$	le monde .	the world .
$C_I A_I$	de par	all over	PP	monde .	world .
$C_I P$	les conflits de par	conflicts all over			

The phrase *"finally ,"* is labelled as an adjunct as it is a sequence of adjuncts with the same governor; *"the world ."* is labelled as an argument sequence as it is a multi-headed sequence containing an argument; *"conflicts all over"* is labelled as a phrase (P) as it is a multi-headed sequence containing an incomplete argument.

3   Model

The model is a SAMT-like, labelled-variant of Hiero (Chiang, 2005). The model is similar to Hiero, but for the fact that the single non-terminal of Hiero is replaced by a set of labels.

Model derivations are scored by a log-linear model over features; our model uses most of the Hiero and SAMT features. Like Hiero, the model features comprehend phrase-translation weights, lexical weights, rule penalty, glue-rule penalty and word penalty; the phrase-translation-weights feature also applies for adjunct/argument-labelled models, and is then computed on unlabelled rule equivalents, i.e., on lexical content only. Like SAMT (Zollmann, 2011), the model uses features for left-hand-side-conditioned rule weights, labelled-rule translation weights, rule-rarity penalty, and flags for lexical-only rules, abstract rules, monotone rules, and abstract-target rules. Unlike SAMT, we do not condition labelled on unlabelled sides: phrase-translation weights are computed on labelled rules on the one hand, and on unlabelled rules on the other hand.

4   Adjunction-label clustering

Hanneman and Lavie (2013) propose a clustering method for SAMT labels to reduce their amount and the resulting computational load. Their method employs source labels next to the usual SAMT target labels: combining source and target labels allows them to compute relative-frequency estimates of source/target labels, which serve to compute distance measures between source labels on one hand, and target labels on the other. The distance measure between two source labels s_1 and s_2 is defined as the marginal difference between $P(t|s_1)$ and $P(t|s_2)$ estimates; the distance between target labels is defined similarly. Clustering proceeds by searching the source or target labels that minimize either one of the source-label and the target-label distances, and collapsing the resulting label pair. Clustering stops after a predefined number of iterations, after which only the clustered target labels are used to extract an SAMT grammar. The resulting model proves superior to SAMT on a Chinese-English task, and generally superior to Hiero.

Even though our bilingual label set is very small, the combination of source and target labels is ad-hoc, and initial experiments show it is misadapted. To correct this, we adapt the method of Hanneman and Lavie (2013) to cluster combined, bilingual labels.

4.1   Label-distance measures

Rather than using a joint distribution of source and target labels to compute label distance, we use a joint distribution of left-hand-side and right-hand-side labels. We define a distance d_{LHS} between left-hand-side label occurrences, and a distance d_{RHS} between right-hand-side label occurrences.

The lhs distance between two non-terminals v_1 and v_2 in the bilingual label set U is computed by marginalizing the difference between non-terminal rewriting probabilities, where probability estimates are obtained by heuristic counting of joint LHS/RHS labels in extracted labelled rules:

$$d_{LHS}(v_1, v_2) = \sum_{v \in U} \left(P_{RHS|LHS}(v|v_1) - P_{RHS|LHS}(v|v_2) \right) \tag{1}$$

This distance captures similarities in the rewriting behaviour of non-terminals.

For the rhs distance, we tested two definitions. The first one, d^m_{RHS}, mirrors the lhs distance, by marginalizing the difference between inverse non-terminal rewriting probabilities:

$$d^m_{RHS}(v_1, v_2) = \sum_{v \in U} \left(P_{LHS|RHS}(v|v_1) - P_{LHS|RHS}(v|v_2) \right) \tag{2}$$

Under this definition, two non-terminals are similar if they have similar generating distributions.

The second one, d^u_{RHS}, marginalizes the difference between joint lhs/rhs probabilities over left-hand-side non-terminal labels:

$$d^u_{RHS}(v_1, v_2) = \sum_{v \in U} \left(P_{LHS,RHS}(v, v_1) - P_{LHS,RHS}(v, v_2) \right) \tag{3}$$

Under this definition, the similarity in right-hand-side label occurrences is not normalized anymore by right-hand-side label probabilities, so this rhs distance is also conditioned on right-hand-side labels having similar frequencies.

We derive a single label distance measure by adding the lhs and rhs distances. Depending on the variant of rhs distance (*normalized* or *unnormalized*), we obtain either d_n or d_u:

$$d_n(v_1, v_2) = d_{LHS}(v_1, v_2) + d^m_{RHS}(v_1, v_2) \tag{4}$$

$$d_u(v_1, v_2) = d_{LHS}(v_1, v_2) + d^u_{RHS}(v_1, v_2) \tag{5}$$

4.2   Clustering

Clustering proceeds by searching at each step for the label pair that minimizes label distance. The two closest labels are clustered into a single label, and probability estimates are updated for the next round. Clustering stops when a predefined label-set size has been reached. The clustered bilingual labels can then be used to extract a new grammar.

5 Experiments

5.1 Experimental set-up

5.1.1 Data

We conduct experiments of French-English data from the Europarl corpus (v7) with in-domain test data from the WMT07 Europarl development and test sets (devtest2006 and test2006).

We use the Berkeley aligner[2] for training word alignments, with 5 rounds of IBM1 and HMM training; the training data consist of the French-English Europarl training set, containing 1.97M sentence pairs with a maximum length of 40 tokens. The data are tokenized with a script adapted from the Moses tokenizer and lowercased. The language model is a 4-gram model with interpolated Kneser-Ney smoothing, and is trained with KenLM[3] on the English side of the training set with a sentence-length limit of 80 tokens; the set contains 52.5M tokens.

The training data consist of 200k sentence pairs of length limited to 40 tokens, taken from the training set used for the language model and the word alignments; the data contain 4.18M English tokens;

5.1.2 Annotations

We parse both sides of the training data with the Berkeley Parser[4]–the data are then true-cased–, and then convert parses to dependency parses: with the Pennconverter of Johansson and Nugues (2007) for English, and the Functional Role Labeller of Candito et al. (2010) for French.

5.1.3 Model Training and decoding

We train models using an in-house grammar extractor, and a decoder based on Joshua[5]. Training and decoding constraints and defaults are the same as for Hiero, but we disallow consecutive non-terminals on both sides, and not only on the source side.

Model parameters are tuned with Mira, allowing up to 20 iterations. Following (Clark et al., 2011) we average results over three rounds of tuning/decoding.

5.2 First results

Table 3 reports tests on adjunct/argument label sets, where we use source-language labels only (AA-Src), target-language labels (AA-Trg), or combined, bilingual labels (AA-Bi).

Table 3: Performance of monolingual and bilingual labelling schemes with regard to Hiero; significant differences are marked with one v for $p = 0.05$ and two for $p = 0.01$

	BLEU		METEOR		TER	
	dev	test	dev	test	dev	test
Hiero	32.1	31.8	34.9	34.8	52.9	53.3
AA-Src	31.9^{vv}	31.3^{vv}	34.8^{v}	34.7^{vv}	53.0	53.5^{vv}
AA-Trg	32.0^{v}	31.6^{vv}	34.9	34.7^{v}	52.9	53.5^{vv}
AA-Bi	31.9^{v}	31.5^{vv}	34.8	34.7^{vv}	53.0	53.5^{v}

All models underperform Hiero, on the test set more than on the development set, and on BLEU more than Meteor or TER. The AA-Src model performs worse: source-labelling models are most known to guide reordering, which is relatively absent in French-English. The AA-Bi model appears to give poorer results than the AA-Trg model, and that while it disposes of more information; argueably, even if the source-language labels are not directly useful, they might serve to refine target labels. We attribute the relatively poor results of the AA-Bi model to the undirected combination of source and target labels, and

---

[2]https://code.google.com/p/berkeleyaligner/
[3]http://kheafield.com/code/kenlm/
[4]https://github.com/slavpetrov/berkeleyparser
[5]http://joshua-decoder.org/

we use label-rewriting statistics on the development set grammar of the `AA-Bi` model to cluster labels as described in section 4.

5.3 Label clustering

We apply both definitions of the rhs distance of Equations 2 and 3 to extract two label sets. In both cases, we limit the final, clustered label-set size to six labels. Table 4 presents the label set obtained with the rhs-normalized distance d_n (equation 4), and Table 5 the label set obtained with the rhs-unnormalized distance d_u (Equation 5).

Table 4: Clusters obtained with normalized (conditional) RHS distance d_n and relative frequency of LHS occurrence

	clustered bilingual labels	$P(LHS)$
1	CA, CA$_I$, CC, CC$_I$, CC$_S$, CP, C$_I$A, C$_I$A$_I$, C$_I$C, C$_I$C$_I$, C$_I$C$_S$, C$_I$P	0.381
2	AA, AA$_I$, AC, AC$_I$, AC$_S$, AP, C$_S$A, C$_S$A$_I$, C$_S$C, C$_S$C$_I$, C$_S$C$_S$, C$_S$P, PA, PA$_I$, PC, PC$_I$, PC$_S$	0.255
3	PP	0.328
4	A$_I$C$_S$	0.024
5	A$_I$C, A$_I$C$_I$	0.012
6	A$_I$A, A$_I$A$_I$, A$_I$P	0.001

Table 5: Clusters obtained with unnormalized (joint) RHS distance d_u and relative frequency of LHS occurrence

	clustered bilingual labels	$P(LHS)$
1	CC, CC$_I$, C$_I$C, C$_I$C$_I$	0.288
2	CA, CA$_I$, CC$_S$, CP, C$_I$A, C$_I$A$_I$, C$_I$C$_S$, C$_I$P, C$_S$C, C$_S$C$_I$, C$_S$C$_S$, C$_S$P, PC, PC$_I$, PC$_S$, PP	0.595
3	AC, A$_I$C, A$_I$C$_I$	0.016
4	AA, AA$_I$, A$_I$A , A$_I$A$_I$	0.050
5	AC$_I$, AC$_S$, AP, A$_I$C$_S$, A$_I$P	0.018
6	C$_S$A, C$_S$A$_I$, PA, PA$_I$	0.032

Clusters obtained with d_n (Table 4) show a dominance of the source-label component: labels with an A_I source component form half of all clusters (clusters 4,5 and 6), and other labels–PP excepted–are clustered by their source component only.

In contrast, clusters obtained with d_u (Table 5) show some symmetry between source and target components, and they group together adjuncts and incomplete adjuncts, arguments and incomplete arguments, and multi-headed dependent sequences and phrases: cluster 1 corresponds to argument/argument translations; cluster 2 to argument/adjunct pairs and phrasal (multi-headed) or semi-phrasal equivalences; cluster 3 to adjunct/argument pairs; cluster 4 to adjunct/adjunct pairs; cluster 5 to adjunct/phrase pairs; and cluster 6 to phrase/adjunct pairs.

These clusters also lead to better translation results, as Table 6 shows.

The model trained with the label set of Table 4, `AA-Cn` performs worse than the original labelled model `AA-Bi`. The second label set leads to a better `AA-Cu` model, which performs significantly better than `AA-Bi` on the test set. Compared to Hiero, `AA-Cu` is still less performant on the development set–at least in terms of BLEU scores–, but achieves comparable results on the test set.

Table 6: Performance of clustered labelling schemes with regard to Hiero and the original bilingual-label model; significant differences with Hiero are marked with one $\triangledown$ for $p = 0.05$ and two for $p = 0.01$; significant differences with the original label-set model are marked with one $\blacktriangle$ for $p = 0.05$ and two for $p = 0.01$;

	BLEU		METEOR		TER	
	dev	test	dev	test	dev	test
Hiero	32.1	31.8	34.9	34.8	52.9	53.3
AA-Bi	31.9	31.5	34.8	34.7	53.0	53.5
AA-Cn	$31.8^{\triangledown\triangledown/\blacktriangledown}$	$31.4^{\triangledown\triangledown}$	34.8	$34.7^{\triangledown}$	$53.1^{\triangledown\triangledown}$	$53.6^{\triangledown\triangledown}$
AA-Cu	$31.9^{\triangledown\triangledown}$	$31.8^{\blacktriangle\blacktriangle}$	34.9	$34.8^{\blacktriangle\blacktriangle}$	53.0	$53.3^{\blacktriangle\blacktriangle}$

6 Discussion

Our first results show that direct matching of source and target labels leads to sub-optimal performance. Our solution uses rule estimates to cluster bilingual labels. This is orthogonal to the approach of Chiang (2010), who applies rule-matching features on both sides of the data, without explicitly matching source and target labels. While using bilingual labels is appealing as these labels are directly interpretable in terms of syntactic correspondence, clustering only allows to merge labels. A more refined method would allow to both split and merge labels, with the original adjunct/argument labels as a starting point for characterizing synchronous recursion linguistically.

As far as the current clustering procedure is concerned, we have shown that a distance based on rewriting patterns of left-hand-side non-terminals and occurrence patterns of right-hand-side non-terminals weighed over left-hand-side contexts leads to meaningful clusters and decent results. The clustered labels pair up labels of type adjunct, argument or (multi-headed) constituent sequence with their incomplete counterparts. This is not surprising: as, e.g., adjunct phrases rewrite largely to the same phrases as the incomplete adjunct phrases, their corresponding labels are close according to the left-hand-side distance; similarly, as both types of phrases are largely extracted from the same phrases, their corresponding labels are close according to the *joint* right-hand-side distance[6]. The results we obtain with these clustered labels suggest that the distinction between full and incomplete constituents is not essential for phrase labelling, which agrees with the labelling method of Li et al. (2012), where phrases are labelled with the highest, undominated head(s).

The translation results we present here are quite limited, both in extent and scores. One can first question whether labelling could increase performance for French-English; we intend to extend the application of the model to other language pairs in future work. Secondly, as we kept the Hiero constraints on phrase length and reordering–using labelled but otherwise standard glue rules–the effect of labelling can only be local. Possible extentions for our model would consist in extending the reordering capacities of Hiero with adjunct/argument reordering rules, or to use adjuncts to restrict recursion, thereby making way to lift Hiero's standard phrase-length constraint.

7 Related Work

Most work on adjunction in SMT takes place in a syntax-based framework, which forms a natural ground for STAG. DeNeefe and Knight (2009) and Liu et al. (2011) for instance have proposed tree-to-string models that differentiate between adjunction and substitution. The only application of adjunction to string-to-string models we know of is that of Arnoult and Sima'an (2012), who exploit the optional character of adjuncts to extract more rules for a Phrase-Based model.

While the first applications of syntax for SMT (Wu, 1997; Poutsma, 2000; Yamada and Knight, 2001)

---

[6]One can also note that, as the right-hand-side distance is not normalized, it takes lower values than the left-hand-side distance; we have not attempted to weigh them differently, but more experiments in this direction might be worth the while.

used constituency trees, recent work has come to use a larger array of linguistic formalisms: besides applications of TAG (DeNeefe and Knight, 2009; Liu et al., 2011), Xie et al. (2011) apply dependency syntax for tree-to-string modelling and Li et al. (2012) for labelling Hiero; Hassan et al. (2007) apply CCG supertags to phrase-based SMT and Almaghout et al. (2011) to Hiero; Xiong et al. (2012) apply predicate-argument structures in a hierarchical phrase-based model and Li et al.(2013) for in Hiero.

Labelling hierarchical models introduces new constraints while providing the opportunity to relax innate Hiero constraints. New constraints are: a limitation of the grammar to observed substitutions, which can be remedied by relaxing matching constraints using features to learn subsitution preferences (Chiang, 2010); an increase of rule sparsity and computational constraints, which can be remedied by label clustering (Hanneman and Lavie, 2013; Mino et al., 2014). The Hiero constraints that one attempts to relax are the monotonic top-level ordering, first and foremost (Huck et al., 2012; Li et al., 2012; Li et al., 2013). Li et al. (2012) also relax the source non-terminal adjacency constraint, while Li et al. (2013) relax the phrase-length constraint for extraction and decoding.

8 Conclusion

We have presented a bilingual labelling scheme for Hiero that is based on the adjunct/argument distinction. Even though our label set is very small, containing only thirty-six labels, we find that clustering these labels is useful. As it is, our model is able to perform similarly to Hiero on in-domain test data for French-English.

For future work, we plan to refine our labelling method, and to extend our model to circumvene the limited reordering capacity of Hiero: either with reordering rules, for which the adjunct/argument distinction should form a good basis, or through restrictions on recursion, which would allow to lift Hiero's phrase-length constraint.

Acknowledgements

We thank Gideon Maillette de Buy Wenniger for his help in using his grammar-extraction and labelling software and for useful discussions. We also thank the reviewers for their comments. This work is supported by The Netherlands Organisation for Scientific Research (NWO), with VC EW grant 612.001.122.

References

Hala Almaghout, Jie Jiang, and Andy Way. 2011. CCG contextual labels in hierarchical phrase-based SMT. In *Proceedings of the 15th conference of the European Association for Machine Translation*, pages 281–288.

Sophie Arnoult and Khalil Sima'an. 2012. Adjunct Alignment in Translation Data with an Application to Phrase-Based Statistical Machine Translation. In *Proceedings of the 16th Annual Conference of the European Association for Machine Translation*, pages 287–294.

Sophie Arnoult and Khalil Sima'an. 2014. How Synchronous are Adjuncts in Translation Data? In *Proceedings of SSST-8, Eighth Workshop on Syntax, Semantics and Structure in Statistical Translation*, page 157?165, Doha, Qatar, October. Association for Computational Linguistics.

Marie Candito, Benoît Crabbé, and Pascal Denis. 2010. Statistical French dependency parsing: treebank conversion and first results. In *Proceedings of The seventh international conference on Language Resources and Evaluation (LREC)*.

David Chiang. 2005. A Hierarchical Phrase-Based Model for Statistical Machine Translation. In *Proceedings of the 43rd Annual Meeting of the Association for Computational Linguistics*, pages 263–270.

David Chiang. 2010. Learning to Translate with Source and Target Syntax. In *Proceedings of the 48th Annual Meeting of the Association for Computational Linguistics*, pages 1443–1452, Uppsala, Sweden, July. Association for Computational Linguistics.

Jonathan H Clark, Chris Dyer, Alon Lavie, and Noah A Smith. 2011. Better hypothesis testing for statistical machine translation: Controlling for optimizer instability. In *Proceedings of the 49th Annual Meeting of the Association for Computational Linguistics: Human Language Technologies: short papers-Volume 2*, pages 176–181. Association for Computational Linguistics.

Steve DeNeefe and Kevin Knight. 2009. Synchronous Tree Adjoining Machine Translation. In *Proceedings of the 2009 Conference on Empirical Methods in Natural Language Processing*, pages 727–736.

Bonnie J. Dorr. 1994. Machine Translation Divergences: A Formal Description and Proposed Solution. *Computational Linguistics*, 20(4):597–633.

Greg Hanneman and Alon Lavie. 2013. Improving Syntax-Augmented Machine Translation by Coarsening the Label Set. In *Proceedings of the 2013 Conference of the North American Chapter of the Association for Computational Linguistics: Human Language Technologies*, pages 288–297, Atlanta, Georgia, June. Association for Computational Linguistics.

Hany Hassan, Khalil Sima'an, and Andy Way. 2007. Supertagged Phrase-Based Statistical Machine Translation. In *Proceedings of the 45th Annual Meeting of the Association of Computational Linguistics*, pages 288–295, Prague, Czech Republic, June. Association for Computational Linguistics.

Matthias Huck, Stephan Peitz, Markus Freitag, and Hermann Ney. 2012. Discriminative Reordering Extensions for Hierarchical Phrase-Based Machine Translation. In *16th Annual Conference of the European Association for Machine Translation*, pages 313–320, Trento, Italy, may.

Rebecca Hwa, Philip Resnik, Amy Weinberg, and Okan Kolak. 2002. Evaluating Translational Correspondence Using Annotation Projection. In *Proceedings of the 40th Annual Meeting on Association for Computational Linguistics*, ACL '02, pages 392–399.

Richard Johansson and Pierre Nugues. 2007. Extended Constituent-to-dependency Conversion for English. In *Proceedings of NODALIDA 2007*, pages 105–112, Tartu, Estonia, May 25-26.

Aravind K. Joshi and Yves Schabes. 1997. Tree-Adjoining Grammars. In G. Rosenberg and A. Salomaa, editors, *Handbook of Formal Languages*. Springer-Verlag, New York, NY.

Aravind K. Joshi, Leon S. Levy, and Masako Takahashi. 1975. Tree Adjunct Grammars. *Journal of Computer and System Sciences*, 10(1):136–163.

Junhui Li, Zhaopeng Tu, Guodong Zhou, and Josef van Genabith. 2012. Using Syntactic Head Information in Hierarchical Phrase-Based Translation. In *Proceedings of the 7th Workshop on Statistical Machine Translation*, pages 232–242.

Junhui Li, Philip Resnik, and Hal Daumé III. 2013. Modeling Syntactic and Semantic Structures in Hierarchical Phrase-based Translation. In *Proceedings of the 2013 Conference of the North American Chapter of the Association for Computational Linguistics: Human Language Technologies*, pages 540–549, Atlanta, Georgia, June. Association for Computational Linguistics.

Yang Liu, Qun Liu, and Yajuan Lü. 2011. Adjoining Tree-to-string Translation. In *Proceedings of the 49th Annual Meeting of the Association for Computational Linguistics: Human Language Technologies - Volume 1*, HLT '11, pages 1278–1287.

Hideya Mino, Taro Watanabe, and Eiichiro Sumita. 2014. Syntax-Augmented Machine Translation using Syntax-Label Clustering. In *Proceedings of the 2014 Conference on Empirical Methods in Natural Language Processing (EMNLP)*, pages 165–171, Doha, Qatar, October. Association for Computational Linguistics.

Arjen Poutsma. 2000. Data-Oriented Translation. In *COLING*, pages 635–641.

Stuart Shieber and Yves Schabes. 1990. Synchronous Tree-Adjoining Grammars. In *Handbook of Formal Languages*, pages 69–123. Springer.

Stuart M. Shieber. 2007. Probabilistic Synchronous Tree-Adjoining Grammars for Machine Translation: The Argument from Bilingual Dictionaries. In Dekai Wu and David Chiang, editors, *Proceedings of the Workshop on Syntax and Structure in Statistical Translation*, Rochester, New York, 26 April.

Mark Steedman. 2000. *The Syntactic Process*. MIT Press, Cambridge, MA.

Dekai Wu. 1997. Stochastic Inversion Transduction Grammars and Bilingual Parsing of Parallel Corpora. *Computational Linguistics*, 23(3):377–404.

Jun Xie, Haitao Mi, and Qun Liu. 2011. A Novel Dependency-to-String Model for Statistical Machine Translation. In *Proceedings of the Conference on Empirical Methods in Natural Language Processing*, EMNLP '11, pages 216–226, Stroudsburg, PA, USA. Association for Computational Linguistics.

Deyi Xiong, Min Zhang, and Haizhou Li. 2012. Modeling the Translation of Predicate-Argument Structure for SMT. In *ACL (1)*, pages 902–911.

Kenji Yamada and Kevin Knight. 2001. A syntax-based statistical translation model. In *Proceedings of the 39th Annual Meeting on Association for Computational Linguistics*, ACL '01, pages 523–530, Stroudsburg, PA, USA. Association for Computational Linguistics.

Andreas Zollmann and Ashish Venugopal. 2006. Syntax Augmented Machine Translation via Chart Parsing. In *Proceedings of NAACL 2006 - Workshop on statistical machine translation*, pages 138–141.

Andreas Zollmann. 2011. *Learning Multiple-Nonterminal Synchronous Grammars for Statistical Machine Translation*. Ph.D. thesis.

Towards Deeper MT - A Hybrid System for German

Eleftherios Avramidis, Maja Popović*, Aljoscha Burchardt and Hans Uszkoreit
German Research Center for Artificial Intelligence (DFKI)
Language Technology Lab
firstname.lastname@dfki.de
* Humboldt University of Berlin
maja.popovic@hu-berlin.de

Abstract

The idea to improve MT quality by using deep linguistic and knowledge-driven information has frequently been expressed. If the goal is to use deep information for building an MT system, there are two extreme options: (1) to start from a purely knowledge-driven approach (RBMT) and try to arrive at the same recall found in current SMT systems; (2) to start from an SMT system and try to arrive at higher precision by modifying it so that more knowledge drives the translation process.

The system architecture we will describe in this paper starts in the middle of these extreme options. It is a hybrid architecture that we take as a starting point for future experiments and extensions to increase MT quality by more knowledge-driven processing.

1 Introduction

Statistical Machine Translation (SMT) based on comparably shallow features can be considered the most successful paradigm in Machine Translation (MT). The processing pipelines and machine learning architectures have become quite sophisticated and complex and allow for many types of optimisations. SMT systems have a (theoretical) high recall in the sense that they provide output for most input and that the pieces that would constitute a good translation are usually present somewhere in a huge search space during the translation process (e.g. in phrase tables or language models). However, it is very difficult to arrive at high precision, i.e., to automatically choose the right pieces and put together a fluent and accurate translation of a given input. The idea to further improve MT quality by adding deeper (i.e., more linguistic and knowledge-driven) information has thus frequently been expressed.

At the same time, rule-based MT systems that primarily apply such knowledge and that are able to control precision much better are used only in certain nieches today. The reason is that they lack recall: for example, parsing failure or gaps in the lexicon typically lead to a dead-end where the only option is to manually code the missing information, which is too resource intensive especially if one wants to take care of those less frequent items and phenomena in the "long tail".

If one has the goal to use deep information for building an MT system with the best possible results, there are two extreme options: (1) to start from a purely knowledge-driven approach and try to arrive at the same (theoretical) recall found in current SMT systems; (2) to start from an SMT system and try to arrive at high precision by modifying it so that knowledge drives the search process. Today, it is an open research question what will lead to the best results in the end.

The system architecture we will describe below starts in the middle of both extreme options. It is a hybrid architecture that we take as starting point for future experiments and extensions to increase MT quality by more knowledge-driven processing. This systems has been developed within the QTLeap project[1] where it serves as a "deeper" baseline system as compared to a pure SMT baseline. The goal of the project is to explore different combinations of shallow and deep processing for improving MT quality. The system presented in this paper is the first of a series of system prototypes developed in the project. We therefore refer to it as System 1 in this paper.

[1] http://qtleap.eu/

Proceedings of the 1st Deep Machine Translation Workshop (DMTW 2015), pages 12–19,
Praha, Czech Republic, 3–4 September 2015.

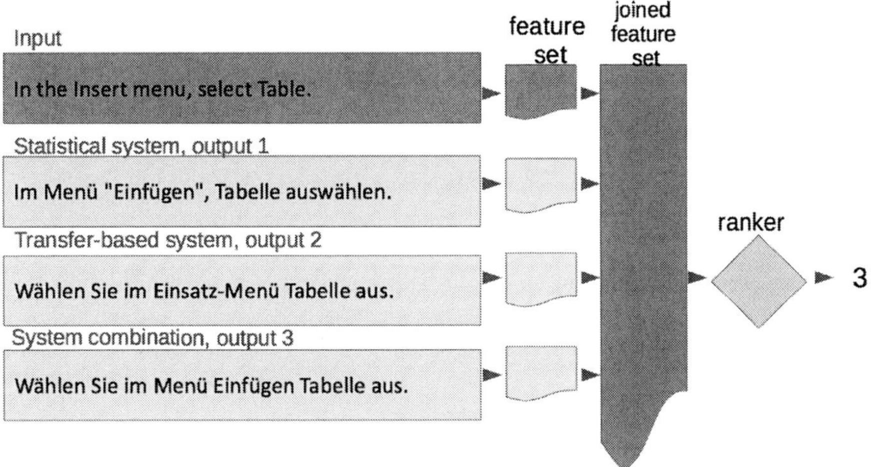

Figure 1: Architecture of System 1.

2   A Hybrid System Combination for German↔English

The fact that German is relatively well-resourced in comparison to other language pairs has allowed MT researchers to build strong statistical systems with very good performance on a lexical or a local level (Bojar et al., 2014). The German-English MT system we present here (System 1) aims to effectively incorporate deep linguistic processing into existing successful machine translation methods for this language pair.

Since our main goal is to achieve a high-quality system that allows for experimentation, competes with state-of-the-art systems, and can be useful in the projects real use-case scenario (translating user queries and expert answers in a chat-based PC helpdesk scenario), we use a system implementation that takes advantage of deep transfer and also includes a statistical mechanism that enhances performance by keeping the best parts from each employed method. Figure 1 shows the overall hybrid architecture that includes:

- A statistical Moses system,

- the commercial transfer-based system Lucy,

- their serial system combination, and

- an informed selection mechanism ("ranker").

The components of this hybrid system will be detailed in the sections below.

2.1   Statistical MT system: Moses

Our statistical machine translation component was based on a vanilla phrase-based system built with Moses (Koehn et al., 2007) trained on the following corpora: Europarl ver. 7, News Commentary ver. 9 (Bojar et al., 2014), Commoncrawl (Smith et al., 2013), and MultiUN (Eisele and Chen, 2010) as well as on the following domain corpora: the Document Foundation (Libreoffice Help – 47K sentence pairs, Libreoffice User Interface – 35K parallel entries), the Document Foundation Terminology (690 translated terms), the Document Foundation Website (226 sentence pairs), Chromium browser (6,3K parallel entries), Ubuntu Documentation (6,3K sentence pairs), Ubuntu Saucy (183K parallel entries), and Drupal web-content management (5K parallel entries). Language models of order 5 have been built and interpolated with SRILM (Stolcke, 2002) and KenLM (Heafield, 2011). For German to English, we also experimented with the method of pre-ordering the source side based on the target-side grammar

(Popovic and Ney, 2006). As a tuning set we used the *news-test 2013*. In our architecture, this system on its own also serves as baseline.

2.2 Transfer-based MT system: Lucy

The transfer-based core of System 1 is based on the Lucy system (Alonso and Thurmair, 2003) that includes the results of long linguistic efforts over the last decades and that has successfully been used in previous projects including Euromatrix+ and QTLaunchPad.

The transfer-based approach has shown good results that compete with pure statistical systems, although its focus is on translating according to linguistic structures sets. Translation occurs in three phases, namely analysis, transfer, and generation. All three phases consist of hand-coded linguistic rules which have shown to perform well for capturing the structural and semantic differences between German and other languages. During the analysis phase, a parsing algorithm constructs a tree of the source language using a monolingual lexicon and the included grammar rules. The analysis algorithm reverts to a shallower analysis at the phrasal level in cases when the engine is not able to process the full tree. The analysis tree is subsequently used for the transfer phase, where deep representations of the source are transferred into deep representations of the target language using a bilingual lexicon based on canonical forms and categories. The generation phase creates the target sentence on the lexical level, using inflection and agreement rules between the dependent target language structures. A RestAPI allows the different processing steps and/or intermediate results to be influenced.

Deep features for empirical enhancement Although deep techniques indicate good coverage of a number of linguistic phenomena, each of the three phases may frequently encounter serious robustness issues and/or the inability to fully process a given sentence. Erroneous analysis from early phases may aggregate along the pipeline and cause further sub-optimal choices in later phases, thus severely deteriorating the quality of the produced translation. Preliminary analysis (Federmann and Hunsicker, 2011) has shown that such is the case for source sentences that are ungrammatical in the first place or that have a very shallow syntax with many specialized lexical entries. To tackle these issues, we combine the transfer-based component with our supportive SMT engine in the following two ways:

(a) train a statistical machine translation to automatically post-edit the output of the transfer-based system ("serial combination")

(b) use the post-edited or the SMT output in cases where the transfer-based system exhibits lower performance. This is done through an empirical *selection mechanism* that performs real-time analysis of the produced translations and automatically selects the output that is predicted to be of a better quality (Avramidis, 2011). Figure 1 shows the overall architecture of System 1 for en→de.

2.3 Serial System Combination: Lucy+Moses

For automatic post-editing of the transfer-based system, a serial Transfer+SMT system combination is used, as described in (Simard et al., 2007) The first stage is translation of the source-language part of the training corpus by the transfer-based system. The second stage is training an SMT system with the transfer-based translation output as a source language and the target-language part as a target language. Later, the test set is first translated by the transfer-based system, and the obtained translation is translated by the SMT system. Figure 2 illustrates the architecture for translation direction en→de. Note that the notion of "German*" in the figure is meant to distinguish the input and output of the SMT system. "German*" is the normal output of the transfer-based system.

In this linear system combination, improvement of up to 6 absolute BLEU points has been achieved for both translation directions in several pilot evaluations. Nevertheless, the method on its own could not outperform the SMT system trained on a large parallel corpus. The example in Figure 1 nicely illustrates how the statistical post-editing operates.

While the original SMT output used the right terminology ("Menü Einfügen" – "insert menu"), the instruction (*Im Menü "Einfügen", Tabelle auswählen*) is stylistically not very polite. In contrast, the output of the transfer-based system (*Wählen Sie im Einsatz-Menü Tabelle aus*) is formulated politely, yet mistranslates the menu type. The serial system combination produces a perfect translation. In this particular case, the machine translation (*Wählen Sie im Einfügen Menü Tabelle aus*) is even better than the human reference (*Wählen Sie im Einfügen Menü die Tabelle aus*) as the latter introduces a determiner for "table" that is not justified by the source.

Figure 2: Serial System Combination en→de.

2.4 Parallel System Combination: Selection Mechanism

The selection mechanism is based on encouraging results of previous projects including Euromatrix Plus (Federmann and Hunsicker, 2011), T4ME (Federmann, 2012), QTLaunchPad (Avramidis, 2013; Shah et al., 2013). It has been extended to include several deep features that can only be generated on a sentence level and that would otherwise blatantly increase the complexity of the transfer or decoding algorithm. In System 1, automatic syntactic and dependency analysis is employed on a sentence level, in order to choose the sentence that fulfills the basic quality aspects of the translation: (a) assert the fluency of the generated sentence, by analyzing the quality of its syntax (b) ensure its adequacy, by comparing the structures of the source with the structures of the generated sentence.

All deep features produced are used to build a ranker based on machine learning against training preference labels. Preference labels are part of the training data and indicate which system output for a given source sentence is of optimal quality. Preference labels are generated either by automatic reference-based metrics or derived from human preferences. The ranker is a result of experimenting with various combinations of feature set and machine learning algorithms and choosing the one that performs best on the project corpus. The selection mechanism is based on the "Qualitative" toolkit that was presented in the MT Marathon, as an open-source contribution (Avramidis et al., 2014).

Feature sets   We started from feature sets that performed well in previous experiments and we experimented with several extensions and modifications. In particular:

- Basic syntax-based feature set: unknown words, count of tokens, count of alternative parse trees, count of verb phrases, parse log likelihood. Parse was done with Berkeley Parser and features were extracted from both source and target. This feature set has performed well as a metric in WMT11 metrics task.

- Basic feature set + 17 QuEst[2] baseline features: this feature set combines the basic syntax-based feature set described above with the baseline feature set of the QuEst toolkit. This feature set combination obtained the best result in the WMT13 quality estimation task.

- Basic syntax-based feature set with Bit Parser: here we replace the Berkeley parser features on the target side with Bit Parser.

- Advanced syntax-based feature set: this augments the basic set by adding IBM model 1 probabilities, full depth of parse trees, depth of the 'S' node, position of the VP and other verb nodes from the beginning and end of the parent node, count of unpaired brackets and compound suggestions (for German, as indicated by LanguageTool.org).

Machine Learning   We tested all suggested feature sets with many machine learning methods, including Support Vector Machines (with both RBF and linear kernel), Logistic Regression, Extra/Decision Trees, k-neighbors, Gaussian Naive Bayes, Linear and Quadratic Discriminant Analysis, Random Forest

---

[2]`http://www.quest.dcs.shef.ac.uk/`

and Adaboost ensemble over Decision Trees. The binary classifiers were wrapped into rankers using the "soft pairwise recomposition" to avoid ties between the systems.

The classifiers were trained on MT outputs of all systems that participated in the translation shared tasks of WMT (years 2008-2014). We also experimented on several sources of sentence level preference labels, in particular human ranks, METEOR and F-score. We chose the label type that maximizes (if possible) all automatic scores, including document-level BLEU.

Best combination The optimal systems used:

1. the *basic syntax-based feature set* for English-German, trained with Support Vector Machines against METEOR scores.

2. the *advanced syntax-based feature set* for German-English, trained with Linear Discriminant Analysis against METEOR scores as well.

Table 1 shows the results of the selection mechanism on a test set used in the QTLeap project that consists of 1000 German questions and English answers to be translated in the respective other language.[3]

The table quantifies the contribution of the three systems: Transfer-based, SMT, and the linear Transfer+SMT combination. It is notable that the mechanism in many cases favors transfer-based output, which is an indication that the deep features are active; one would have expected a bias towards SMT for a shallower selection mechanism. However, this first hypothesis needs to be confirmed by further studies.

	Transfer	SMT	Transfer+SMT
de→en questions	45.2%	33.3%	23.8%
en→de answers	42.5 %	16.3%	50.5%

Table 1: Percentages chosen automatically by the selection mechanism from each of the systems. Percentages which sum more than 100% indicate ties. When ties occur, there is a preset order of preference SMT, Transfer, Transfer+SMT.

3   Evaluation

3.1   Automatic Evaluation

Translation results were evaluated using three automatic metrics: BLEU,[4] word-level F-score (wordF) and character-level F-score (charF) using `rgbF.py` (Popovic, 2012). F-scores are calculated on 1-grams, 2-grams, 3-grams and 4-grams and then averaged using the arithmetic mean. The final score is obtained in the usual way and is the harmonic mean of precision and recall. Although BLEU is certainly the most used automatic metric, F-score has been shown to correlate better with human judgments, especially if n-grams are averaged using arithmetic instead of geometric mean. We also calculated character level F-score because the target language is morphologically rich.

As baseline, we used the Moses SMT system described above on its own. Following the evaluation scenario in the project, we evaluate on the translation of questions for the direction German into English and on the answers only for the direction from English to German. Table 2 shows the scores for the baseline (Moses) and contrasts them with the results for System 1.

The results show that System 1 performs comparably to the baseline for translation of questions into English while the translation of answers into German still poses more problems. In addition to the scores discussed above, the translation errors were analyzed using Hjerson (Popović, 2011), an automatic tool for error analysis that provides a categorization into five classes:

- word form (agreement errors, tense, capitalization, part of speech)

---

[3]The corpus is available for Basque, Bulgarian, Czech, Dutch, English, German, Portuguese and Spanish and can be downloaded from the META-SHARE portal (`http://metashare.metanet4u.eu/`) under the name "QTLeap Corpus".

[4]We used the official BLEU script `mteval-v13a.pl --international-tokenization`.

		questions de→en	answers en→de
	BLEU	43.0	41.7
Moses	wordF	44.6	42.2
	charF	64.9	64.7
	BLEU	43.3	33.0
System 1	wordF	43.8	30.2
	charF	63.4	57.4

Table 2: BLEU scores, word-level and character-level F-scores for Moses baseline and System 1 translation outputs.

- word order

- omission

- addition

- mistranslation (general mistranslations, terminology errors, style, punctuation and any changes to wording)

For each error class, the tool provides raw error counts together with error rates (raw counts normalized over the total number of words in the translation output). Block error counts and block error rates are calculated as well, where the block refers to a group of successive words belonging to the same error class.

The tool is language independent. It requires the translation output and a reference, both in full form and lemmatized. During the evaluation experiments, it has been observed that there are a number of capitalization errors (or inconsistencies between the reference and the translation), such as "OpenOffice" vs. "openOffice", "VLC" vs "vlc", etc. Therefore we subsequently calculated capitalization error rates as difference between word form error rate of true-cased texts and word form error rates of lower-cased texts that are displayed in the table below. The pure morphological errors are those obtained with lower-cased texts. In order to arrive at a fair treatment of the prevalent items in the input such as "File > Save As" or URLs, we have reported block error rates instead of word-level error rates.

The results are presented in Table 3. The error classification results are presented below, in the form of block error rates (lower is better). The error rates read as follows, taking Moses de→enas an example: 12.2% of the word groups in the translation output are mistranslated in comparison to the human reference (i.e. these words are different than the reference words). So, if the system has translated 100 words, ca. 12 (consecutive blocks of) words consist of other words than found in the reference.

		questions de→en	answers en→de
	form	1.2	4.4
	order	6.5	5.7
Moses	omission	4.4	4.6
	addition	2.8	3.7
	mistranslation	12.2	11.9
	form	1.1	4.0
	order	5.6	5.6
System 1	omission	3.4	3.0
	addition	3.6	7.4
	mistranslation	12.8	13.5

Table 3: Class error rates for Moses and System 1 translation outputs.

When going from Moses to System 1, this automatic analysis indicates that the number of morphological errors, reordering errors and omissions goes down slightly while the number of mistranslations (lexical errors) goes up. The most striking difference is the increase in additions when translating into German which almost doubles. The reason for this might be that deeper systems produce structurally different translations that do not match the reference translations. This needs to be analysed in more detail.

3.2 User Evaluation

Finally, we also evaluated the performance of System 1 compared to the Moses baseline in a task-based user evaluation performed by volunteers that will be published in this volume (Del Gaudio et al.). Explained briefly, users were presented a technical question (in German) in a web interface, a German reference answer and answers translated from English by Moses and System 1 in random order. They had to indicate which MT answer is better or if both are the same given these options (where A and B are the two systems, respectively):

  i A is a better answer than B

  ii B is a better answer than A

  iii A and B are equally good answers

  iv A and B are equally bad answers

100 question-answer pairs were judged by three volunteers. If we lump ties (i.e., iii and iv) together, the central (averaged) results of the user evaluation are:

- System 1 has been judged better than Moses in 17.3% of cases (i)

- System 1 has been judged better or same as Moses in 75.5 % of cases (i+iii+iv)

Given that, for translation into German, the BLEU score of System 1 is more than 8 points worse than that of Moses, further detailed investigation is needed to interpret these results.

4 Summary and outlook

In this paper, we've described a first experimental systems that combines deep and shallow MT components in different hybrid combinations. The goal is to explore various ways of using "deeper" information for translation between English and German. Evaluation has shown that the hybrid system performs comparably to an SMT baseline for some tasks, yet shows worse performance on others. A small user evaluation has shown promising results. In the future, various experiments and improvements are possible and foreseen, starting from improving the transfer-based system (handling of lexical items such as terminology, MWEs, untranslatables, and robustness of parsing), the serial combination (e.g., improved disambiguation), and moving up to more detailed analysis and testing and improvement of the selection mechanism (e.g., integrating more linguistic information from external parsing).

Acknowledgments

This paper has received funding from the European Union's Seventh Framework Programme for research, technological development and demonstration under grant agreement no 610516 (QTLeap: Quality Translation by Deep Language Engineering Approaches). We are grateful to the anonymous reviewers for their valuable feedback.

References

Juan A. Alonso and Gregor Thurmair. 2003. The comprendium translator system. In *Proceedings of the Ninth Machine Translation Summit*, New Orleans, LA, September.

Eleftherios Avramidis, Lukas Poustka, and Sven Schmeier. 2014. Qualitative: Open source python tool for quality estimation over multiple machine translation outputs. *The Prague Bulletin of Mathematical Linguistics*, 102(1):5–16.

Eleftherios Avramidis. 2011. DFKI System Combination with Sentence Ranking at ML4HMT-2011. In *Proceedings of the International Workshop on Using Linguistic Information for Hybrid Machine Translation (LIHMT 2011) and of the Shared Task on Applying Machine Learning Techniques to Optimising the Division of Labour in Hybrid Machine Translation (ML4HMT-11)*, Barcelona, Spain. Center for Language and Speech Technologies and Applications (TALP), Technical University of Catalonia.

Eleftherios Avramidis. 2013. Sentence-level ranking with quality estimation. *Machine Translation (MT)*, 28(Special issue on Quality Estimation):1–20.

Ondřej Bojar, Christian Buck, Christian Federmann, Barry Haddow, Philipp Koehn, Johannes Leveling, Christof Monz, Pavel Pecina, Matt Post, Herve Saint-Amand, Radu Soricut, Lucia Specia, and Aleš Tamchyna. 2014. Findings of the 2014 Workshop on Statistical Machine Translation. In *Proceedings of the Ninth Workshop on Statistical Machine Translation*, pages 12–58, Baltimore, Maryland, USA, June. Association for Computational Linguistics.

Andreas Eisele and Yu Chen. 2010. MultiUN: A Multilingual Corpus from United Nation Documents. In Daniel Tapias, Mike Rosner, Stelios Piperidis, Jan Odjik, Joseph Mariani, Bente Maegaard, Khalid Choukri, and Nicoletta Calzolari (Conference Chair), editors, *Proceedings of the Seventh conference on International Language Resources and Evaluation. International Conference on Language Resources and Evaluation (LREC-2010), May 19-21, La Valletta, Malta*, pages 2868–2872. European Language Resources Association (ELRA).

Christian Federmann and Sabine Hunsicker. 2011. Stochastic Parse Tree Selection for an Existing RBMT System. In *Proceedings of the Sixth Workshop on Statistical Machine Translation*, pages 351–357, Edinburgh, Scotland, July. Association for Computational Linguistics.

Christian Federmann. 2012. Can Machine Learning Algorithms Improve Phrase Selection in Hybrid Machine Translation? In *Proceedings of the 13th Conference of the European Chapter of the Association for Computational Linguistics. Joint Workshop on Exploiting Synergies between Information Retrieval and Machine Translation (ESIRMT) and Hybrid Approaches to Machine Translation*, pages 113–118, Avignon, France, April. European Chapter of the Association for Computational Linguistics (EACL).

Kenneth Heafield. 2011. KenLM : Faster and Smaller Language Model Queries. In *Proceedings of the Sixth Workshop on Statistical Machine Translation*, number 2009, pages 187–197, Edinburgh, Scotland, July. Association for Computational Linguistics.

Philipp Koehn, Hieu Hoang, Alexandra Birch, Chris Callison-Burch, Marcello Federico, Nicola Bertoldi, Brooke Cowan, Wade Shen, Christine Moran, Chris Zens, Richard a nd Dyer, Ondřej Bojar, Alexandra Constantin, and Evan Herbst. 2007. Moses: open source toolkit for statistical machine translation. In *Proceedings of the 45th Annual Meeting of the ACL on Interactive Poster and Demonstration Sessions*, ACL '07, pages 177–180, Stroudsburg, PA, USA. Association for Computational Linguistics.

Maja Popovic and Hermann Ney. 2006. Pos-based word reorderings for statistical machine translation. In *International Conference on Language Resources and Evaluation*, pages 1278–1283.

Maja Popović. 2011. Hjerson: An Open Source Tool for Automatic Error Classification of Machine Translation Output. *The Prague Bulletin of Mathematical Linguistics*, (96):59–68, October.

Maja Popovic. 2012. rgbf: An open source tool for n-gram based automatic evaluation of machine translation output. *The Prague Bulletin of Mathematical Linguistics*, 98:99–108, 10.

Kashif Shah, Eleftherios Avramidis, Ergun Biçici, and Lucia Specia. 2013. QuEst: Design, Implementation and Extensions of a Framework for Machine Translation Quality Estimation. *The Prague Bulletin of Mathematical Linguistics (PBML)*, 100:19–30.

Michel Simard, Cyril Goutte, and Pierre Isabelle. 2007. Statistical phrase-based post-editing. In *Proceedings of The North American Chapter of the Association for Computational Linguistics Conference (NAACL-07)*, pages 508–515, Rochester, NY, April.

Jason R Smith, Herve Saint-Amand, Magdalena Plamada, Philipp Koehn, Chris Callison-Burch, and Adam Lopez. 2013. Dirt Cheap Web-Scale Parallel Text from the Common Crawl. In *Proceedings of the 51st Annual Meeting of the Association for Computational Linguistics (Volume 1: Long Papers)*, pages 1374–1383, Sofia, Bulgaria, August. Association for Computational Linguistics.

Andreas Stolcke. 2002. Srilm — an Extensible Language Modeling Toolkit. In *System*, volume 2, pages 901–904. ISCA, September.

Splitting Compounds by Semantic Analogy

Joachim Daiber[*]   **Lautaro Quiroz**[†]   **Roger Wechsler**[†]   **Stella Frank**[*]

[*]Institute for Logic, Language and Computation
University of Amsterdam
Science Park 107, 1098 XG Amsterdam
{J.Daiber,S.C.Frank}@uva.nl

[†]Graduate School of Informatics
University of Amsterdam
Science Park 904, 1098 XH Amsterdam
first.last@student.uva.nl

Abstract

Compounding is a highly productive word-formation process in some languages that is often problematic for natural language processing applications. In this paper, we investigate whether distributional semantics in the form of word embeddings can enable a deeper, i.e., more knowledge-rich, processing of compounds than the standard string-based methods. We present an unsupervised approach that exploits regularities in the semantic vector space (based on analogies such as "bookshop is to shop as bookshelf is to shelf") to produce compound analyses of high quality. A subsequent compound splitting algorithm based on these analyses is highly effective, particularly for ambiguous compounds. German to English machine translation experiments show that this semantic analogy-based compound splitter leads to better translations than a commonly used frequency-based method.

1   Introduction

In languages such as German, compound words are a frequent occurrence leading to difficulties for natural language processing applications, and in particular machine translation. Several methods for dealing with this issue—from shallow count-based methods to deeper but more complex neural network-based processing methods—have been proposed. The recent surge in practical models for distributional semantics has enabled a multitude of practical applications in many areas, most recently in morphological analysis (Soricut and Och, 2015). In this paper, we investigate whether similar methods can be utilized to perform deeper, i.e. more knowledge-rich, processing of compounds. A great asset of word embeddings are the regularities that their multi-dimensional vector space exhibits. Mikolov et al. (2013) showed that regularities such as "*king* is to *man* what *queen* is to *woman*" can be expressed and exploited in the form of basic linear algebra operations on the vectors produced by their method. This often-cited example can be expressed as follows: $v(\text{king}) - v(\text{man}) + v(\text{woman}) \approx v(\text{queen})$, where $v(.)$ maps a word into its word embedding in vector space.

In a very recent approach, Soricut and Och (2015) exploit these regularities for unsupervised morphology induction. Their method induces vector representations for basic morphological transformations in a fully unsupervised manner. String prefix and suffix replacement rules are induced directly from the data based on the idea that morphological processes can be modeled on the basis of *prototype* transformations, i.e. vectors that are good examples of a morphological process are applied to a word vector to retrieve its inflected form. A simple example of this idea is $\uparrow d_{cars} = v(\text{cars}) - v(\text{car})$ and $v(\text{dogs}) \approx v(\text{dog}) + \uparrow d_{cars}$, which expresses the assumption that the word *car* is to *cars* what *dog* is to *dogs*. The direction vector $\uparrow d_{cars}$ represents the process of adding the plural morpheme *-s* to a noun.

While this intuition works well for frequently occurring inflectional morphology, it is not clear whether it extends to more semantically motivated derivational processes such as compounding. We study this question in the present paper. Our experiments are based on the German language, in which compounding is a highly productive phenomenon allowing for a potentially infinite number of combinations of words into compounds. This fact, coupled with the issue that many compounds are observed infrequently in data, leads to a data sparsity problem that hinders the processing of such languages. Our

20

Proceedings of the 1st Deep Machine Translation Workshop (DMTW 2015), pages 20–28,
Praha, Czech Republic, 3–4 September 2015.

contributions are as follows: After reviewing related work (Section 2), we study whether the regularities exhibited by the vector space also apply to compounds (Section 3). We examine the relationship between the components within compounds, as illustrated by the analogical relationship "*Hauptziel* is to *Ziel* what *Hauptader* is to *Ader*."[1] By leveraging this analogy we can then analyze the novel compound *Hauptmann* (captain) by searching for known string prefixes (e.g. *Haupt-*) and testing whether the resulting split compound (*Haupt|mann*) has a similar relation between its components (*haupt, mann*) as the prototypical example (*Haupt|ziel*). We induce the compound components and their prototypes and apply them in a greedy compound splitting algorithm (Section 4), which we evaluate on a gold standard compound splitting task (Section 4.3) and as a preprocessing step in a machine translation setup (Section 5).

2 Related work

Our methodology follows from recent work on morphology induction (Soricut and Och, 2015), which combines string edits with distributional semantics to split words into morphemes. In this model, morphemes are represented as string edits plus vectors, and are linked into derivation graphs. The authors consider prefix and suffix morphemes up to six characters in length; in contrast, our approach to noun compound splitting only considers components at least four characters long.

2.1 Splitting compounds for SMT

Dealing with word compounding in statistical machine translation (SMT) is essential to mitigate the sparse data problems that productive word generation causes. There are several issues that need to be addressed: *splitting* compound words into their correct components (i.e. disambiguating between split points), *deciding* whether to split a compound word at all, and, if translating into a compounding language, *merging* components into a compound word (something we do not address, but see Fraser et al. (2012) and Cap et al. (2014) for systems that do). Koehn and Knight (2003) address German compound splitting using a straightforward approach based on component frequency. They also present splitting approaches based on word alignments and POS tag information, but find that while the more resource-intensive approaches give better splitting performance (measured by gold-standard segmentations) the frequency-based method results in the best SMT performance (measured by BLEU). This is attributed to the fact that phrase-based MT system do not penalize the frequency-based method for over-splitting, since it can handle components as a phrase.

Nießen and Ney (2000), Popović et al. (2006) and Fritzinger and Fraser (2010) explore using morphological analyzers for German compound splitting, with mixed results. Since these approaches use heavy supervision within the morphological analyzer, they are orthogonal to our unsupervised approach.

It may be advantageous to split only compositional compounds, and leave lexicalized compounds whole. Weller et al. (2014) investigate this question by using distributional similarity to split only words that pass a certain threshold (i.e., where the parts proposed by the morphological analyzer are similar to the compound). Contrary to their hypothesis, they find no advantage in terms of SMT, again indicating that oversplitting is not a problem for phrase-based SMT. The use of distributional similarity as a cue for splitting is similar to the work presented in this paper. However, the approach we follow in this paper is fully unsupervised, requiring only word embeddings estimated from a monolingual corpus. Additionally, it stands out for its simplicity, making it easy to understand and implement.

2.2 Semantic compositionality

Noun compounding has also been treated within the field of distributional semantics. Reddy et al. (2011) examine English noun compounds and find that distributional co-occurrence can capture the relationship between compound parts and whole, as judged by humans in terms of 'literalness'. Schulte im Walde et al. (2013) replicate this result for German, and also show that simple window-based distributional vectors outperform syntax-based vectors.

---

[1] In vector algebra: $\uparrow d_{\mathrm{Hauptziel}} = v(\mathrm{Hauptziel}) - v(\mathrm{Ziel})$ and $v(\mathrm{Hauptader}) \approx v(\mathrm{Ader}) + \uparrow d_{\mathrm{Hauptziel}}$. The compounds translate to main goal (*Hauptziel*) and main artery (*Hauptader*). As a separate noun, *Haupt* means head.

3 Towards deeper processing of compound words

3.1 Unsupervised morphology induction from word embeddings

Our approach is based on the work of Soricut and Och (2015), who exploit regularities in the vector space to induce morphological transformations. The authors extract morphological transformations in the form of prefix and suffix replacement rules up to a maximum length of 6 characters. The method requires an initial candidate set which contains all possible prefix and suffix rules that occur in the monolingual corpus. For English, the candidate set contains rules such as `suffix:ed:ing`, which represents the suffix *ed* replaced by *ing* (e.g. *walked→walking*). This candidate set also contains overgenerated rules that do not reflect actual morphological transformations; for example `prefix:S:ϵ`[2] in *scream→cream*.

The goal is to filter the initial candidate set to remove spurious rules while keeping useful rules. For all word pairs a rule applies to, word embeddings are used to calculate a vector representing the transformation. For example, the direction vector for the rule `suffix:ing:ed` based on the pair (*walking*, *walked*) would be $\uparrow d_{walking \rightarrow ed} = v(walked) - v(walking)$. For each rule there are thus potentially as many direction vectors as word pairs it applies to. A direction vector is considered to be meaning-preserving if it successfully predicts the affix replacements of other, similar word pairs. Specifically, each direction vector is applied to the first word in the other pair and an ordered list of suggested words is produced. For example, the direction vector $\uparrow d_{walking \rightarrow ed}$ can be evaluated against (*playing*, *played*) by applying $\uparrow d_{walking \rightarrow ed}$ to *playing* to produce the predicted word form: $v(played*) = v(playing) + \uparrow d_{walking \rightarrow ed}$. This prediction is then compared against the true word embedding $v(played)$ using a generic evaluation function $E(v(played), v(playing) + \uparrow d_{walking \rightarrow ed})$.[3] If the evaluation function passes a certain threshold, we say that the direction vector *explains* the word pair. Some direction vectors explain many word pairs while others might explain very few. To judge the explanatory power of a direction vector, a *hit rate* metric is calculated, expressing the percentage of applicable word pairs for which the vector makes good predictions.[4] Each direction vector has a hit rate and a set of word pairs that it explains (its evidence set). Apart from their varying explanatory power, morphological transformation rules are also possibly ambiguous. For example, the rule `suffix:ϵ:s` can describe both the pluralization of a noun (one *house→*two *houses*) and the 3rd person singular form of a verb (I *find→*she *finds*). Different direction vectors might explain the nouns and verbs separately.

Soricut and Och (2015) retain only the most explanatory vectors by applying a recursive procedure to find the minimal set of direction vectors explaining most word pairs. We call this set of direction vectors *prototypes*, as they represent a prototypical transformation for a rule and other words are formed *in analogy to* this particular word pair. Finally, Soricut and Och (2015) show that their prototypes can be applied successfully in a word similarity task for several languages.

3.2 Compound words and the semantic vector space

According to Lieber and Štekauer (2009), compounds can be classified into several groups based on whether the semantic head is part of the compound (*endocentric* compounds; a doghouse is a also a house) or whether the semantic head is outside of the compound (*exocentric* compounds; a skinhead is not a head). In this paper, we focus on endocentric compounds, which are also the most frequent type in German. Endocentric compounds consist of a modifier and a semantic head. The semantic head specifies the basic meaning of the word and the modifier restricts this meaning. In German, the modifiers come before the semantic head; hence, the semantic head is always the last component in the compound. When applying the idea of modeling morphological processes by semantic analogy to compounds, we can represent either the semantic head or the modifier of the compound as the transformation (like the morpheme rules above). Since the head carries the compound's basic meaning, we add the modifier's vector representation to the head word in order to restrict its meaning. We expect the resulting compound to be in the neighborhood of the head word in the semantic space (e.g., a *doghouse* is close to *house*).

---

[2]ϵ denotes the empty string.

[3]We follow Soricut and Och (2015) in defining E as either the *cosine* distance or the *rank* (position in the predictions).

[4]A transformation is considered a *hit* if the evaluated score is above a certain threshold for each evaluation method E.

[5]Gloss for modifiers: (a) main, (b) federal, (c) children, (d) finance. Heads: (e) piece of work, (f) ministry, (g) man, (h) city.

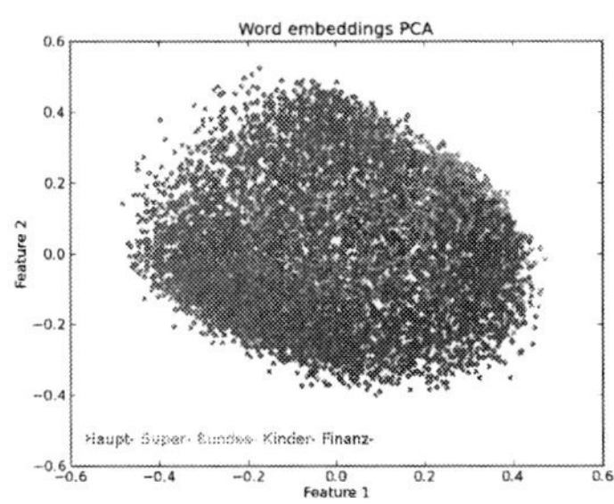 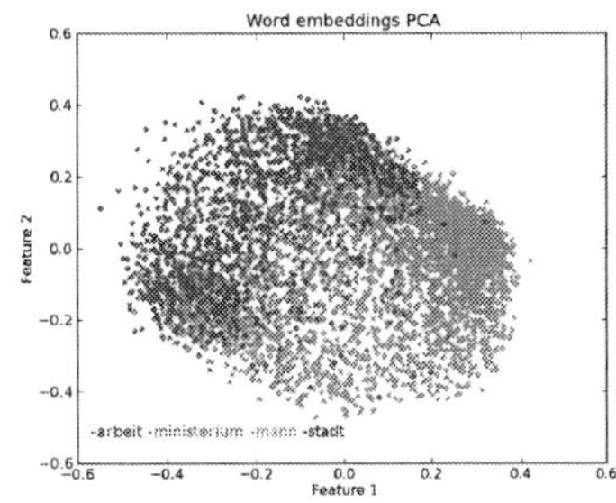

(a) Compounds with the same modifier. (b) Compounds with the same head.

Figure 1: Semantic representations of compounds based on (a) their modifiers and (b) their heads.

We illustrate this intuition by visualizing compound words and their parts in the vector space. All visualizations are produced by performing principal component analysis (PCA) to reduce the vector space from 500 to 2 dimensions. Figure 1 presents the visualization of various compounds with either the same head or the same modifier. For Figure 1a, we plot all German compounds in our dataset that have one of the modifiers *Haupt-*,[5a] *Super-*, *Bundes-*,[5b] *Kinder-*[5c] or *Finanz-*.[5d] Figure 1b, on the other hand, shows a plot for all German compounds that have one of the heads *-arbeit,*[5e] *-ministerium,*[5f] *-mann*[5g] or *-stadt*.[5h] Hence, the two plots illustrate the difference between learning vector representations for compound modifiers or heads. Words with the same modifier do not necessarily appear in close proximity in the embedding space. This is particularly true for modifiers that can be applied liberally to many head words, such as *Super-* or *Kinder-*.[5c] On the other hand, compounds with the same head are close in the embedding space. This observation is crucial to our method, as we aim to find direction vectors that generalize to as many word pairs as possible.

4 Compound induction from word embeddings

4.1 Compound extraction

Candidate extraction We compile an initial set of modifier candidates by extracting all possible prefixes with a minimum length of 4 characters.[6] We retain a modifier as a candidate if both the modifier and the rest of the word, i.e. the potential head of the compound, occur in the vocabulary. The initial candidate set contains 281K modifiers, which are reduced to 165K candidates by removing the modifiers occurring in only one word. The length of the average support set (i.e., the set of all compounds the modifier applies to) is 13.5 words. Table 1a shows the ten candidate modifiers with the biggest support sets. At this stage, the candidate set contains any modifier-head split that can be observed in the data, including candidates that do not reflect real compound splits.[7] Compound splits are not applied recursively here, as we assume that internal splits can be learned from the occurrences of the heads as individual words.[8]

Prototype extraction To find the prototype vectors that generalize best over the most words in the support set, we apply the same recursive algorithm as Soricut and Och (2015). The algorithm initially computes the direction vector for each *(modifier, compound)* pair in the support set by subtracting the embedding of the head from the embedding of the compound, e.g. $\uparrow d_{doghouse} = v(doghouse) - v(house)$. Each direction vector is then evaluated by applying it to all the word pairs in the support set, for example $v(owner) + \uparrow d_{doghouse} \overset{?}{=} v(dogowner)$ for the word pair *dog|owner*. If the resulting vector is close (according to $\overrightarrow{E}$) to the vector of the actual target compound, we add it to the evidence set of the vector. The direction vector with the largest evidence set is selected as a prototype. All pairs this prototype explains are then removed and the algorithm is applied recursively until no direction vector explains

---

[6]For efficient computation, we use a directed acyclic word graph: `https://pypi.python.org/pypi/pyDAWG`.

[7]For example, as *Para* (a river) and *dies* (this) occur in the data, an incorrect candidate split occurs for *Para|dies* (paradise).

[8]For example, for *Haupt|bahn|hof* (main train station), we observe both *Haupt|bahnhof* and *Bahn|hof*.

23

	Modifier	Support		Modifier	Support
1.	*Land-*	8387	6.	*Landes-*	5189
2.	*Kinder-*	6249	7.	*Schul-*	5011
3.	*Haupt-*	5855	8.	*Jugend-*	4855
4.	*Lande-*	5637	9.	*Ober-*	4799
5.	*Stadt-*	5327	10.	*Groß-*	4656

(a) Modifiers by size of support set.

Prototype	Evidence words
v-Zeiger	-Bewegung -Klicks -Klick -Tasten -Zeiger
v-Stämme	-Mutanten -Gene -Hirnen -Stämme
v-Kostüm	-Knopf -Hirn -Hirns -Kostüm
v-Steuerung	-Ersatz -Bedienung -Steuerung

(b) Prototypes and evidence words for *Maus-*.[9]

Table 1: Overall most common modifiers and the prototypes extracted for the modifier *Maus-*.

at least t_{evd} compounds. As the evaluation function E we use the rank of the correct word in the list of predictions and experiment with $t_{\mathrm{evd}} = \{10, 6, 4\}$. Lastly, for efficient computation we sample the evidence set down to a maximum number of 500 words.

4.2 Implementation considerations

We now turn to implementation considerations and perform an intrinsic evaluation of the prototypes.

Word embeddings   We use the German data of the *News Crawl Corpora* (2007-2014).[10] The text is truecased and tokenized, and all punctuation characters are removed, resulting in approximately 2B tokens and a vocabulary size of 3M. We use *word2vec* to estimate the word embeddings.[11] We train 500-dimensional word embeddings using the skip-gram model, a window size of 5 and a minimum word frequency threshold of 2. The latter ensures that we find word embeddings for all words that occur at least twice in the corpus, which is useful as long compounds may occur only very few times.

Treatment of interfixes (Fugenelemente)   For mostly phonetic reasons, German allows the insertion of a limited set of characters between the modifier and the head. As learning this set is not the aim of our work, we simply allow the fixed set of interfixes {*-s-*, *-es-*} to occur. For any combination of interfix and casing of the head word, we add the tuple of the two to the support set of the corresponding modifier.

What do the prototypes encode?   An inspection of the prototypes for each modifier shows that the differences between them are not always clear cut. Often, however, each prototype expresses one specific sense of the modifier. Table 1b illustrates this on the example of the German modifier *Maus-* (Engl. *mouse*), which can refer to both the animal and the computer device. Although there are more than two prototype vectors, it is interesting to observe that the two word senses are almost fully separated.

Calculating the hit rate   To evaluate the quality of the prototypes, we use the hit rate metric defined by Soricut and Och (2015). A direction vector's hit rate is the percentage of relevant word pairs that can be explained by the vector. A prediction is explainable if the actual target word is among the top t_{rank} predictions and, optionally, if the cosine similarity between the two is at least t_{sim}.

The implementation of this evaluation function E requires the calculation of the cosine distance between a newly created vector and the word vector of every item in the vocabulary. Since this score is calculated N times for every of the N word pairs (i.e., N^2 times), this is a computationally extremely expensive process. For more efficient computation, we use an approximate k-nearest neighbor search method.[12] While this is not a lossless search method, it offers an adjustable trade-off between the model's prediction accuracy and running time.[13] For a standard setting ($t_{\mathrm{evd}} = 6, t_{\mathrm{rank}} = 80$), the hit rates using approximate and exact rank are 85.9% and 60.9% respectively. This shows that the hit rates obtained with the approximate method are more optimistic, which will affect how the prototype vectors are extracted. Additionally, restricting both *rank* and *similarity* ($t_{\mathrm{rank}} = 80, t_{\mathrm{sim}} \geq 0.5$) leads to lower hit rates (25.9% for approximate and 15% for exact rank).

---

[9] Words are related to mouse pointer (*Zeiger*), biological genus (*Stämme*), mouse costume (*Kostüm*) and control (*Steuerung*).

[10] http://www.statmt.org/wmt15/translation-task.html

[11] https://code.google.com/p/word2vec/

[12] https://github.com/spotify/annoy

[13] With this fast approx. search method the total training time would be just below 7 days if run on a single 16 core machine.

	(a) Mean hit rate		(b) Mean cosine sim.		(c) % with prototypes		(d) Mean # of prototypes	
$t_{\mathrm{rank}} =$	80	100	80	100	80	100	80	100
$t_{\mathrm{evd}} = 4$	26%	22%	0.39	0.39	8.93%	9.52%	4.20	4.16
$t_{\mathrm{evd}} = 6$	31%	26%	0.43	0.43	5.13%	5.47%	3.29	3.30
$t_{\mathrm{evd}} = 10$	36%	31%	0.45	0.45	2.91%	3.14%	2.25	2.29

Table 2: Overview of the influence of the hyperparameters on prototype extraction.

Influence of thresholds Table 2 compares the parameters of our model based on (a) the mean hit rate, (b) cosine similarity, (c) the percentage of candidate modifiers with at least one prototype and (d) the mean number of prototypes per rule. Higher values of t_{evd} (minimum evidence set size) lead to better quality in terms of hit rate and cosine similarity as prototypes have to be able to cover a larger number of word pairs in order to be retained. The rank threshold t_{rank} also behaves as expected. Reducing t_{rank} to 80 means that the predicted vectors are of higher quality as they need to be closer to the true compound embeddings. Tables (c) and (d) illustrate that the more restrictive parameter settings reduce the amount of modifiers for which prototypes can be extracted. From a total of 165399 candidate prefixes, only 3%-10% are retained in the end for our settings. Similarly, the average number of prototypes per modifier also decreases with more restrictive settings. Interestingly, however, for the most restrictive setting ($t_{\mathrm{evd}} = 10$, $t_{\mathrm{rank}} = 80$), this number is still a relatively high 2 prototypes per vector.

4.3 Compound splitting

To obtain a clearer view of the quality of the extracted compound representations, we apply the prototypes to a compound splitting task.

Splitting compounds by semantic analogy The extracted compound modifiers and their prototypes can be employed directly to split a compound into its components. Algorithm 1 presents the greedy algorithm applied to every word in the text. V is the word embedding vocabulary, M is the set of extracted modifiers with their prototypes, and PREFIXES(.) is a function returning all string prefixes.

1: **procedure** DECOMPOUND($word$, V, M)
2:     $modifiers \leftarrow \{m \mid p \leftarrow$ PREFIXES$(word)$ if $p \in M\}$
3:     **if** $modifiers = \emptyset$ OR $word \notin V$ **then**
4:         **return** $word$
5:     $bestModifier \leftarrow \emptyset$
6:     **for** $modifier \in modifiers$ **do**
7:         $head \leftarrow word$ without $modifier$ ▷ e.g. house $\leftarrow$ doghouse without dog-
8:         **if** $head \in V$ **then**
9:             **for** $(head_{proto}, word_{proto}) \in modifier$ **do**
10:                Evaluate "$word$ is to $head$ what $word_{proto}$ is to $head_{proto}$"
11:                ▷ e.g. doghouse is to house what dogowner is to owner
12:                Update $bestModifier$ if this is the best match so far
13:     **return** $word$ split based on $bestModifier$

Algorithm 1: Greedy compound splitting algorithm.

Compounds may only be split if (a) the full compound word is in the vocabulary V, i.e. it has been observed at least twice in the training data (Line 3), (b) it has a string prefix in the modifier set and this modifier has at least one prototype (Line 3), (c) the potential head word resulting from splitting the compound based on the modifier is also in our vocabulary (Line 8). The last case, namely that the compound head candidate is not in the vocabulary can occur for two reasons: either this potential head is a valid word that has not been observed frequently enough or, the more common reason, the substring is not a valid word in the language.[14] The algorithm's coverage can be increased by backing off to a frequency-based method if conditions (a) or (c) are violated. The core of the algorithm is the evaluation of meaning

---

[14] For example, when applying the algorithm to *Herrengarderobe* (male cloak room), two possible prefixes apply: *Herr* and *Herren*. In the first case, the remaining slice is *engarderobe*, which is not a valid word and thus the candidate prefix is discarded.

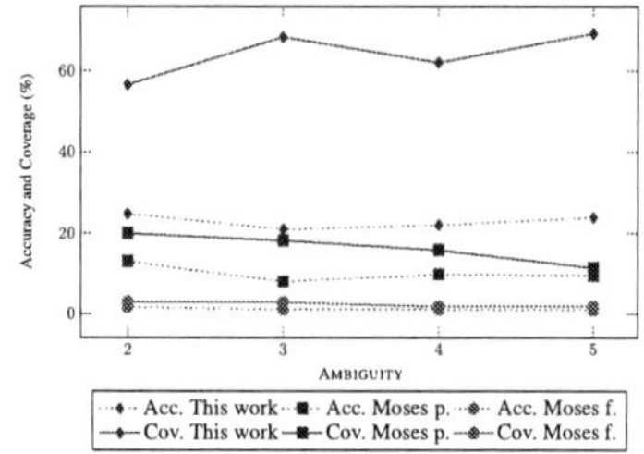

| | This work | | Moses (partial) | | Moses (full) | |
Scenario	Acc.	Cov.	Acc.	Cov.	Acc.	Cov.
Full test set	27.43	58.45	18.04	31.41	6.57	13.75
2 splits	24.94	56.75	13.13	20.13	1.79	3.11
3 splits	21.10	68.37	8.04	18.35	1.21	2.92
4 splits	22.09	62.11	9.98	15.91	1.19	1.90
5 splits	24.04	69.23	9.62	11.54	0.96	1.92

(a) Evaluation of highly ambiguous compounds.   (b) Evaluation of all compounds and highly ambiguous compounds only.

Table 3: Gold standard evaluation of compound splitting.

preservation in Line 10. This evaluation is performed using the *rank*-based and *cosine similarity*-based evaluation functions. Modifiers that do not pass the thresholds defined for these functions are discarded as weak splits. To split compounds with more than two components, the algorithm is applied recursively.

General evaluation   We use the test set from Henrich and Hinrichs (2011), which contains a list of 54569 compounds annotated with binary splits. As we only consider prefixes with a minimal length of 4 characters, we filter the test set accordingly, leaving 50651 compounds. Moses (Koehn et al., 2007) offers a compound splitter that splits a word if the geometric average of the frequencies of its components is higher than the frequency of the compound. We trained two instances of this compound splitter to use as references: one using the German monolingual dataset used to train the Word2Vec models and a second using a subset of the previous dataset.[15] Unlike our method, the two baseline systems do not consider the meaning preservation criteria of the compound splitting rules that are applied. Results for the full test set (accuracy and coverage, i.e. $\frac{|\text{correct splits}|}{|\text{compounds}|}$ and $\frac{|\text{compounds split}|}{|\text{compounds}|}$) are presented in the first row of Table 3b.

Evaluation of highly ambiguous compounds   The strength of our method resides in the capacity to discriminate good candidate splits from bad ones. By capturing the meaning relation between compounds and their components, we are able to decide for a given word which splitting rule is the most appropriate. With this in mind, our approach should stand out in contexts where multiple split points may apply to a compound. We simulate different ambiguity scenarios based on Henrich and Hinrich's gold standard dataset: We extract compounds for which we find 2, 3, 4, and 5 potential split points.[16] The resulting test sets consists of 18571, 1815, 842 and 104 compounds, respectively. For all compound splitting experiments, we use the prototype vectors extracted with the parameters $t_{\text{evd}} = 6$ and $t_{\text{rank}} = 100$.

Table 3b presents accuracy and coverage for the compounds within the different ambiguity scenarios. To better visualize the trends for highly ambiguous compounds, we plot the accuracy and coverage scores in relation to the ambiguity of the compounds in Table 3a. The analogy-based method outperforms the frequency-based baselines in both coverage and accuracy. While for the Moses splitter, the coverage decreases with increasing ambiguity, the opposite behavior is shown by our approach, as having more possible splits results in a higher number of direction vectors increasing the likelihood of obtaining meaning-preserving splits. This experiment shows that the analogy-based compound splitter is advantageous for words that can potentially be explained by several candidate splits.

5   Compound splitting for machine translation

Translation setup   We use the Moses decoder (Koehn et al., 2007) to train a phrase-based MT system on the English–German *Common crawl* parallel corpus and *WMT news test* 2010 (tuning). Word alignment is performed with Giza++ (Och and Ney, 2003). We use a 3rd order language model estimated using IRSTLM (Federico et al., 2008), as well as lexicalized reordering. The test data set is *WMT news*

---

[15] Subset: *News Crawl 2007-2009* (275M tokens, 2.09M types). Full set: *News Crawl 2007-2014* (2B tokens, 3M types).

[16] Each string prefix which occurs as a separate word produces a potential split point (indicated by ǀ). The potential split points may not be linguistically motivated and can lead to correct (*general|stabs*) or incorrect splits (*gene|rals|tabs*). Examples include Einkaufǀsǀwagen, Eisǀenǀbahnǀunternehmen, Wissenǀsǀchaftǀsǀpark and Geneǀraǀlǀsǀtabǀs.

	(a) No comp. splitting			(b) OOV only			(c) Rare: $c(w) < 20$			(d) All words		
	Splits	BLEU	MTR	Splits	BLEU	MTR	Splits	BLEU	MTR	Splits	BLEU	MTR
Moses splitter	0	17.6	25.5	226	17.6	25.7[A]	231	17.6	25.7	244	17.9	25.8[A]
This work				317	17.6	25.8[A]	744	**18.2**[ABC] **26.1**[ABC]		1616	17.7	26.3[A]

[A] Stat. sign. against (a) at $p < 0.05$ [B] Stat. sign. against Moses splitter at same c(w) at $p < 0.05$ [C] Stat. sign. against best Moses splitter (d) at $p < 0.05$

Table 4: Translation results for various integration methods.

test 2015,[17] which contains approx. 2100 de-en sentence pairs and 10000 tokens (with one reference translation). We compare our method against a baseline translation system with no compound splitter, and the same system implementing Moses' default compound splitting tool. The test set contains 2111 out-of-vocabulary word types (natural OOV words), which yields a total of 2765 unknown tokens, consisting mostly of compounds, brand names, and city names. This implies that 22.16% (word types) resp. 7.15% (tokens) of the test corpus are unknown to the baseline system.

Translation experiments To test the analogy-based compound splitter on a realistic setting, we perform a standard machine translation task. We translate a German text using a translation baseline system with no compound handling (a), a translation system integrating the standard Moses compound splitter tool trained using the best-performing settings, and a translation system using our analogy-based compound splitter. We test the following basic methods of integration: Splitting only words that are OOV to the translation model (b), splitting all words that occur less than 20 times in the training corpus (c),and applying the compound splitters to every word in the datasets (d). Table 4 shows the results of these translation experiments. For each experiment, we report BLEU (Papineni et al., 2002), METEOR (Denkowski and Lavie, 2014), and the number of compound splits performed on the test set. Statistical significance tests are performed using bootstrap resampling (Koehn, 2004).

Discussion The results show that when applied without restrictions, our method splits a large number of words and leads to minor improvements. When applied only to rare words the splitter produces statistically significant improvements in both BLEU and METEOR over the best frequency-based compound splitter. This difference indicates that a better method for deciding which words the splitter should be applied to could lead to further improvements. Overall, the output of the analogy-based compound splitter is more beneficial to the machine translation system than the baseline splitter.

6 Conclusion

In this paper, we have studied whether regularities in the semantic word embedding space can be exploited to model the composition of compound words based on analogy. To approach this question, we made the following contributions: First, we evaluated whether properties of compounds can be found in the semantic vector space. We found that this space lends itself to modeling compounds based on their semantic head. Based on this finding, we discussed how to extract compound transformations and prototypes following the method of Soricut and Och (2015) and proposed an algorithm for applying these structures to compound splitting. Our experiments show that the analogy-based compound splitter outperforms a commonly used compound splitter on a gold standard task. Our novel compound splitter is particularly adept at splitting highly ambiguous compounds. Finally, we applied the analogy-based compound splitter in a machine translation task and found that it compares favorably to the commonly used shallow frequency-based method.

Acknowledgements Joachim Daiber is supported by the EXPERT (EXPloiting Empirical appRoaches to Translation) Initial Training Network (ITN) of the European Union's Seventh Framework Programme. Stella Frank is supported by funding from the European Unions Horizon 2020 research and innovation programme under grant agreement Nr. 645452.

---

[17] http://www.statmt.org/wmt15/translation-task.html

References

Fabienne Cap, Alexander Fraser, Marion Weller, and Aoife Cahill. 2014. How to produce unseen teddy bears: Improved morphological processing of compounds in SMT. In *Proceedings of the 14th Conference of the European Chapter of the Association for Computational Linguistics (EACL)*.

Michael Denkowski and Alon Lavie. 2014. Meteor universal: Language specific translation evaluation for any target language. In *Proceedings of the Ninth Workshop on Statistical Machine Translation*.

Marcello Federico, Nicola Bertoldi, and Mauro Cettolo. 2008. IRSTLM: An open source toolkit for handling large scale language models. In *Proceedings of Interspeech 2008 - 9th Annual Conference of the International Speech Communication Association*.

Alexander Fraser, Marion Weller, Aoife Cahill, and Fabienne Cap. 2012. Modeling inflection and word-formation in SMT. In *Proceedings of the 13th Conference of the European Chapter of the Association for Computational Linguistics (EACL)*.

Fabienne Fritzinger and Alexander Fraser. 2010. How to avoid burning ducks: Combining linguistic analysis and corpus statistics for German compound processing. In *Proceedings of the ACL 2010 Joint Fifth Workshop on Statistical Machine Translation and Metrics (MATR)*.

Verena Henrich and Erhard W. Hinrichs. 2011. Determining immediate constituents of compounds in GermaNet. In *Proceedings of the International Conference on Recent Advances in Natural Language Processing 2011*.

Philipp Koehn and Kevin Knight. 2003. Empirical methods for compound splitting. In *Proceedings of the 10th Conference of the European Chapter of the Association for Computational Linguistics (EACL)*.

Philipp Koehn, Hieu Hoang, Alexandra Birch, Chris Callison-Burch, Marcello Federico, Nicola Bertoldi, Brooke Cowan, Wade Shen, Christine Moran, Richard Zens, Chris Dyer, Ondrej Bojar, Alexandra Constantin, and Evan Herbst. 2007. Moses: Open source toolkit for statistical machine translation. In *Proceedings of the 45th Annual Meeting of the Association for Computational Linguistics (ACL)*.

Philipp Koehn. 2004. Statistical significance tests for machine translation evaluation. In *Proceedings of the 9th Conference on Empirical Methods in Natural Language Processing (EMNLP)*.

Rochelle Lieber and Pavol Štekauer. 2009. *The Oxford handbook of compounding*. Oxford University Press.

Tomas Mikolov, Wen-tau Yih, and Geoffrey Zweig. 2013. Linguistic regularities in continuous space word representations. In *Proceedings of the 2013 Conference of the North American Chapter of the Association for Computational Linguistics (NAACL)*.

Sonja Nießen and Hermann Ney. 2000. Improving SMT quality with morpho-syntactic analysis. In *Proceedings of the 18th International Conference on Computational Linguistics (COLING)*.

Franz Josef Och and Hermann Ney. 2003. A systematic comparison of various statistical alignment models. *Computational Linguistics*, 29(1):19–51.

Kishore Papineni, Salim Roukos, Todd Ward, and Wei-Jing Zhu. 2002. BLEU: A method for automatic evaluation of machine translation. In *Proceedings of the 40th Annual Meeting of the Association for Computational Linguistics (ACL)*.

Maja Popović, Daniel Stein, and Hermann Ney. 2006. Statistical machine translation of German compound words. In *Proceedings of FinTal - 5th International Conference on Natural Language Processing*.

Siva Reddy, Diana McCarthy, and Suresh Manandhar. 2011. An empirical study on compositionality in compound nouns. In *Proceedings of the 5th International Joint Conference on Natural Language Processing*.

Sabine Schulte im Walde, Stefan Müller, and Stephen Roller. 2013. Exploring vector space models to predict the compositionality of German noun-noun compounds. In *Proceedings of the 2nd Joint Conference on Lexical and Computational Semantics (*SEM)*.

Radu Soricut and Franz Och. 2015. Unsupervised morphology induction using word embeddings. In *Proceedings of the 2015 Conference of the North American Chapter of the Association for Computational Linguistics (NAACL)*.

Marion Weller, Fabienne Cap, Stefan Müller, Sabine Schulte im Walde, and Alexander Fraser. 2014. Distinguishing degrees of compositionality in compound splitting for statistical machine translation. In *Proceedings of the First Workshop on Computational Approaches to Compound Analysis (ComaComa) at COLING*.

Delimiting Morphosyntactic Search Space
with Source-Side Reordering Models

Joachim Daiber and **Khalil Sima'an**
Institute for Logic, Language and Computation
University of Amsterdam
Science Park 107, 1098 XG Amsterdam, The Netherlands
{j.daiber,k.simaan}@uva.nl

Abstract

Source-side reordering has recently seen a surge in popularity in machine translation research, often providing enormous reductions in translation time and showing good empirical results in translation quality. For many language pairs, however—especially for translation into morphologically rich languages—the assumptions of these models may be too crude. But while such language pairs call for more complex models, these could increase the search space to an extent that would diminish their benefits. In this paper, we examine the question whether purely syntax-oriented adaptation models (i.e., models only considering word order) can be used as a means to delimit the search space for more complex morphosyntactic models. We propose a model based on a popular preordering algorithm (Lerner and Petrov, 2013). This novel preordering model is able to produce both n-best word order predictions as well as distributions over possible word order choices in the form of a lattice and is therefore a good fit for use by richer models taking into account aspects of both syntax and morphology. We show that the integration of non-local language model features can be beneficial for the model's preordering quality and evaluate the space of potential word order choices the model produces.

1 Introduction

A significant amount of research in machine translation has recently focused on methods for effectively restricting the often prohibitively large search space of statistical machine translation systems. One popular method providing a crude but theoretically motivated restriction of this space is preordering (also pre-reordering or source-side reordering). In preordering, the source sentence is rearranged to reflect the assumed word order in the target language. This provides an effective method for handling word and phrase movements caused by long-range dependencies, which usually enlarge the search space significantly. After preordering, decoding can be performed in fully monotone or close to monotone fashion, making the method applicable to a wide range of translation systems, including ngram-based translation (Marino et al., 2006) and recent approaches to neural machine translation (Bahdanau et al., 2015, inter alia). While systems using this approach have in the past not always been able to show improvements in translation quality over systems using more exhaustive search algorithms or specialized reordering models, preordering provides several benefits: Apart from facilitating the integration of additional information sources such as paraphrases, preordering approaches provide significant improvements in runtime performance. Jehl et al. (2014), for example, report an 80-fold speed improvement using their preordering system compared to a standard system producing translations of the same quality.

Preordering systems can be compared along several dimensions. The main distinctions are whether the reordering rules are specified manually (Collins et al., 2005) or automatically learnt from data (Lerner and Petrov, 2013; Khalilov and Sima'an, 2012). Furthermore, approaches differ in the types of syntactic structures they assume. Systems may use either source or target syntax (Lerner and Petrov, 2013; Khalilov and Sima'an, 2012), both source and target syntax or no syntax at all (e.g. DeNero and Uszkoreit (2011)). In this paper, we focus on approaches using only source-side syntax. Dependency grammar offers a flexible and light-weight syntactic framework that can cover a large number of languages and

Proceedings of the 1st Deep Machine Translation Workshop (DMTW 2015), pages 29–38,
Praha, Czech Republic, 3–4 September 2015.

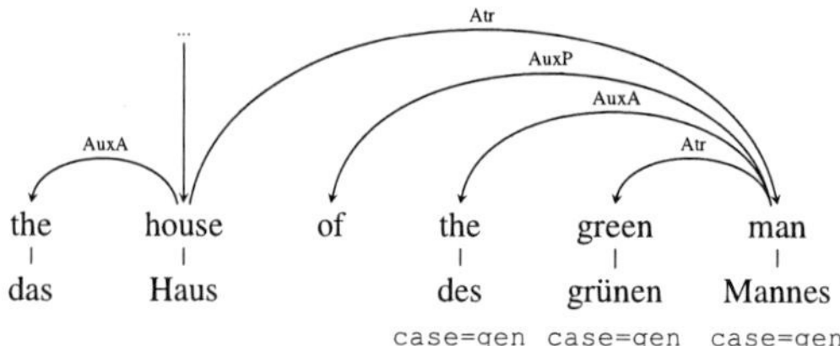

Figure 1: Translation of an English prepositional phrase as a genitive noun phrase in German.

provides suitable syntactic representations for reordering. Hence, we follow Lerner and Petrov (2013), in using dependency trees for the representation of source syntax. After reviewing related work in Section 2, we propose a model and general framework for producing the space of potential word order choices in Section 3. Since the possible reorderings in source-syntax approaches to preordering are often restricted by the source trees, the annotation conventions of the training treebank and hence the form of the predicted dependency trees play a significant role for the preordering system. We will briefly describe the treebank format and other details of the experimental setup in Section 4.1. Section 4.2 and 4.3 present results of the experimental evaluation and a discussion of these results. We conclude in Section 5.

2   Related work

Various approaches to preordering have been explored in the literature. A brief overview of the work establishing the background for the presented method will be given in this section.

2.1   Gold experiments

To investigate the upper bounds of preordering in terms of quality and integration with translation systems, several researchers have performed studies with gold reorderings. Khalilov and Sima'an (2012), as well as Herrmann et al. (2013) compare various systems and provide oracle scores for syntax-based preordering models. These studies show that *perfect gold* reorderings estimated via automatic alignments enable translation systems enormous jumps in translation quality and further provide improvements in the size of the downstream translation models. Additionally, it was found that properties of the source syntax representation, such as how deeply phrase structure trees are nested, can significantly hamper the quality of these approaches.

2.2   Preordering with source syntax

Jehl et al. (2014) learn order decisions for sibling nodes of the source-side parse tree and explore the space of possible permutations using a depth-first branch-and-bound search. In later work, this model is further improved by replacing the logistic regression classifier with a feed-forward neural network (de Gispert et al., 2015). This modification shows both improved empirical results and eliminates the need for feature engineering. Similarly, Lerner and Petrov (2013) learn classifiers to permute the tree nodes of a dependency tree. The main difference here is that the permutation of up to 6 tree nodes is predicted directly instead of predicting the orientation of individual node pairs. Figure 1 shows an example dependency tree that can serve as input to such systems.

2.3   Preordering without source syntax

Tromble and Eisner (2009) apply machine learning techniques to learn ITG-like orientations (straight or inverted order) for each pair of input words in the sentence. The best reordering is then determined using a standard $O(n^3)$ chart parsing algorithm. Generally, systems not relying on syntactic information fill the full spectrum from simple to advanced approaches. A simple approach is the application of multiple MT systems (Costa-jussà and Fonollosa, 2006): one MT system learns the preordering (i.e. the translation of the source sentence to its preordered form, $s \rightarrow s'$) and the second MT system learns to translate the preordered form into the target sentence ($s' \rightarrow t$). More advanced approaches include the automatic induction of parse trees from aligned data (DeNero and Uszkoreit, 2011).

3 Generating the space of potential word order choices

3.1 Going beyond first-best predictions

Our work is related to the work of Lerner and Petrov (2013), in which feature-rich discriminative classifiers are trained to directly predict the target-side word order based on source-side dependency trees. This is done by traversing the dependency tree in a top-down fashion and predicting the target order for each tree family (a family consists of a syntactic head and its children). To address sparsity issues, two models are introduced. For each subtree, the 1-step model directly predicts the target order of the child nodes. Unlike other preordering models, which often restrict the space of possible permutations, e.g. by the permutations permissible under the ITG constraint (Wu, 1997), the space of possible permutations for each subtree is restricted to the k permutations most commonly observed in the data. The blow-up in permutation space with growing numbers of children is addressed by a second model, the 2-step model. This model decreases the number of nodes involved in any single word order decision. A binary classifier (pivot classifier, in analogy to quicksort) first predicts whether a child node should occur to the left or to the right of the head of the subtree. The order of the set of nodes to the left and to the right of the head is then directly predicted as in the 1-step model. In total, the 2-step approach requires one pivot classifier, 5 classifiers for the children on the left and 5 classifiers for the children on the right.

The cascade-of-classifiers approach used by this method (i.e. first predict the pivot, then predict the left and right orders, then recurse) exhibits the problematic characteristic that classification errors occurring near the top of the tree will propagate disproportionately to later decisions. The goal of the present work is to enable the preordering model to pass its decisions to a more complex morphosyntactic model. Hence, this error propagation issue may become problematic. In order to address this problem, we extract n-best word order predictions from the classifier decisions. A distribution over the n-best preordered sentences can then be passed to the subsequent model or directly to a machine translation decoder either as a list of options or in the form of a lattice. Similar to the practice of n-best list extraction in MT decoders such as Moses, the preordering problem likewise allows the extraction of n-best preordering options either with or without additional integration of non-local features such as a language model.

General model   We define a model over the possible orders of the tokens in the source sentence. Given a source sentence $\mathbf{s}$ and a corresponding dependency tree τ, π is the permutation of source tokens and π_h is a local permutation of a single tree family under head h. The score of a source word order $\mathbf{s}'$ is:

$$P(\mathbf{s}' \mid \mathbf{s}, \tau) = \prod_{h \in \tau} P_T(\pi_h \mid \mathbf{s}, h, \tau) \tag{1}$$

$$P_T(\pi \mid \mathbf{s}, h, \tau) = P(\psi \mid \mathbf{s}, h, \tau) P_L(\pi_L \mid \mathbf{s}, h, \tau) P_R(\pi_R \mid \mathbf{s}, h, \tau)$$

For each dependency tree family, the generative story of this model is as follows: First, decide on the positions of the child nodes relative to the head, i.e. $P(\psi \mid \mathbf{s}, h, \tau)$. Then, decide the order of the nodes on the left, $P_L(\pi_L \mid \mathbf{s}, h, \tau)$, and on the right, $P_R(\pi_R \mid \mathbf{s}, h, \tau)$.

Preordering algorithm   Based on this model, we introduce the following preordering algorithm. For each source dependency tree family with head h, we extract the best k_T local word order predictions using the function PREORDERFAMILY in Algorithm 1. $\Psi(cs)$ is the set of possible choices when distributing nodes using the pivot classifier. Given a set of child nodes cs, $\Pi(cs)$ is the set of their possible permutations. The best permutations for the left and right side are extracted by the following methods:

$$\hat{\pi}_L \leftarrow \underset{\pi_L \in \Pi(cs_L)}{\arg \operatorname{best} k} P_L(\pi_L \mid \mathbf{s}, h, \tau) \quad (2) \qquad \hat{\pi}_R \leftarrow \underset{\pi_R \in \Pi(cs_R)}{\arg \operatorname{best} k} P_R(\pi_R \mid \mathbf{s}, h, \tau) \quad (3)$$

Since this model is implemented using multi-class classifiers, finding the best k_O permutations for the nodes to the left and right of the head, i.e. Equation 2 and 3, only require one multi-class classification. Following Lerner and Petrov (2013), we restrict the set of allowed permutations $\Pi(cs)$ to the 20 most common permutations observed in the training data. Given a pivot decision $\hat{\psi}$ (which children go left and which go right of the head?), LEFT($\hat{\psi}$) returns the children to the left and RIGHT($\hat{\psi}$) returns the children to the right of the head. The function PERMUTATION($\hat{\psi}, \hat{\pi}_L, \hat{\pi}_R$) returns the word order permutation resulting from the pivot decision, the left children order and the right children order.

Algorithm 1 n-best preordering of a source tree family

> **procedure** PREORDERFAMILY(h, τ)
> $cs \leftarrow$ CHILDREN(h, τ)
> $topk \leftarrow$ PRIORITYQUEUE()
>
>   **for** $\hat{\psi} \leftarrow \arg\text{bestk}_{\psi \in \Psi(cs)} P(\psi \mid \mathbf{s}, h, \tau)$ **do** $\triangleright$ Pivot decisions
> $cs_L \leftarrow$ LEFT($\hat{\psi}$)
> $cs_R \leftarrow$ RIGHT($\hat{\psi}$)
>   **for** $\hat{\pi}_L \leftarrow \arg\text{bestk}_{\pi_L \in \Pi(cs_L)} P_L(\pi_L \mid \mathbf{s}, h, \tau)$ **do** $\triangleright$ Left order decisions
>   **for** $\hat{\pi}_R \leftarrow \arg\text{bestk}_{\pi_R \in \Pi(cs_R)} P_R(\pi_R \mid \mathbf{s}, h, \tau)$ **do** $\triangleright$ Right order decisions
> $p \leftarrow$ PERMUTATION($\hat{\psi}, \hat{\pi}_L, \hat{\pi}_R$)
>   TOPK.PUSH($P(\hat{\psi} \mid \mathbf{s}, h, \tau) \times P_L(\hat{\pi}_L \mid \mathbf{s}, h, \tau) \times P_R(\hat{\pi}_R \mid \mathbf{s}, h, \tau), p$)
>   **return** TOPK.TAKE(k_T)

For n children, there are $S(n, 2)$ possible pivot decisions, where $S(n, k)$ is the Stirling number of the second kind. Since this number grows exponentially with n, it would be extremely expensive, if not infeasible, to consider all possible pivot decisions. Hence, similar to the extraction of $\hat{\pi}_L$ and $\hat{\pi}_R$, the extraction of the possible choices for the pivot decision, i.e. $\hat{\psi}$, is implemented as k-best Viterbi extraction from a conditional random field classifier: $\hat{\psi} \leftarrow \arg\text{bestk}_{\psi \in \Psi(cs)} P(\psi \mid \mathbf{s}, h, \tau)$.

This approximation means that only the best k_P pivot decisions are considered. Hence, for each of the maximally k_P possible ways to distribute the child nodes when taking the pivot decision, two classifications have to be performed: one for the nodes on the left and one for the nodes on the right. The extraction of n-best word order predictions therefore requires $2 \times k_P$ classifications for each source-side tree family. With the best k_T local permutations for each source tree family, we can then extract n-best permutations for the whole tree. If all order decisions in this model are local to their tree family, extracting the best permutations for the whole sentence is straight-forward. In the next section, we will discuss how this assumption changes with the introduction of non-local features.

3.2 Integration of non-local features

While the basic model introduced by Lerner and Petrov (2013) shows promising empirical performance, it also makes fairly strong independence assumptions. The generative process assumes that the local order decisions occur only within individual tree families defined by the dependency tree. Hence, a local word order decision at any point in the dependency tree is fully independent from any other decision in the tree. For languages such as German, this independence assumption can be problematic because the position of a constituent in the sentence bracket influences the internal word order (Müller, 2015). For example, certain positions allow for scrambling, i.e. more or less free movement of some constituents within a specific area of the sentence. Previous work on preordering (Khalilov and Sima'an, 2012) has shown that the integration of even a weak trigram language model estimated over the gold word order predictions s′ can improve preordering performance. Since we use projective dependency trees, which are internally converted to a flat phrase structure representation, the model can be expressed in the form of a weighted context-free grammar in which labels encode the order of the constituents. One method to weaken the independence assumptions of this grammar is the direct integration of a language model (LM). This idea is reminiscent of the integration of the finite state language model with the synchronous context-free grammar used in hierarchical phrase-based machine translation (Chiang, 2007).

Hence, instead of searching for $\hat{s}' = \arg\max_{s'} P(s' \mid s, \tau)$, the search will now include the ngram language model, such that: $\hat{s}' = \arg\max_{s'} P(s' \mid s, \tau) P_{LM}(s')$. This integration can be performed in three ways: the simplest form of integration, which is fast but allows for significant search errors, is to generate an n-best list of word order predictions using the $-$LM preordering model (i.e., without the LM or other non-local features) and re-score this list using the language model. On the other end of the spectrum, the language model can be integrated by performing a full intersection between the preordering CFG and the finite state automaton that defines the language model (Bar-Hillel et al., 1961). While this would allow for exact search, this method is found to be too slow in practice. A compromise between these two extremes is cube pruning (Chiang, 2007), in which the inner LM cost as well as the left and right LM states are stored on each node, so that it is possible to perform bottom-up dynamic programming to efficiently determine the total LM cost by combining the intermediate node costs. Keeping the properties required for performing cube pruning, we use the more general log-linear model formulation (Och and Ney, 2002) by defining the search for the best word order prediction $\hat{s}'$ as follows:

$$\hat{s}' = \arg\max_{s'} P(s' \mid s, \tau)^{\lambda_{RM}} P_{LM}(s)^{\lambda_{LM}} \ldots = \arg\max_{s'} \prod_i \phi_i(s')^{\lambda_i} = \arg\max_{s'} \sum_i \lambda_i \log \phi_i(s')$$

On every source tree node, cube pruning is performed with a beam size of $k_{+\text{LM}}$ word order predictions. The best $k_{-\text{LM}}$ preordering labels are considered for expansion. Additionally, we prune all preordering labels for which the language model cost is higher than the language model cost of the original source tree order (i.e., performing no reordering). To make individual configurations comparable, we follow Chiang (2007) in adding a heuristic cost that approximates the cost of the first $m - 1$ words: $\log P_{\text{LM}}(e_1 \ldots e_l)$ where $l = \min\{m - 1, |e|\}$ for an m-gram language model. In our case, e is the vector of preordered source-side words at a specific tree node. We add the heuristic cost of all relevant feature functions ϕ_i for the set of language model feature functions Φ_{LM} as $\sum_{i \in \Phi_{\text{LM}}} \lambda_i \log \phi_i(e_1 \ldots e_l)$.

Feature functions

The log-linear model formulation makes the addition of arbitrary local and non-local features possible; i.e., any suitable feature function can be added to this model. We use the following initial features:

Lexicalized preordering model The most important feature is the lexicalized preordering model $P(s' \mid s, \tau)$ introduced in Section 3.1. It is lexicalized since it makes decisions based on the source words while other models might make predictions based on non-lexical information (e.g., POS tags).

Language models To weaken the strong independence assumptions of this model, we add a generic ngram language model over the gold word order predictions s', a language model over part-of-speech tags and a class-based language model.

Unlexicalized preordering model As the lexicalized preordering model might run into sparsity issues, we add as a further feature function a weaker model $P_W(\pi \mid h, cs)$, where cs is the set of children represented by their dependency label and by whether they have children, and h is the head represented by its POS tag. The model is estimated via maximum likelihood estimation from the oracle word order choices restricted by the source-side dependency trees (*oracle tree reorderings*). These tree-restricted oracle word order choices differ from the free oracle word order choices in that words are not allowed to move out of the constituents of the dependency tree. For example, in the English sentence "the house of the green man" in Figure 1, the word "green" would always be on the same side of "house" as "man" since as a dependent of "man", it will always move with "man" in relation to its grandparent "house".

3.3   Applicability of the model

While we focused on one particular n-best preordering method in Section 3.1, the general model introduced in Section 3.2 is applicable to any preordering model over source trees for which n-best candidates can be extracted. For example, the pairwise neural network-based method by de Gispert et al. (2015) can be used either by extracting n-best decisions directly from the graph or, more efficiently, by applying the CKY algorithm on the space of permutations permissible under ITG (Tromble and Eisner, 2009).

4 Experiments

We perform various experiments to evaluate these ideas. Before providing experimental results and evaluation, we will describe selected details of the preordering system and the experimental setup. Further, we highlight assumptions and decisions that were necessary for training the system.

4.1 Implementation and experimental setup

Source-side syntax For preordering to work reliably, the dependency representation should fulfill certain requirements: *Flatter* trees increase the space of covered permutations while the information in the left-out segmentations may be recoverable by the preordering model. Additionally, whenever reasonable, content-bearing elements should be treated as the head.[1] We use a customized version of the treebank collection and transformation tool HamleDT (Zeman et al., 2012) for this purpose.

Model training For training the model, we mostly follow the process from Lerner and Petrov (2013). Training instances are extracted from the automatically aligned training data based on a small set of manually defined rules. To ensure high quality training data, only subtrees that are fully connected by high confidence alignments are considered. The preordering classifiers are trained on the intersection of high-confidence word alignments and the first-best output of the TurboParser dependency parser (Martins et al., 2009). The alignments are created using the Berkeley aligner[2] with the hard intersection setting. This setting ensures that only high confidence alignment links are produced. While this will lead to a reduction in the number of alignment links, it creates more reliable training data for the preordering model. The dependency parser is trained to produce pseudo-projective dependency trees (Nivre and Nilsson, 2005).[3] Appropriate values for $k_{+\text{LM}}$ and $k_{-\text{LM}}$ are determined using grid search. We found that beam sizes above $k_{+\text{LM}} = 15$ and $k_{-\text{LM}} = 5$ did not improve first-best preordering quality.

Model tuning The set of weights λ for the combination of the preordering model and the language models are optimized for a selected target metric on heldout data. The straight-forward choice for this metric is Kendall τ, which indicates the similarity of the word order of both sides. The Kendall τ distance $d_\tau(\pi, \sigma)$ between two permutations π and σ is defined as (Birch et al., 2010):

$$d_\tau(\pi, \sigma) = 1 - \frac{\sum_{i=1}^{n} \sum_{j=1}^{n} z_{ij}}{Z}$$

$$\text{where } z_{ij} = \begin{cases} 1 & \text{if } \pi(i) < \pi(j) \text{ and } \sigma(i) > \sigma(j) \\ 0 & \text{otherwise} \end{cases} \quad \text{and } Z = \frac{(n^2 - n)}{2}$$

The metric indicates the ratio of pairwise order differences between two permutations. An alternative to this ordering measure is the simulation of a full machine translation system, as first proposed by Tromble and Eisner (2009). To ensure that the changes in word order do not affect this mock translation system and to limit its complexity, the system is limited to phrases of length 1.

Tuning is performed using the *tuning as ranking* (PRO) framework (Hopkins and May, 2011). At tuning time, $k_{-\text{LM}}$ and $k_{+\text{LM}}$ are set to 15 and 100 respectively. *PRO* requires the unweighted values of all feature functions; hence, during tuning only, we remember the unweighted feature values on each node and sum over intermediate values to arrive at the overall scores. Training instances for ranking are sampled from the best 100 word order predictions for each sentence in the tuning set. We perform 6 iterations and interpolate the weights of each iteration with the weights from the previous iteration by the recommended factor of $\Psi = 0.1$.

Translation setup To evaluate the model in a full translation setup, we follow the standard approach to preordering. Given the source side **s** and the target side **t** of the parallel training corpus, we first perform

---

[1] For example, auxiliary verbs should modify the finite verb and prepositions depend on the head of the noun phrase.
[2] https://code.google.com/p/berkeleyaligner/
[3] Projectivization was performed using MaltParser version 1.8; http://www.maltparser.org/.

Model	Kendall τ	BLEU ($\hat{\text{s}}' \rightarrow \text{s}'$)
First-best $-$LM	92.16	68.1
First-best $+$LM (cube pruned)	92.27	68.7
Best out of n-best $+$LM (cube pruned, $n = 5$)	93.33	–
Best out of n-best $+$LM (cube pruned, $n = 10$)	93.72	–

Table 1: LM integration tested on first-best prediction (*en–de*, scores from predicted to gold-ordered *en*).

word alignment using MGIZA++ (Gao and Vogel, 2008). We perform 6 iterations of IBM model 1 training followed by 6 iterations of HMM word alignment and 3 iterations each of IBM model 3 and 4.

After initial training, the preordering model is applied to s, obtaining the preordered corpus $\hat{\text{s}}'$. Since the word order differences between $\hat{\text{s}}'$ and t should be less acute, less computationally expensive word alignment tools are sufficient to re-align the corpus. We align $\hat{\text{s}}'$ and t using `fast_align`,[4] an efficient re-parameterization of IBM model 2 (Dyer et al., 2013). Improvements in word order can lead to improvements in alignments and hence the training and word alignment process can be performed repeatedly. Lerner and Petrov (2013) report no significant improvements after the initial re-alignment. Accordingly, we do not iterate the training process either. The underlying translation system is Moses (Koehn et al., 2007) using the standard feature setup and using only the distortion-based reordering model. Tuning is performed using MERT (Och, 2003). The system is trained on the full parallel sections of the Europarl corpus (Koehn, 2005) and tuned and tested on the WMT 2009 and WMT 2010 newstest sets respectively. The language model is a 5-gram ngram model trained on the target side of Europarl and the news commentary corpus.[5]

4.2 Testing the effectiveness of non-local features

While our preliminary results showed that the integration of a language model might be helpful, we now consider this question in more detail. To test whether the language model features are beneficial to the reordering model, we compare two versions of the same system: *first-best* $-$LM is the reordering system without a language model and *first-best* $+$LM is the same system with the language model integrated via cube pruning. Results are presented in Table 1. While Kendall τ gives an impression of the overall word order quality, the BLEU metric gives an indication of the quality of reorderings within the more restricted space of the length of the ngrams used in the metric. The results show that the integration of the language model helps the system improve the quality of the reorderings. We expected the language model to provide benefits mostly on the borders between tree nodes. The BLEU score indicates an improvement in the ordering of short word sequences, which hints at the presence of this benefit.

In the n-best $+$LM setup, we produce the top n word order predictions and select the prediction that provides the most Kendall τ improvement. These results hint at the potential improvement contained in the best n predictions of the model. Next, we turn to examining the quality of the space of word order predictions in more detail by applying them in a machine translation task.

4.3 Evaluating the quality of the word order predictions

Our goal in this work has been to use a syntax-oriented preordering model to delimit the search space for a subsequent, more complex model. Hence, in order to examine the model presented in Section 3, we determine the quality of the n-best predictions the model produces. We perform the following experiment for the language pair English–German: Using the preordering system, we produce the 10 best word order predictions for each sentence in the test set. We then translate each sentence arranged according to each of the word order predictions using a standard phrase-based machine translation system trained on the corpus produced by the first-best preordering system. After the translation is performed, one translation is selected based on the best sentence-level BLEU score. Table 2 shows results for this setup and for a baseline system without preordering. Both systems use a distortion limit of 7 and use only the standard

---

[4] http://github.com/clab/fast_align
[5] http://statmt.org/wmt13/translation-task.html

	Distortion limit	BLEU	METEOR	TER
Baseline		15.20	35.43	66.62
Best out of k ($k = 10$)	7	17.26*	37.97*	62.64*

* Result is statistically significant against baseline at $p < 0.05$.

Table 2: Estimation of the quality of the k best word order predictions.

distance-based reordering model. Statistical significance tests are performed using bootstrap resampling (Koehn, 2004) and statistically significant results ($p < 0.05$) are marked with an asterisk. These results show that significant improvements in translation quality measured in terms of BLEU, METEOR and TER are possible based on the space of word order choices provided by our model.

4.4 Discussion

Having introduced our preordering method and having evaluated the influence of non-local features, we are now interested in two basic aspects of the output space provided by this system:

The first aspect is the quality of the space of the space delimited by the preordering system. Since we plan to pass the output space to a richer model, it has to be ensured that a sufficient number of good candidates are contained in this space. This question is answered by the translation experiments performed in Section 4.3, which indicate that even within the first 10 word order predictions, there are enough good instances to enable a significant improvement in translation quality. Since the evaluation of our translation experiments is performed using only automatic evaluation metrics, it is difficult to pinpoint the exact source of these potential improvements. In order to examine the gains in more detail and to determine how much the fluency of the output increased, we therefore intend to perform manual evaluation in future work. The second question is whether the size of the space of potential word order choices is manageable for subsequent models. Since the previous experiments showed that even with only 10 word order predictions, a significant improvement can be observed, it is clear that this very small space can be used by a subsequent model. In addition to this, the output in the form of a lattice allows for using more options and efficient processing using dynamic programming algorithms. Since the model from Section 3.1 works on local tree families in a chart, it may be able to work with a parse forest instead of a tree, possibly alleviating parse errors on the source. We plan to explore this direction in future work.

5 Conclusion

Source-side reordering provides a significant potential for improvements in translation quality and translation performance in machine translation, which was shown in previous studies and is further supported by the method's recent surge in popularity. It is therefore an attractive model to extend to morphosyntax beyond pure word order patterns. Most of the benefits of source-side reordering are due to enabling the modeling of much larger reordering spaces in a more reliable manner than it would be possible within the underlying machine translation system. For languages such as German or Arabic, however, word order and morphology are interconnected and should not be treated in isolation. As a first step towards broader morphosyntactic processing beyond word order only, this paper has explored how a preordering model can be utilized to produce a space of sensible word order predictions. We have presented a novel preordering model for this purpose and have evaluated its outputs with translation experiments using a common system setup. The experiments also show that non-local language model features integrated via cube pruning improve the preordering quality for the language pair English–German. Further, our translation experiments show that this preordering system, when optimized for producing n-best predictions, provides an output space that is valuable for further processing both in its compactness and in the potential improvement in translation quality it enables.

Acknowledgements   We thank the three anonymous reviewers for their constructive comments and suggestions. The first author is supported by the EXPERT (EXPloiting Empirical appRoaches to Translation) Initial Training Network (ITN) of the European Union's Seventh Framework Programme.

References

Dzmitry Bahdanau, Kyunghyun Cho, and Yoshua Bengio. 2015. Neural machine translation by jointly learning to align and translate. *Proceedings of the International Conference on Learning Representations.*

Yehoshua Bar-Hillel, M. Perles, and E. Shamir. 1961. On formal properties of simple phrase structure grammars. *Zeitschrift für Phonetik, Sprachwissenschaft und Kommunikationsforschung*, 14:143–172. Reprinted in Y. Bar-Hillel. (1964). *Language and Information: Selected Essays on their Theory and Application*, Addison-Wesley 1964, 116–150.

Alexandra Birch, Miles Osborne, and Phil Blunsom. 2010. Metrics for MT evaluation: Evaluating reordering. *Machine Translation*, 24(1):15–26, March.

David Chiang. 2007. Hierarchical phrase-based translation. *Computational Linguistics*, 33(2):201–228.

Michael Collins, Philipp Koehn, and Ivona Kucerova. 2005. Clause restructuring for statistical machine translation. In *Proceedings of the 43rd Annual Meeting of the Association for Computational Linguistics (ACL'05)*, pages 531–540, Ann Arbor, Michigan, June. Association for Computational Linguistics.

Marta R. Costa-jussà and José A. R. Fonollosa. 2006. Statistical machine reordering. In *Proceedings of the 2006 Conference on Empirical Methods in Natural Language Processing*, pages 70–76, Sydney, Australia, July. Association for Computational Linguistics.

Adrià de Gispert, Gonzalo Iglesias, and William Byrne. 2015. Fast and accurate preordering for SMT using neural networks. In *Proceedings of the Conference of the North American Chapter of the Association for Computational Linguistics - Human Language Technologies (NAACL HLT 2015)*, June.

John DeNero and Jakob Uszkoreit. 2011. Inducing sentence structure from parallel corpora for reordering. In *Proceedings of the 2011 Conference on Empirical Methods in Natural Language Processing*, pages 193–203, Edinburgh, Scotland, UK., July. Association for Computational Linguistics.

Chris Dyer, Victor Chahuneau, and Noah A. Smith. 2013. A simple, fast, and effective reparameterization of IBM model 2. In *Proceedings of the 2013 Conference of the North American Chapter of the Association for Computational Linguistics: Human Language Technologies*, pages 644–648, Atlanta, Georgia, June. Association for Computational Linguistics.

Qin Gao and Stephan Vogel. 2008. Parallel implementations of word alignment tool. In *Software Engineering, Testing, and Quality Assurance for Natural Language Processing*, pages 49–57. Association for Computational Linguistics.

Teresa Herrmann, Jochen Weiner, Jan Niehues, and Alex Waibel. 2013. Analyzing the potential of source sentence reordering in statistical machine translation. In *Proceedings of the International Workshop on Spoken Language Translation (IWSLT 2013)*.

Mark Hopkins and Jonathan May. 2011. Tuning as ranking. In *Proceedings of the 2011 Conference on Empirical Methods in Natural Language Processing*, pages 1352–1362, Edinburgh, Scotland, UK., July. Association for Computational Linguistics.

Laura Jehl, Adrià de Gispert, Mark Hopkins, and Bill Byrne. 2014. Source-side preordering for translation using logistic regression and depth-first branch-and-bound search. In *Proceedings of the 14th Conference of the European Chapter of the Association for Computational Linguistics*, pages 239–248, Gothenburg, Sweden, April. Association for Computational Linguistics.

Maxim Khalilov and Khalil Sima'an. 2012. Statistical translation after source reordering: Oracles, context-aware models, and empirical analysis. *Natural Language Engineering*, 18:491–519, 10.

Philipp Koehn, Hieu Hoang, Alexandra Birch, Chris Callison-Burch, Marcello Federico, Nicola Bertoldi, Brooke Cowan, Wade Shen, Christine Moran, Richard Zens, et al. 2007. Moses: Open source toolkit for statistical machine translation. In *Proceedings of the 45th annual meeting of the ACL on interactive poster and demonstration sessions*, pages 177–180. Association for Computational Linguistics.

Philipp Koehn. 2004. Statistical significance tests for machine translation evaluation. In *Proceedings of the 2004 Conference on Empirical Methods in Natural Language Processing*, pages 388–395. Association for Computational Linguistics.

Philipp Koehn. 2005. Europarl: A parallel corpus for statistical machine translation. In *MT summit*, volume 5, pages 79–86.

Uri Lerner and Slav Petrov. 2013. Source-side classifier preordering for machine translation. In *Proceedings of the 2013 Conference on Empirical Methods in Natural Language Processing*, pages 513–523, Seattle, Washington, USA, October. Association for Computational Linguistics.

José B Marino, Rafael E Banchs, Josep M Crego, Adria de Gispert, Patrik Lambert, José AR Fonollosa, and Marta R Costa-Jussà. 2006. N-gram-based machine translation. *Computational Linguistics*, 32(4):527–549.

Andre Martins, Noah Smith, and Eric Xing. 2009. Concise integer linear programming formulations for dependency parsing. In *Proceedings of the Joint Conference of the 47th Annual Meeting of the ACL and the 4th International Joint Conference on Natural Language Processing of the AFNLP*, pages 342–350, Suntec, Singapore, August. Association for Computational Linguistics.

Stefan Müller. 2015. *Grammatical Theory: From Transformational Grammar to Constraint-Based Approaches*. Number 1 in Lecture Notes in Language Sciences. Language Science Press, Berlin. Open Review Version.

Joakim Nivre and Jens Nilsson. 2005. Pseudo-projective dependency parsing. In *Proceedings of the 43rd Annual Meeting of the Association for Computational Linguistics (ACL'05)*, pages 99–106, Ann Arbor, Michigan, June. Association for Computational Linguistics.

Franz Josef Och and Hermann Ney. 2002. Discriminative training and maximum entropy models for statistical machine translation. In *Proceedings of the 40th Annual Meeting on Association for Computational Linguistics*, ACL '02, pages 295–302, Stroudsburg, PA, USA. Association for Computational Linguistics.

Franz Josef Och. 2003. Minimum error rate training in statistical machine translation. In *Proceedings of the 41st Annual Meeting on Association for Computational Linguistics-Volume 1*, pages 160–167. Association for Computational Linguistics.

Roy Tromble and Jason Eisner. 2009. Learning linear ordering problems for better translation. In *Proceedings of the 2009 Conference on Empirical Methods in Natural Language Processing*, pages 1007–1016, Singapore, August. Association for Computational Linguistics.

Dekai Wu. 1997. Stochastic inversion transduction grammars and bilingual parsing of parallel corpora. *Computational Linguistics*, 23(3):377–403.

Daniel Zeman, David Mareček, Martin Popel, Loganathan Ramasamy, Jan Štěpánek, Zdeněk Žabokrtský, and Jan Hajič. 2012. HamleDT: To parse or not to parse? In Nicoletta Calzolari (Conference Chair), Khalid Choukri, Thierry Declerck, Mehmet Uğur Doğan, Bente Maegaard, Joseph Mariani, Jan Odijk, and Stelios Piperidis, editors, *Proceedings of the Eight International Conference on Language Resources and Evaluation (LREC'12)*, Istanbul, Turkey, may. European Language Resources Association (ELRA).

Evaluating a Machine Translation System in a Technical Support Scenario

Rosa Del Gaudio*, Aljoscha Burchardt and Arle Lommel
* Higher Functions – Sistemas Inteligentes
Lisbon, Portugal
`rosa.gaudio@pcmedic.pt`
German Research Center for Artificial Intelligence (DFKI)
Language Technology Lab - Berlin, Germany
`aljoscha.burchardt@dfki.de`
`arle.lommel@dfki.de`

Abstract

In this document we report on a user scenario based evaluation aiming at assessing the performance of a machine translation (MT) system in a real context of use. This extrinsic evaluation exemplifies a framework that makes it possible to estimate MT performance and to verify if improvements of MT technology lead to better performance in a real usage scenario. We report on the evaluation of Moses baselines for several languages in a cross-lingual IT helpdesk scenario.

1 Introduction

Extrinsic evaluation of MT, i.e., assessment of MT quality within a task other than translation, has not (yet) been established as a major research topic. Reasons may include the prevalent focus of MT research on translation of newspaper texts, which does not readily lend itself to task-based evaluation. In industrial applications of MT, task-based evaluation is certainly performed more frequently, but the results are typically not published. The evaluation reported in this paper joins together general research and industrial applications. The focus is to find the best procedure for evaluating a machine translation system in a real-world application using a user-based scenario methodology.

This evaluation is based on the integration of MT services in a helpdesk application developed by the company Higher Functions as part of its business (see Section 3) to make it cross-lingual. It has been performed within the QTLeap project[1], which aims to investigate an articulated methodology for machine translation based on deep language engineering approaches and evaluates several different MT approaches in a usage scenario.

In general, the focus of this evaluation is to assess the added value of the translations in terms of their impact on the performance of the QA system of the helpdesk in a multilingual environment. The main goals are to i) assess the impact of the MT services on the application, ii) find out to what extent the inclusion of MT can generate business opportunities, and iii) set a baseline that makes it possible to see if future improvements of the MT technology lead to better performance in the usage scenario.

In order to reach this objective, the evaluation was split in two distinctive parts. The first part focuses on evaluating how the translation affects the answer retrieval component of the question and answer (QA) algorithm. The second part focuses on outbound translation to evaluate to what extent it delivers a clear and understandable answer to final customers without the intervention of a human operator. In this paper we report on the second part of the evaluation covering seven different languages: Basque, Bulgarian, Czech, Dutch, German, Portuguese and Spanish.

Section 2 reports on the state of the art, while Section 3 describes the real user scenario. Section 4 explains in details how the evaluation was carried out. Section 5 presents the results for each of the seven languages. Finally we draw some conclusions in Section 6.

---

[1]`www.qtleap.eu`

Proceedings of the 1st Deep Machine Translation Workshop (DMTW 2015), pages 39–47,
Praha, Czech Republic, 3–4 September 2015.

2 State of the art

Previous work includes extrinsic evaluation of machine translation through several MT applications: cross-lingual patent retrieval, cross-lingual sentiment classification, collaborative work via idea exchange, speech-to-speech translation, and dialogue.

The Patent Translation Task at the Seventh NTCIR Workshop employed search topics for cross-lingual patent retrieval, which was used to evaluate the contribution of machine translation for retrieving patent documents across languages (Fujii et al., 2008). They also analysed the relationship between the accuracy of MT and its effects on retrieval accuracy (Fujii et al., 2009), which comes closest to the evaluation of answer retrieval in our scenario.

Duh et al. (2011) investigated the effect of Machine Translation on Cross-lingual Sentiment classification and suggested improvements to the adaptation problems that have been identified. Yamashita and Ishida (2006) started research on collaborative work using machine translation. Similarly, Wang et al. (2013) evaluated MT through idea exchange: in this scenario, pairs of one English and one Chinese speaker performed brainstorming tasks assisted by MT, which helped the non-native English speakers produce ideas; nevertheless comprehension problems were identified with MT output.

In the early years of NLP, the Verbmobil project (Jekat and Hahn, 2000) performed end-to-end Machine-Translation as part of a longer pipeline with several modules, and evaluation of MT via speech-to-speech translation has been conducted in the frame of a yearly shared task (e.g., Cellotolo *et al.* (2013)). In another example on dialogue systems, Schneider *et al.* (2010) employed a "Wizard of Oz" technique in order to assess the quality of translations in the context of a dialogue application. A human operator (the "wizard") who is not visible to the user, takes the role of the system. In that scenario, German speakers have to find a good offer on Internet connections in Ireland. The extrinsic evaluation measuring elapsed time, shows different results to the intrinsic error-specific MT evaluation. The questionnaire we use in our evaluation is based on the one used in this task.

3 Tech support scenario

The scenario used in our evaluation is based on a real service developed by the Portuguese company Higher Functions to support their clients. This service, named PcWizard, offers technical support by chat. Usually technical support can be divided into three levels based on the difficulty of the request: first-level, second-level, and third-level. Most of the first-level inquiries are straightforward and simple, and can be easily handled. Literature has shown that the majority of user requests can be answered by the front-line level, as they are "simple and routine", and do not require specialized knowledge (Leung and Lau, 2007). At the same time, these kinds of requests represent the majority of all requests and are responsible for long waiting times, leading to user dissatisfaction. The PcWizard application attempts to address this specific context, trying to automate the process of answering first-level user requests. The area of specialization of this service is basic computer and IT troubleshooting for both hardware and software.

The process of providing support to end-users involves remote, written interaction via chat channels through a call centre. This process of problem solving can be made efficient by using a Question Answering (QA) application that helps call centre operators prepare replies for clients.

Using techniques based on natural language processing, each query for help is matched against a memory of previous questions and answers (QAs) and a list of possible replies from the repository is displayed, ranked by relevance according to the internal heuristics of the support system. If the top reply scores above a certain threshold, it is returned to the client. If the reply does not score over the threshold, the operator is presented with the list of possible answers delivered by the system and he can (a) pick the most appropriate reply, (b) modify one of the replies, or (c) write a completely new reply. In the last two cases, the new reply is used to further increase the QA memory.

Figure 1 shows the application workflow with the embedded MT services. As the memory of previous question answering is in English, there are two distinct places where MT services are used in the application. The first time occurs when the incoming user request is translated from the original language to English. This translation is used by the QA search algorithm for retrieving a possible answer.

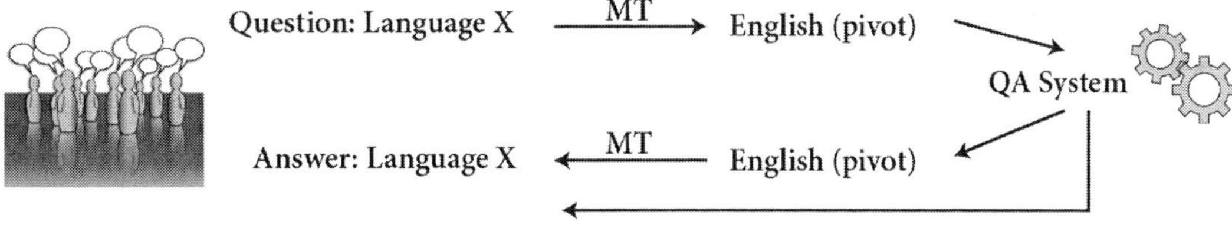

Figure 1: The workflow with the MT services

Once an answer is found in English, MT services are used to translate the answer back to the users original language. This means that the MT services interact with the system in two different moments and for two very different purposes. In the first, inbound retrieval step, the translation is not presented to a human, but it is only used by an algorithm. By contrast, in the second, outbound presentation step the translation is presented to the final user. (In this case all the translations are done to or from English.)

4 The experimental settings

This evaluation was carried out in a controlled setting in order to avoid dealing with different variables that interfere with the real objective of this evaluation, such as having a relatively small multilingual database and no previous data on a multilingual scenario. Furthermore a direct field test would lead to the problem that the questions would differ between evaluations and complicate comparison of the results. For these reasons 100 question/answer pairs from the corpus were selected and volunteers were recruited for this in-vitro experiment. Where possible, IT experts were avoided as evaluators in order to simulate the typical user of the PcWizard application.

4.1 The corpus

A corpus was collected to develop and evaluate different MT systems. This corpus is composed of 4000 question and answer pairs in the domain of computer and IT troubleshooting for both hardware and software. As this corpus was collected using the PcWizard application, it is composed of naturally occurring utterances produced by users while interacting with the service. The corpus was collected by selecting the data contained in the database of the application, in which all client interactions are saved. For this corpus, only interactions composed of one question and a respective answer were considered.

The corpus consists of short sentences (usually a request of help) followed by an answer, and each conversation thread involves only two persons (the user and the operator). The request for help is often a well-formed question or a declarative sentence reporting a problem, but in a significant number of cases, the question is not grammatically correct, presenting problems with coordination, missing verbs, etc. In some cases, the request is composed of a list of key words. This kind of utterance is representative of informal communication via chats. On the other hand, a more formal register characterizes the answers, as they are produced by well-trained operators and they need to be very precise and concise in order to clarify the user request and to avoid generating more confusion.

The corpus, available for Basque, Bulgarian, Czech, Dutch, English, German, Portuguese and Spanish, can be downloaded from the META-SHARE portal [2] under the name "QTLeap Corpus".

4.2 Evaluation workflow

At a basic level, this evaluation exposes the human evaluator first to the machine translated (MT) answer and then to the reference answer. In this way, the subject evaluates the MT answer first on its own and then with respect to the reference.

Using a web interface, a question is presented to the evaluator in the target language and then he/she is asked to provide a self-estimation of his/her knowledge level (high, medium, or low) on the subject involved in the question.

---

[2] http://metashare.metanet4u.eu/

	A	SA	N	SD	D
I have serious problems in understanding this answer	-	-		+	+
These sentences are fluent	+	+		-	-
There are awkward words and expressions	-	-		+	+
I would rate the sentences as comprehensible	+	+		-	-
Some words appear in a strange order	-	-		+	+
The instructions/information in the answer are not clear	-	-		+	+
I would consider using a similar system for technical support in a similar context	+	+		-	-

Table 1: List of the statements used in the final questionnaire

Then the same question is presented, followed by the automatically translated answer (A). In this step the subject assesses on the usefulness of this answer, according to the following options:

- It would clearly help me solve my problem / answer my question

- It might help, but would require some thinking to understand it

- It is not helpful / I don't understand it

After answering, the evaluator is presented again with the question, the MT answer (A), and the reference answer (B). This time the subject is asked to compare answers A and B. Taking into account that the second answer B is giving the correct information, he/she is asked to re-evaluate the first answer A, selecting one of the following options:

- A gives the right advice.

- A gets minor points wrong.

- A gets important points wrong

Finally, evaluators are asked to give a closer look at the automatically translated answer and provide a more fine-grained evaluation on seven different aspects using a questionnaire with answers based on a 5-point Likert scale: agree (A), slightly agree (SA), neither agree nor disagree (N), slightly disagree (SD), disagree (D). At this point evaluators have also the possibility to leave a comment on the interaction evaluated.

The statements used for this questionnaire were developed using the questionnaire presented in (Schneider et al., 2010) for evaluating an MT dialogue system as a starting point. Following the literature, the statements in the questionnaire were designed in order to balance the number of negative and positive statements to avoid getting the same judgment and to force evaluators to read each statement carefully.

Table 1 shows the list of the statements used in the questionnaire. The plus and minus symbols represent the value of the statement. A positive judgment is represented by the plus, a negative by minus. For instance, if the evaluator agrees with the first statement, it means that the sentence presents some kind of problem, so it is negative for the performance of the system. For the second statement (which presents a positive judgment) the situation is inverted: if the evaluator agrees, it means that, for that specific aspect, the answer present a positive score.

All the question/answer pairs were evaluated at least by 3 volunteers for each of the seven languages, with a global average of 3.3.

5   Results

To clarify the framework, this section presents the results of evaluating Moses baselines for the project languages mentioned above. Is is important to note that it is not our goal to compare performance between languages, even if the presentation of results might raise this expectation. The Moses systems that have been set up for the different languages have been trained on different general and domain corpora depending on availability of resources. Table 2 shows the evaluation results when the evaluator is asked to assess on the usefulness of the automatically translated answer. Based on these results, the quality of the response is very different across the languages.

	EU	BG	CS	NL	DE	PT	ES	Avg.
It would clearly help me solve my problem / answer my question	30.7%	48.1%	49.5%	24.7%	37.3%	12.4%	65.3%	38.3%
It might help, but would require some thinking to understand it	47.7%	43.6%	35.2%	43.4%	41.4%	35.3%	26.3%	39.0%
It is not helpful / I don't understand it	21.7%	8.3%	15.3%	31.6%	21.3%	52.3%	8.3%	22.7%

Table 2: Assessment of the usefulness of the translated answers

Bulgarian and Spanish received the best evaluation with only 8.3% of answers judged as not helpful/not understandable, versus 52.3% for Portuguese. Czech also demonstrated good performance, with almost 50% of the answers considered clearly helpful in answering the question.

Table 3 reports on the results when the evaluator was asked to compare the automatically translated answers (A) with the reference answer (B) giving the correct information.

When the reference answer is presented, very different results were obtained compared to the previous table. In particular, the evaluations are more homogeneous among all the languages and among the three different options.

It is interesting to note that the positive evaluation obtained when only the MT answer is presented decreases for four of the seven languages (Basque, Bulgarian, Czech and Spanish), but increases for the other three (Dutch, German, Portuguese). Subjects using Dutch and Portuguese were the ones providing the worst evaluation of MT answers.

Based on this scenario, a metric was elaborated. This metric attempts to determine the probability of final users making a phone call to get a satisfactory answer to their questions. What it is relevant for this metric is the perception of the user about the correctness of the answer. This means that if the evaluator checked that the automatically translated answer would "clearly help to solve my problem/answer the question" the probability of asking for further help would very low. This would be the case especially if the answer, when compared to a reference answer, is judged as giving the right advice or just some minor points wrong.

Cases when an evaluator thinks that the translated answer would require some thinking to understand it and gets important points wrong are rather different: in this case the probability of calling an operator would be higher.

Table 4 shows the probability of calling an operator for each different possibility. The results for each language are presented in Table 5.

In order to draw some considerations, the aggregates results are presented in Table 6.

As noticed in the previous tables, there is a high degree of variance between the different languages. For example, Spanish or Czech present a much smaller probability of users calling an operator than do Portuguese and Dutch.

	EU	BG	CS	NL	DE	PT	ES	Avg.
A gives the right advice.	25.7%	35.0%	42.2%	25.6%	43.2%	22.9%	45.3%	34.3%
A gets minor points wrong	37.7%	44.3%	31.9%	35.9%	33.4%	23.2%	22.3%	32.7%
A gets important points wrong	36.7%	20.7%	25.9%	38.4%	23.4%	54.0%	32.3%	33.1%

Table 3: Assessment of the translated answer against the reference answer

	MT answer	Reference Answer	Probability
A	Solves my problem	Gets the right advice	low
B	Solves my problem	Gets minor points wrong	low
C	Would require some thinking to understand it	Gets the right advice	low
D	Would require some thinking to understand it	Gets minor points wrong	medium
E	Solves my problem	Gets important points wrong	high
F	Would require some thinking to understand it	Gets important points wrong	high
G	Is not helpful / I don't understand it	Gets the right advice	high
H	Is not helpful / I don't understand it	Gets minor points wrong	high
I	Is not helpful / I don't understand it	Gets important points wrong	high

Table 4: The metric with the probability of calling an operator

	Probability	EU	BG	CS	NL	DE	PT	ES	Avg.
A	low	20.8%	28.6%	34.9%	14.4%	29.0%	8.8%	39.7%	25.2%
B	low	7.9%	14.8%	12.6%	8.8%	7.2%	2.5%	15.0%	9.8%
C	low	4.6%	4.0%	7.0%	7.2%	11.6%	10.2%	5.7%	7.2%
D	medium	28.1%	30.6%	17.9%	21.9%	22.0%	15.8%	7.0%	20.5%
E	high	1.7%	1.3%	2.0%	1.6%	1.4%	1.1%	10.7%	2.8%
F	high	14.9%	11.7%	10.3%	14.4%	7.8%	9.3%	13.7%	11.76%
G	high	0.3%	0.0%	0.3%	4.1%	3.2%	4.0%	0.0%	1.7%
H	high	1.3%	1.5%	1.3%	5.3%	3.8%	4.8%	0.3%	2.6%
I	high	20.5%	7.5%	13.6%	22.3%	13.9%	43.5%	8.0%	18.5%

Table 5: Results of the metric considering each case

Probability	EU	BG	CS	NL	DE	PT	ES	Avg.
low	33.3%	47.4%	54.5%	30.4%	47.8%	21.5%	60.4%	42.2%
medium	28.1%	30.6%	17.9%	21.9%	22.0%	15.8%	7.0%	20.5%
high	37.0%	22.0%	27.5%	47.7%	30.1%	62.7%	32.7%	37.1%

Table 6: Aggregated results of the metric

The following graphics report on the results obtained with the final questionnaire where the MT answers were evaluated on seven different aspects: understanding, fluency, awkwardness, word order, clarity, use of this type of system.

The agree/disagree evaluation are normalised into positive/negative judgments and then calculated as a weighted average where the slightly positive/negative cases get a lower weight of .5 and neutral values are simply ignored: (positive - negative) + 0.5*(slightly positive - slightly negative).

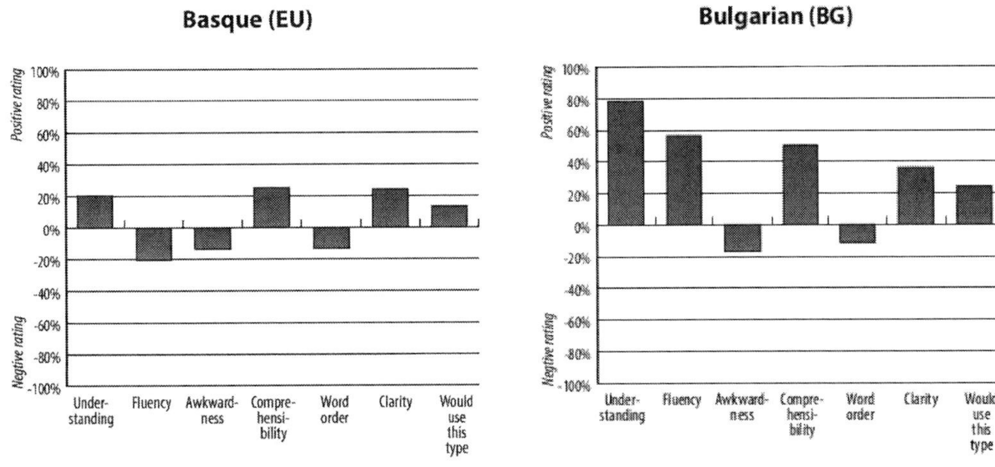

Figure 2: Basque   Figure 3: Bulgarian

As show in Figure 2, the Basque speaking subjects provide positive evaluation in four out of seven statements. In particular evaluators agree in the 54.5% of the cases that they do not have serious problems in understanding the answer, that it was comprehensible (56.5%), and the instructions were clear (54.5%), and they would consider using a similar system (47.8%). The problems come up with the lack of fluency of the sentences (51.5%), the presence of awkward expressions (58.6%) and the order of the words (61.8%).

For Bulgarian (Figure 3) the outcome was more positive than for Basque. The positive dimensions go from four to five. The sentences are also considered fluent in 78.3% of the cases. In general the positive dimension obtains higher values. For example, in 89.2% of the cases the evaluators have no problems in understanding the answer. The problem again is the presence of awkward expressions (58.6%) and the order of the words (54.5%).

For Czech, Figure 4, all the dimensions are positives with the exception of the fluency of the sentences where positive and negative judgments present almost the same weight (41.7% and 42.7% respectively).

Figure 5 shows a very opposite evaluation for Dutch speaking subjects. All the statements get a negative evaluation.

German-speaking evaluators provided positive evaluation on three dimensions: the understandability of the answer (50.6%), the clarity of instructions (49.1%) and use of the system in a similar situation (34.6%).

Portuguese speaking evaluators, similarly to Dutch, provide negative evaluation on all the seven statements.

Finally, Spanish-speaking subjects evaluated six of the seven dimensions positively. The only problem is given by the presence of awkward words and expressions reported in 63.1% of the evaluations.

6 Conclusions

In this paper we presented an innovative method to evaluate MT systems, taking into consideration real user context.

Czech (CS)

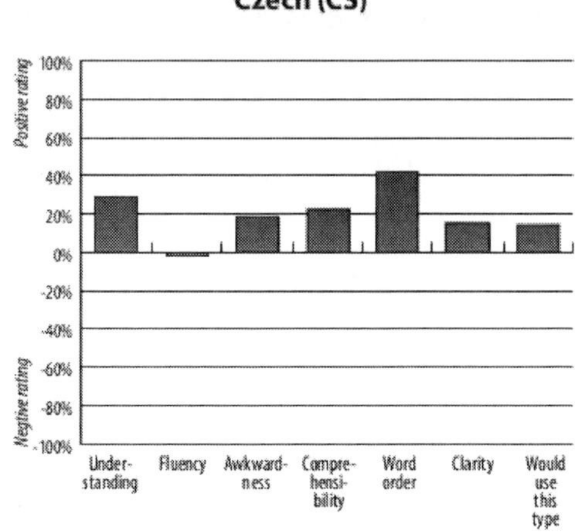

Figure 4: Czech

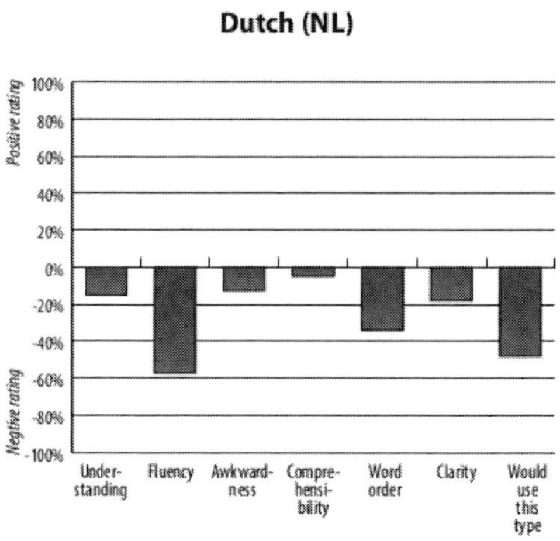

Dutch (NL)

Figure 5: Dutch

German (DE)

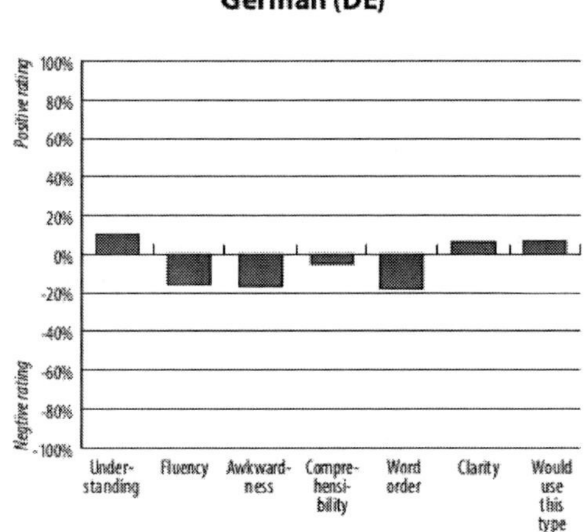

Figure 6: German

Portuguese (PT)

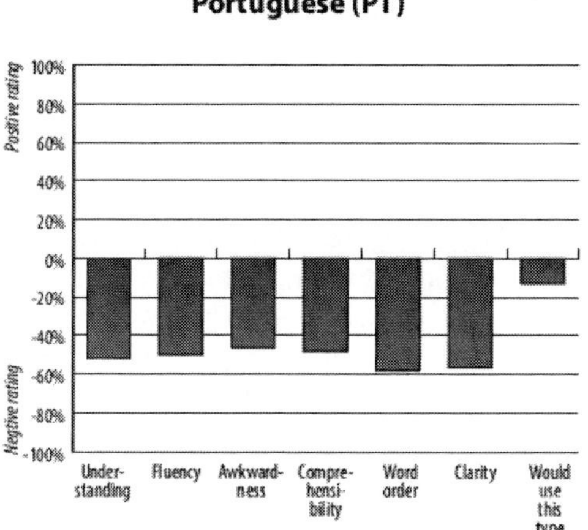

Figure 7: Portuguese

With this evaluation we show that although the translations of answers presented to the real user were produced by baseline systems, results are promising from a business perspective and could result in a real-world reduction in service calls. Even if there are many flaws in the translations, a considerable part of the test users would use a system like this again and the approximated chance of calling an operator is lower than expected (even allowing for the fact that the numbers are approximations).

The results reported in this paper provide the basis for the extrinsic evaluation of the impact of MT system to the QA system where it was embedded.

Acknowledgements

This work has received support by the ECs FP7 (FP7/2007-2013) under grant agreement number 610516: "QTLeap: Quality Translation by Deep Language Engineering Approaches".

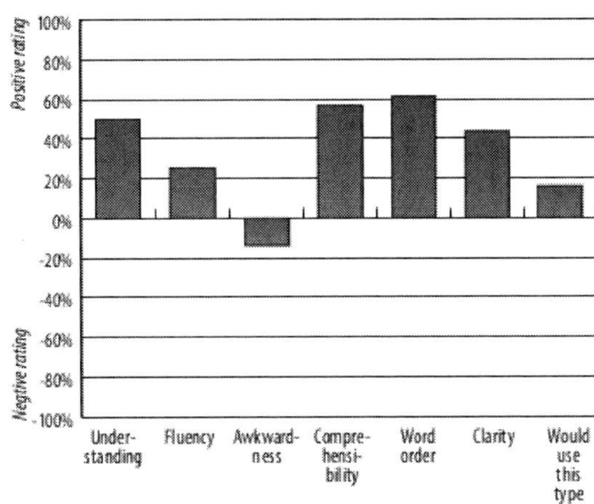

Figure 8: Spanish

References

Mauro Cettolo, Jan Niehues, Sebastian Stker, and Luisa Bentivogli andMarcello Federico. 2013. Report on the 10th iwslt evaluation campaign. In *Proceedings of the International Workshop for Spoken Language Translation (IWSLT 2013)*, pages 29–38.

Kevin Duh, Akinori Fujino, and Masaaki Nagata. 2011. Is machine translation ripe for cross-lingual sentiment classification? In *Proceedings of the 49th Annual Meeting of the Association for Computational Linguistics: Human Language Technologies: Short Papers - Volume 2*, HLT '11, pages 429–433, Stroudsburg, PA, USA. Association for Computational Linguistics.

Atsushi Fujii, Masao Utiyama, Mikio Yamamoto, Takehito Utsuro, Terumasa Ehara, Hiroshi Echizen-ya, and Sayori Shimohata. 2008. Overview of the patent translation task at the ntcir-7 workshop. In *In Proceedings of the 7th NTCIR Workshop Meeting*, pages 349–400.

Atsushi Fujii, Masao Utiyama, Mikio Yamamoto, and Takehito Utsuro. 2009. Evaluating effects of machine translation accuracy on cross-lingual patent retrieval. In *Proceedings of the 32Nd International ACM SIGIR Conference on Research and Development in Information Retrieval*, SIGIR '09, pages 674–675, New York, NY, USA. ACM.

SusanneJ. Jekat and Walther Hahn. 2000. Multilingual verbmobil-dialogs: Experiments, data collection and data analysis. In Wolfgang Wahlster, editor, *Verbmobil: Foundations of Speech-to-Speech Translation*, Artificial Intelligence, pages 575–582. Springer Berlin Heidelberg.

Nelson K. Y. Leung and Sim Kim Lau. 2007. Information technology help desk survey: To identify the classification of simple and routine enquiries. *Journal of Computer Information Systems*, 47(4):70–81.

Anne Schneider, Ielka van der Sluis, and Saturnino Luz. 2010. Comparing intrinsic and extrinsic evaluation of mt output in a dialogue system. In *IWSLT*, pages 329–336.

Hao-Chuan Wang, Susan Fussell, and Dan Cosley. 2013. Machine translation vs. common language: Effects on idea exchange in cross-lingual groups. In *Proceedings of the 2013 Conference on Computer Supported Cooperative Work*, CSCW '13, pages 935–944, New York, NY, USA. ACM.

Naomi Yamashita and Toru Ishida. 2006. Effects of machine translation on collaborative work. In *Proceedings of the 2006 20th Anniversary Conference on Computer Supported Cooperative Work*, CSCW '06, pages 515–524, New York, NY, USA. ACM.

Development of Telugu-Tamil Transfer-Based Machine Translation system: With Special reference to Divergence Index

K. Parameswari

Centre for Applied Linguistics and Translation Studies
University of Hyderabad
`pksh@uohyd.ernet.in, parameshkrishnaa@gmail.com`

Abstract

The existence of translation divergence precludes straightforward mapping in machine translation (MT) system. An increase in the number of divergences also increases the complexity, especially in linguistically motivated transfer-based MT systems. In other words, divergence is directly proportional to the complexity of MT. Here we propose a divergence index (DI) to quantify the number of parametric variations between languages, which helps in improving the success rate of MT. This paper deals with how to build divergence index for a given language pair by giving examples between Telugu and Tamil, the major Dravidian languages spoken in South India. It also proposes handling strategies to overcome these divergences. The presentation of the paper also includes a live demo of Telugu-Tamil MT.

1 Introduction

In MT, there are a number of methods that are being practiced all over the world, chiefly, they are direct, interlingual, transfer-based methods and a combination of these beside the statistical and corpus based methods. This paper discusses the development of transfer-based Telugu-Tamil MT system with a special reference to divergences. In the development of MT[1], linguistically-grounded classification of divergence types need to be formally defined and systematically resolved. Identifying such divergences is the most significant part that facilitates the design and implementation of MT systems. As divergences are encountered as the specific problem in MT, identifying these are also the most crucial to obtain qualitatively a better output.

Divergence between languages may vary from one language pair to another. An increase in the number of divergence also increases the complexity in building an MT. In other words, it can be stated that divergence is directly proportional to the complexity of MT. Measuring divergence between languages supports to ascertain effort justification to build an MT for the proposed languages. Here we propose a divergence index (DI) to quantify the number of parametric variations between languages. DI also classifies divergence exhaustively into different levels in order to understand its depth. It facilitates MT in proposing where to put efforts for the given language pair to attain a better result.

2 Telugu-Tamil MT

Telugu and Tamil are major Dravidian languages with rich literary tradition sharing indubitable linguistic similarities and dissimilarities. An MT between them may be viewed as a bridge to understand and share the richness of both the languages. The MT system demonstrated here is a completely automatic translation system without human interference for the first time involving Telugu and Tamil. It is one of the successfully implemented systems under Indian language to Indian language(IL-IL) MT[2].

---

[1]In this paper, MT refers to linguistically motivated transfer-based machine translation.

[2]IL-IL MT is a consortium funded by the Department Of Electronics and Information Technology (DeitY), Ministry Of Communications and Information Technology, Government of India under the project name *Sampark*. Telugu-Tamil MT is

Proceedings of the 1st Deep Machine Translation Workshop (DMTW 2015), pages 48–54,
Praha, Czech Republic, 3–4 September 2015.

The Telugu-Tamil MT system is an assembly of various linguistic modules run on specific engines whose output is sequentially maneuvered and modified by a series of modules till the output is generated. It employs three stage architecture:

Stage 1: Source language analysis

Stage 2: Source language to target language transfer

Stage 3: Target language generation

The most crucial linguistic modules in Source Language analysis include a Morphological Analyzer (MA), Parts of Speech Tagger (POS), Chunker, Named Entity Recognizer (NER), Simple Parser (SP) and the Source Language to Target Language Transfer Module includes Multi Word Expression (MWE) component, Transfer Grammar (TG) Component, Lexical Transfer component consisting of a synset and bilingual lexicons and in Target Language Generation includes Agreement (AGR) modules and a Morphological Generator (MG). All the modules have been integrated on the platform called *Dashboard* based on black board architecture (Pawan et al, 2010) which configures data flow in a specified pipeline.

The architecture of Telugu-Tamil MT system is given below:

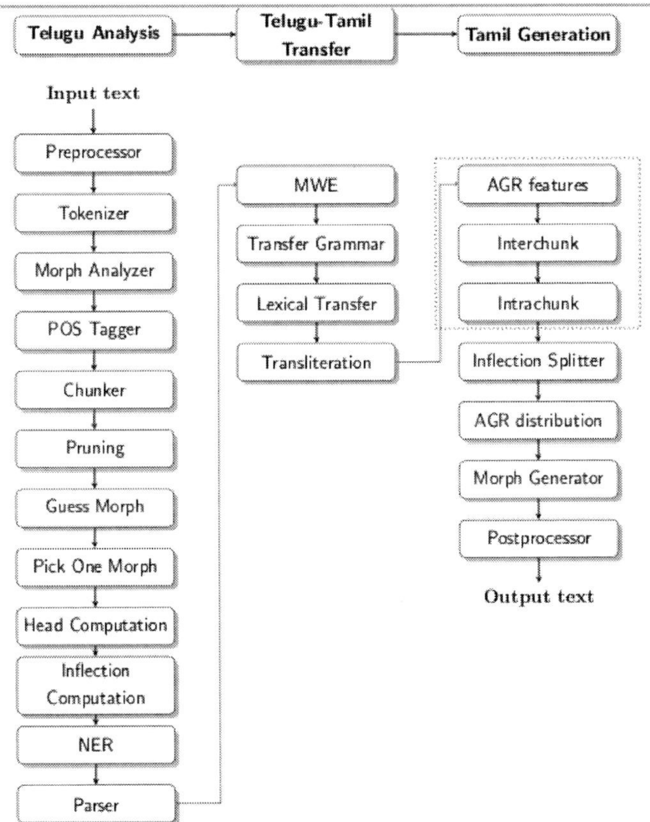

3 Translation Divergence

The term 'Translation Divergence' refers to distinctions or differences that occur between languages when they are translated. It is realized when the source language content is decoded differently in the target language and affects the 'well-formedness' of the target language. According to Dorr (1993), the translation divergence occurs when the underlying concept or 'gist' of a sentence is distributed over dif-

being developed as part of a larger project of IL-ILMT (with Prof. G. Uma Maheshwar Rao as the chief investigator) at Language Technology Laboratory, Centre for Applied Linguistics and Tanslation Studies(CALTS), University of Hyderabad. For more details see: http://caltslab.uohyd.ernet.in/. This system is also available at TDIL website for public access: http://tdil-c.in/components/com_mtsystem/CommonUI/homeMT.php.

ferent words or in different configurations for different languages. The notion of divergence in MT is comparable to the linguistically motivated notion of *parameteric variation* i.e. cross-linguistic distinctions.

Telugu and Tamil in spite of being cognate languages, exhibit considerable amount of divergences in various levels affecting the quality of output. In most of the cases, Dorr's divergences are noticed as rare phenomena and do not pose much problem as far as Telugu and Tamil are considered. However, these language pairs do pose problems at various other levels displaying different divergences. The current research attempts to classify these divergences into three major kinds, such as morphological, syntactic and lexical-semantic divergences.

4 Divergence Index

Divergence index (DI) represents a measure of the differences that occur between languages. The variations of linguistic features can be seen at any levels (L) in terms of surface, shallow and deep levels of languages. These levels are identified as L1, L2, L3 etc., according to its depth of variation. Identifying the divergence with its level between a pair of languages enables one to compute and quantify the effort that is required to build an MT. DI uses a table that attributes to features to identify and classify divergences exhaustively into different levels in order to understand its depth. It facilitates MT in proposing where to put effort for the given language pair to obtain a better result.

4.1 Divergence Index Table

Languages may share certain features or differ with each other. When they differ, it indicates that a certain feature is encoded differently or not available in one of the languages. This is a cause for divergence. Table 1 provides instances where divergences are possible with reference to a given feature in the said languages. Y indicates that the feature is available in a language and N indicates not. When both the languages share similar features (see Table 1 (1.) and (2.)), it means no divergence (indicated by 0). When they differ (see Table 1 (3.) and (4.)), there arises divergence (indicate by 1).

S.No	SL feature	TL feature	Divergence Index
1.	Y	Y	0
2.	N	N	0
3.	Y	N	1
4.	N	Y	1
5.	Y/N	Y/N	0
6.	Y/N	Y	1
7.	Y/N	N	1
8.	Y	Y/N	0
9.	N	Y/N	0

Table 1: **Divergence Index Table**

In certain cases, Y/N is given to indicate optional in the use of a feature. When both source language (SL) and target language (TL) show optional, it means no divergence (see Table 1 (5.)). When only SL shows optional, it is counted as divergence because TL element may not be directly mapped when the option differs (see Table 1 (6.) and (7.)). When the option occurs only in TL, it is counted as no divergence (see Table 1 (8.) and (9.)) because TL optionally behaves like SL, hence SL features can be directly mapped to TL.

4.2 Morphological Divergence Index

Morphological divergences, here, we refer to divergences that occur due to inflectional and productive derivational devices of words between Telugu and Tamil. Open word class categories such as nouns, verbs and adjectives and closed word classes such as pronouns, number words and nouns of space and time (NST) are studied to find out morphological divergences. Functional elements on these categories need to be carefully matched from the source language to the target language to attain well-formed wordforms in the output. Uninflected word classes i.e. indeclinables and non-productive derivational wordforms are excluded here because they are listed in the lexicon and straightforward mapping between them solves the problem in MT.

For example , nouns in Telugu and Tamil are major word classes inflecting for number and case. The major inflectional differences occur due to two reasons i.e. (1) the choice of items in terms of inflections viz., the oblique stem formation, case and postposition and (2) the order of their presentation. For instance, the Table 2 explicates the differences.

No.	PSP	Telugu	Tamil	Gloss
1.	Comparitive	*iMṭi- kaMṭē* house.OBL- than	*vīṭṭ- ai- viṭa/* *vīṭṭ- ai.k- kāṭṭilum* house- ACC- than	'compared to the house'
2.	Semblative	*iMṭi- lāMṭi/* *iMṭi- vaMṭi/* house.OBL- like *iMṭi- ni- pōlina* house- ACC- like	*vīṭṭ- ai.p- pōnra* house- ACC- like	'like the house' (adnominal usage)
3.	Locative: Circumferential	*iMṭi- cuṭṭū* *iMṭi- cuṭṭūtā* house.OBL- around	*vīṭṭ- ai.c- cuṟṟiyum/* *vīṭṭ- ai.c- cuṟṟilum* house- ACC- around	'around the house'
4.	Locative:Interior:Direction	*iMṭi- lōpali- ki/* *iMṭi- lō- ki* home.OBL- inside- DAT	*vīṭṭ- ukk- ul(lē)/* home.OBL- DAT- inside *vīṭṭ- in- ul(lē)* home.OBL- GEN- inside	'to inside the house'

Table 2: **Postpositions**

As seen in the table 2 (No. 1-3), certain postpositions require their complement nouns differently case marked between Telugu and Tamil. Also as shown in Table 2 (No. 4) the order of suffixes in Telugu and Tamil may differ. The difference is explicated as below:

Te. Noun- ±Number suffix- ±Stem-formative- ±Postposition- ±Case Suffix

Ta. Noun- ±Number suffix- ±Stem-formative- ±Case Suffix- ±Postposition

The divergence index for Table 2 is built as below:

No.	PSP	Telugu	Tamil	DI/Level
1.	Comparative	Y	Y	0/L1
	Accusative case marker	N	Y	1/L2
2.	Semblative	Y	Y	0/L1
	Accusative case marker	Y/N	Y	1/L2
3.	Locative: Circumferential	Y	Y	0/L1
	Accusative case marker	N	Y	1/L2
4.	Locative:Interior:Direction	Y	Y	0/L1
	Dative case marker with PSP	Y	N	1/L2

Table 3: **Divergence Index for Table 2**

In predicative positions, nouns in Telugu agree with their subjects in the first person singular and plural, and in the second person singular and exhibit explicit overt markings unlike Tamil. Consider the following in Table 4.

S.No.	GNP	Telugu	Tamil	Gloss	DI/Level
1.	1.SG.	*manisi- **ni*** human.SG.OBL-**1.SG.**	*manitan- ø* human.SG	'(I am) a human'	1/L1
2.	1.PL.	*manuṣula- **mu*** human.PL.OBL-**1.PL.**	*manitar- kaḷ- ø* human- PL	'(we are) humans'	1/L1
3.	2.SG.	*manisi- **vi***	*manitan- ø*	'(You are) a human'	1/L1

Table 4: Nominal predicates in Telugu and Tamil

These kind of divergences need to be noticed and handled strategically in the target language Tamil since it does not express these details on nominal predicates. Morphological divergences are mainly handled by the morphological generator (MG), the target language (TL) generation module. MG is equipped with inbuilt morphological features of TL which generates acceptable TL. Other modules such as parser, transfer grammar (TG), lexical transfer (LT) and agreement (AGR) modules do involve in handling morphological divergence.

4.3 Syntactic Divergence Index

Syntactic divergence here we refer to syntactic structural differences that occur between pairs of languages. It is obvious to find out similar constructions in Telugu and Tamil in majority of cases but still there are lots of variations arise due to case mismatches, agreement, anaphora, negation, subordination and clitics. Various syntactic processing and a robust transfer grammar are obviously required to overcome syntactic divergence.

For example, each case marker has a number of functions and it is obvious that they lead to case mismatches in MT. The difference in form and function of a case in the source language precludes the straightforward mapping of it in the target language. For instance, Telugu and Tamil agree in using the dative case marker in various functions viz., beneficiary of an action, goal of motion, experiencer subject (Cf. Krishnamurti, 2003:434; Verma and Mohanan, 1990:27) among other functions. However, to express a possessive relationship between two inanimate nouns, one of the nouns of inanimate category carries the dative marker to express the locative function in Telugu. On the contrary, the locative case marker is in use in Tamil. Example:

Te. gōḍa- ku kiṭikī̄   uM-   di.
    wall- DAT window.NOM be.PRS- 3.SG.N.

Ta. cuvaṟṟ- il jaṉṉal   iru- kkiṟ- atu.
    wall-   LOC window.NOM be- PRS- 3.SG.N.
    'The wall has a window.'

Syntactic divergences are mainly handled by TG. TG is equipped with performing certain tasks such as insertion, deletion, modification and re-ordering of words and chunks. It also has the ability to handle files where it is possible to operate a single rule over a list of items.

4.4 Lexical-Semantic Divergence Index

Lexical-semantic translation divergences are characterized by properties that are entirely lexically determined between languages. A concept expressed by a lexeme may not have the similar meaning in all contexts. The major lexical-semantic divergences that occur between Telugu and Tamil are due to the nature of its semantic compositions and their formal collocation in their expression.

For example, a lexeme, used to express a concept in a language may not have the same meaning in all contexts. When it has multiple meanings, word sense disambiguation is required to overcome lexical ambiguity and to select an appropriate sense with its form in the target language.

For instance, the lexeme *kuṭṭu* in Telugu is ambiguous and expresses three different senses as given below:
Sense 1: *kuṭṭu* 'to bite' as in the context of *cīma* 'an ant' and etc. The equivalent word in Tamil is *kaṭi* 'to bite'.
Sense 2: *kuṭṭu* 'to stitch' as in the context of *baṭṭalu* 'clothings'. The equivalent word in Tamil is *tai* 'to stitch'.

Sense 3: *kuṭṭu* 'to pierce' as in the context of *cevulu* 'ears' or body parts and etc. The equivalent word in Tamil is *kuttu* 'to pierce'.

Lexical-semantic divergences are handled by MWE component and LT. MWE component contains a lexical database consisting words of co-occurrence. When a group of words are identified as MWE, this module transfers them into the acceptable target language expression. Lexical ambiguities are handled by TG. An exhaustive set of transfer grammar rules operating on identification of the ambiguous words and disambiguating them by looking at the subject or the object nouns as suggested above are built. For instance, the following TG rules are samples to handle the different senses of Telugu word *kuṭṭu* in Tamil.

```
V1:R1::"$x=animate.txt"
R1:   NP<root="$x",lcat="n"> VGF<root="kuṭṭu",lcat="v"> =>
NP<root="$x", lcat="n"> VGF<root="kaṭi",lcat="v">
V2:R2::"$y=inanimate.txt"
R2:   NP<root="$y",lcat="n"> VGF<root="kuṭṭu",lcat="v"> =>
NP<root="$y", lcat="n"> VGF<root="tai",lcat="v">
V3:R3::"$z=bodyparts.txt"
R3:   NP<root="$z",lcat="n"> VGF<root="kuṭṭu",lcat="v"> =>
NP<root="$z", lcat="n"> VGF<root="kuttu",lcat="v">
```

5 Conclusion

Though Tamil and Telugu belong to the same language family (Dravidian language family), some major and minor differences are found in their linguistic behavior which preclude any straightforward mapping. To avoid this, it is essential to formalize the divergent patterns and develop a certain number of rules as the case demands to have a successful system with broad coverage. Building divergence Index is proved to be a useful activity to identify and handle divergences effectively in transfer-based MT.

References

Annamalai, E. 2000. 'Lexical Anaphors and Pronouns in Tamil'. In Lust et al (ed.), *Lexical Anaphors and Pronouns in Selected South Asian Languages: A Principled Typology*, 169–216.

Arokianathan, S. 1981. *Tamil Clitics*. Trivandrum: Dravidian Linguistics Association.

Bharati, Akshar, Rajeev Sangal & Dipti M Sharma. 2007. 'SSF: Shakti Standard Format Guide' 1–25.

Dash, Niladri Sekhar. 2013. 'Linguistic Divergences in English to Bengali Translation'. *International Journal of English Linguistics* 3(1).

Dave, Shachi, Jignashu Parikh & Pushpak Bhattacharyya. 2001. 'Interlingua-based English–Hindi Machine Translation and Language Divergence'. *Machine Translation* 16(4). 251–304.

Dorr, Bonnie Jean. 1993. *Machine Translation: a View from the Lexicon*. Massachusetts: MIT press.

Dorr, Bonnie Jean. 1994. 'Classification of Machine Translation Divergence and a Proposed Solution'. *Computational Linguistics* 20(4). 597–633.

Emeneau, Murray B. 1956. 'India as a Linguistic Area'. *Language* 3–16.

Goyal, Pawan & R Mahesh K Sinha. 2009. 'Translation divergence in English-Sanskrit-Hindi Language Pairs'. In *Sanskrit Computational Linguistics*, vol. 5406, 134–143. Springer.

Gupta, Deepa & Niladri Chatterjee. 2003. 'Identification of Divergence for English to Hindi EBMT. In *Proceeding of MT Summit-IX*, 141–148.

Hockett, Charles F. 1954. 'Two Models of Grammatical Description'. *Word 10*. 210–234.

Krishnamurti, Bh. & J. P. L. Gwynn. 1985. *A Grammar of Modern Telugu*. Delhi: Oxford University Press.

Lehmann, Thomas. 1993. *A Grammar of Modern Tamil*. Pondicherry: Pondicherry Institute of Linguistics and Culture.

Masica, Colin P. 1976. *'Defining a Linguistic Area: South Asia'*. Chicago: University of Chicago Press, 1976.

Mishra, Vimal & R. B. Mishra. 2008. 'Study of Example Based English to Sanskrit Machine Translation'. *Polibits* (37). 43–54.

Mitkov, Ruslan. 1999. *Anaphora Resolution: the State of the Art. http://clg.wlv.ac.uk/papers/mitkov-99a.pdf.*

Pawan, Kumar, A. K. Rathaur, Ahmad Rashid, K Sinha Mukul & Sangal Rajeev. 2010. 'Dashboard: An Integration & Testing Platform Based on Black Board Architecture for NLP Applications'. *Proceedings of 6th International Conference on Natural language Processing and Knowledge Engineering (NLP-KE)*, Beijing, China, August.

Shukla, Preeti, Devanand Shukl & Amba Kulkarni. 2010. Vibhakti Divergence between Sanskrit and Hindi. In *Proceedings of the International Sanskrit Computational Linguistics Symposium*, 198–208. Springer.

Subbarao, K. V. 2012. *South Asian Languages: A Syntactic Typology*. Cambridge: Cambridge University Press.

Subbarao, K. V. & B. Lalitha Murthy. 2000. 'Lexical Anaphors and Pronouns in Telugu'. In Lust et al (ed.), *Lexical Anaphors and Pronouns in Selected South Asian Languages: A Principled Typology*, 217–276.

Verma, Manindra K. & Mohanan K. P. (eds.). 1990. *'Experiencer Subjects in South Asian Languages'*. Stanford: Center for the Study of Language (CSLI).

Whitman, Neal. 2002. 'A Categorial Treatment of Adverbial Nouns'. *Journal of Linguistics* 38. 561–597.

Weaver, Warren. 1955. 'Translation'. *Machine Translation of Languages* 14. 15–23.

Deep-syntax TectoMT for English-Spanish MT

**Gorka Labaka, Oneka Jauregi, Arantza Díaz de Ilarraza,
Michael Ustaszewski, Nora Aranberri and Eneko Agirre**
IXA Group
Faculty of Computer Science
University of the Basque Country
Spain
{gorka.labaka, ojauregi002, a.diazdeilarraza,
mustaszewski001, nora.aranberri, e.agirre}@ehu.eus

Abstract

Deep-syntax approaches to machine translation have emerged as an alternative to phrase-based statistical systems, which seem to lack the capacity to address essential linguistic phenomena for translation. As an alternative, TectoMT is an open source framework for transfer-based MT which works at the deep tectogrammatical level and combines linguistic knowledge and statistical techniques. This work describes the development of machine translation systems for English-Spanish in both directions, leveraging on the modules for the English-Czech TectoMT system. We show that it is feasible to develop basic systems with relatively low effort in 9 months. Our evaluation shows that despite not yet being able to beat a phrase-based statistical system, the TectoMT architecture offers flexible customization options, which considerably increase the BLEU scores.

1 Introduction

Phrase-based machine translation (MT) systems have difficulty in capturing linguistic phenomena, such as long-distance grammatical cohesion. Syntax-based approaches have appeared as an alternative that can overcome this barrier more easily. Shallow approaches, however, seem still too restrictive and methods of deep linguistic analysis have been put forward as a tool to capture all the important parts of the meaning of the text. Efforts to build translation models around deep syntactic structure often move the level of linguistic abstraction a step deeper into semantic roles and relations, which should entail a simpler transfer step because of the greater structural similarity between the deep structures of the source and target languages as compared to the surface realizations; better generalization of the language as it operates on lemmas of content words and grammatical constructions are abstracted with their meaning captured by language-independent attributes; and improved grammaticality of the output given the explicit representation of target-side sentence structure.

TectoMT (Žabokrtský et al., 2008; Popel and Žabokrtský, 2010) has emerged as a potential architecture to develop such an approach, together with other deep-transfer systems such as Matxin (Mayor et al., 2011) and the one proposed by Gasser (2012). In contrast to those systems, TectoMT combines linguistic knowledge and statistical techniques, particularly during transfer, and it aims at transfer on the so-called tectogrammatical layer (Hajičová, 2000), a layer of deep syntactic dependency trees.

In this paper we present a description of the work done to develop a TectoMT system for both directions of English-Spanish, based on the existing English-Czech TectoMT system. In Section 2 we give an overview of the TectoMT architecture and the key linguistic concepts it is based on; in Section 3 we describe the analysis, transfer and synthesis stages, and highlight the upgrades and modifications carried out to develop the new language pair; in Section 4 we show an initial evaluation of the new prototypes; and finally, in Section 5 we draw conclusions and comment on the planned future work.

Proceedings of the 1st Deep Machine Translation Workshop (DMTW 2015), pages 55–63,
Praha, Czech Republic, 3–4 September 2015.

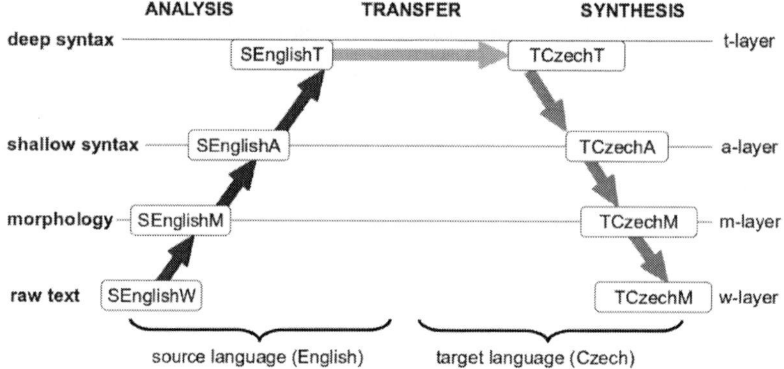

Figure 1: The general TectoMT architecture (from (Popel and Žabokrtský, 2010, :298)).

2 TectoMT architecture

As with most rule-based systems, TectoMT consists of an analysis, transfer and synthesis stages. The system works on different levels of abstraction (cf. Figure 1) and uses Blocks and Scenarios to process the information across the architecture.

2.1 Tecto layers

TectoMT works on an stratification approach to language, that is, it defines four layers of language, in increasing level of abstraction: raw text (word layer or w-layer), morphological layer (m-layer), shallow-syntax layer (analytical layer or a-layer), and deep-syntax layer (tectogrammatical layer or t-layer). This strategy is adopted from the Functional Generative Description theory (Sgall, 1967), which has been further elaborated and implemented in the Prague Dependency Treebank (PDT) (Hajič et al., 2006). As explained by (Popel and Žabokrtský, 2010, :296), each layer contains the following representation:

- **Morphological layer (m-layer)**

  Each sentence is tokenized and each token is annotated with a lemma and morphological tag.

- **Analytical layer (a-layer)**

  Each sentence is represented as a shallow-syntax dependency tree (a-tree). There is one-to-one correspondence between m-layer tokens and a-layer nodes. Each a-node is annotated with the type of dependency relation to its governing node or parent.

- **Tectogrammatical layer (t-layer)**

  Each sentence is represented as a deep-syntax dependency tree (t-tree). Autosemantic (meaningful) words are represented as t-layer nodes (t-nodes). Information conveyed by functional words (such as auxiliary verbs, prepositions and subordinating conjunctions) is represented by attributes of t-nodes. Most important attributes of t-nodes are:

  - tectogrammatical lemma;
  - functor: represents the semantic value of syntactic dependency relations, e.g. causal adjunct, conditional adjunct, actor, effect;
  - grammatemes: semantically oriented counterparts of morphological categories present at the higher level of abstraction, e.g. tense, number, verb modality, deontic modality, negation;
  - formemes: the morphosyntactic form of a t-node in the surface sentence. The set of formeme values compatible with a given t-node is limited by its semantic part of speech, e.g. subject noun, direct object noun, verb as a head of a relative clause (Dušek et al., 2012).

2.2 Blocks and Scenarios

Blocks are reusable components of subsequent steps into which NLP tasks can be decomposed. Each block has a well defined input and output specification and, in most cases, also a linguistically interpretable functionality. When developing new applications, blocks can be listed in a specific sequence and applied to the relevant data. These sequences are called scenarios.

TectoMT includes over a thousand blocks; approximately 224 blocks specific for English, 237 for Czech, over 57 for English-to-Czech transfer, 129 for other languages and 467 language-independent blocks.[1] Blocks vary in lengths, as they can consist of a few lines of code or tackle complex linguistic phenomena. To avoid code duplications, many routines are implemented separately and used in several blocks.

3 Development of a new language pair

We set to port the TectoMT system to work for the English-Spanish language pair in both directions. Because the original system covers both directions for the English-Czech pair, English analysis and synthesis were ready to use and our work mainly focused on Spanish analysis and synthesis, and on the transfer stages. In the following subsections we describe the work done on each step, analysis, transfer and synthesis, for each translation direction in our attempt to build tecto-level MT systems.

TectoMT is integrated within Treex,[2] a highly modular open source NLP framework implemented in Perl programming language. The framework includes modules for the English-Czech and Czech-English pairs, which are divided into language-specific and language independent blocks, thus facilitating the work to build the systems for the new language pair. As we will see in what follows, a good number of resources were reused, mainly those setting the general architecture and those specific to English; others were adapted, mainly those involving training of new language and translation models; and several new blocks were created to enable language-pair-specific features.

3.1 Analysis

The analysis stage aims at getting raw input text and analyzing it up to the tectogrammatical level so that transfer can be performed (cf. figs. 2 and 3). For English, the modules needed for analysis were already developed and running, and therefore little effort had to be put on it.

For Spanish, however, new analysis tools had to be integrated into Treex. For tokenization and sentence splitting, we adapted the modules of Treex to Spanish. Treex integrates tokenization and sentence splitting based on non-breaking prefixes. Therefore, we added a list of Spanish non-breaking prefixes in the module.

For the remaining tasks, we opted for the `ixa-pipes tools`.[3] These tools consist of a set of modules that perform linguistic analysis from tokenization to parsing, as well as several external tools that have been adapted to interact with them, adding extra functionality. We integrated the lemmatization and POS tagging (`ixa-pipe-pos`) and the dependency parsing (`ixa-pipe-srl`) tools in Treex. The first provides Perceptron (Collins, 2002) and Maximum Entropy (Ratnaparkhi, 1999) POS tagging models trained and evaluated using the AnCora corpus via 10-fold cross-validation, dictionary-based lemmatization, multiword detection and post-processing of probabilistic model pos tags using monosemic dictionaries. The second provides constituent parsing trained on the AnCora corpus and HeadFinders based on Collins head rules (Collins, 1999).

The tools were already developed, with accurate models for Spanish, and ready to use. Our efforts focused on their integration within Treex. We did this by adding them as wrapper blocks that, given a set of already tokenized sentences, creates the appropriate input in the corresponding format and calls the relevant tool. Once the tools complete their work, the output of the system is read and loaded in Treex documents.

---

[1] Statistics taken from: `https://github.com/ufal/treex.git` (27/08/2015)

[2] `https://ufal.mff.cuni.cz/treex`, `https://github.com/ufal/treex`

[3] `http://ixa2.si.ehu.es/ixa-pipes/`

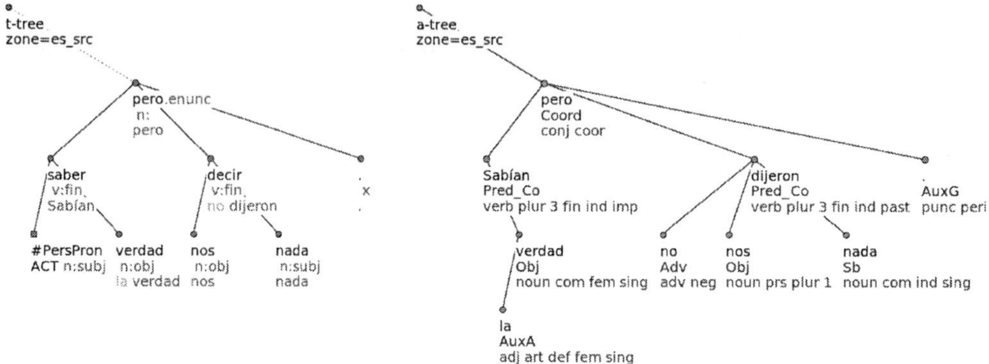

Figure 2: a-level and t-level Spanish analysis.

All `ixa-pipes tools` read NAF documents (with word forms and term elements) via standard input and output NAF through standard output. The NAF format is a linguistic annotation format designed for complex NLP pipelines (Fokkens et al., 2014).

The analyses generated by the `ixa-pipes tools` follow the AnCora guidelines both for morphological tags and dependency tree structures. This mostly equates to the a-layer in the TectoMT stratification. Therefore, to fully integrate the analyses into Treex and generate the expected a-tree, the analyses had to be mapped to a universal PoS and dependency tags. TectoMT currently uses the Interset tagset (Zeman, 2008) and HamleDT guidelines (Zeman et al., 2014). To implement this mapping, we used existing modules such as the Interset driver for Spanish AnCora Treebank tagset[4] by Dan Zeman and Zdenek Zabokrtsky, and the Harmonization Treex block for Spanish AnCora-style dependencies[5] by Dan Zeman, Zdenek Zabokrtsky and Martin Popel. On top of these, and in order to form the t-level tree, we used 16 additional blocks:

1. **Language-independent blocks.** 11 of the blocks were simply reused from the language-independent set already available in Treex. These mainly re-arrange nodes, mark heads (coordinations, clauses, coreference) and set node types.

2. **Adapted blocks.** 4 blocks were adapted from blocks originally used for English or Czech analysis. These include how to mark edges to collapse nodes into a single t-level node, how to annotate a number of functions words, sentence mood and grammateme values.

3. **New language-specific blocks.** 1 block was specifically written to set the grammatemes based on the Interset tagset features (and formemes) of the corresponding auxiliary a-level nodes.

3.2 Transfer

The transfer stage uses a statistical transfer dictionary together with a set of manually written blocks. The transfer dictionary is trained on parallel corpora analyzed up to the t-level in both languages. Learning equivalences at this level of representation enriches the model and simplifies the complexity of translation: it is not word-form equivalences that are learned, but rather the final dictionary includes the translation of lemmas, formemes and grammatemes (Žabokrtský, 2010). This approach is based on the assumption that t-tree structures in different languages are shared. Although this is not always true (Popel, 2009), it allows to model the working language pair as source-target one-to-one mapping.

For each t-lemma and formeme in a source t-tree, the translation model (TM) assigns a score to all possible translations observed in the training data. This score is a probability estimate of the translation

---

[4]`https://metacpan.org/source/ZEMAN/Lingua-Interset-2.041/lib/Lingua/Interset/Tagset/ES/Conll2009.pm`

[5]`https://github.com/ufal/treex/blob/master/lib/Treex/Block/HamleDT/ES/Harmonize.pm`

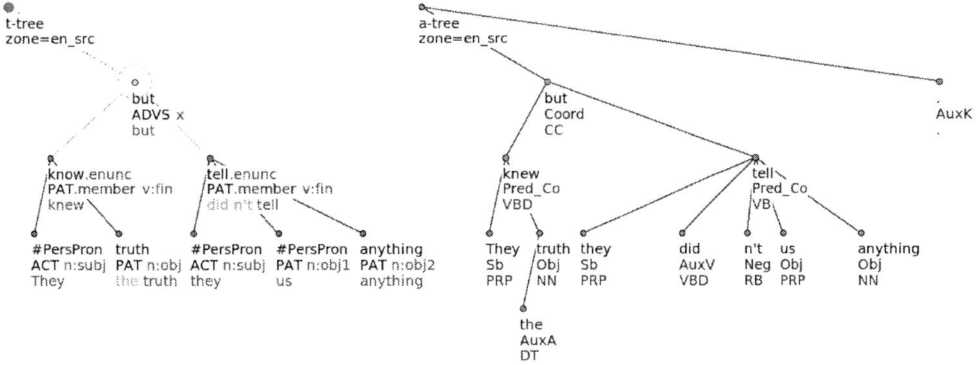

Figure 3: a-level and t-level English analysis.

variant given the source t-lemma and formeme, and other contextual information, and it is calculated as a linear combination of two main components:

- **The discriminative TM** (Mareček et al., 2010) is a set of maximum entropy (MaxEnt) models (Berger et al., 1996) trained for each specific source t-lemma and formeme, where the prediction is based on features extracted from the source tree (Crouse et al., 1998; Žabokrtský and Popel, 2009).

- **The dictionary TM** is a bilingual dictionary that contains a list of possible translation equivalents based on relative frequencies and no contextual features.

Both components are trained on the parallel corpora at the t-level. The final score assigned to each t-lemma and formeme in the TMs is calculated through interpolation. For the t-lemmas, weights of 0.5 and 1 are assigned to the dictionary TM and the discriminative TM, respectively. In the case of formemes, the values are reversed. Using these two TMs, we obtain a weighted n-best list of translation variants for each t-lemma and each formeme. The lists are jointly re-ranked by Hidden Markov Tree Models (HMTM), similarly to standard chains but operating on trees (Crouse et al., 1998; Žabokrtský and Popel, 2009). This setting was taken as-is from the one used for English-Czech.

The hybrid architecture of TectoMT, where both statistical transfer models and manually defined blocks can be combined, allows the integration of domain specific human dictionaries. Our development targets a question-and-answer (Q&A) scenario in the information technology (IT) domain. Therefore, in order to customize the systems to this domain, we integrated the Microsoft Terminology Collection as preprocessing (so the two TMs serve as a backoff for this human in-domain dictionary). The Microsoft Terminology Collection is freely available[6] and contains 22,475 entries.

The equivalence of grammatemes is assigned by manually written rules. The information they contain is linguistically more abstract, e.g. tense and number, and it is usually paralleled in the target language. Therefore, a set of relatively simple rules (with a list of exceptions) is sufficient for this task. These rules are inherently language-specific. At the time of writing, we use 5 blocks specifically written for the English-to-Spanish direction. These blocks address the lack of gender in English nouns (necessary in Spanish), differences in definiteness and articles, differences in structures such as *There is...* and relative clauses.

3.3 Synthesis

The output from transfer is a t-level tree that must be interpreted during the synthesis stage to generate the a-tree, which is used to create the final raw text (cf. figs. 4 and 5). The English synthesis was already developed and therefore, once again, our work mainly focused on preparing the Spanish synthesis, as we explain below.

---

[6] http://www.microsoft.com/Language/en-US/Terminology.aspx

We distinguish three steps during synthesis. On a first step, the t-tree generated using the information obtained during transfer must be transformed into an a-tree. At the time of writing, we use a total of 24 blocks.

1. **Language-independent blocks.** 9 of the blocks were reused from the language-independent set already available in Treex. Among these are blocks to mark subjects, impose subject-predicate and attribute agreements, add separate negation nodes, add specific punctuation for coordinate clauses, or impose capitalization at the beginning of sentence.

2. **Adapted blocks.** 12 blocks were adapted from the blocks in the English and Czech synthesis, or generic ones. For example, after acquiring the tree structure, the morphological categories are filled with values derived from the grammatemes and formemes. Whereas this is done for all languages, Spanish requires information coming from English grammatemes to be further distinguished. This is the case of the imperfect tense (a subcategory of past tense) and imperfect aspect, for instance, which we set on a block. Another block deals with articles. Knowing the definiteness of a noun or noun phrase is not always enough to decide whether to generate a determiner in the target language, and when necessary, to generate the appropriate one. Similarly, we adapted blocks for prepositions, subordinate conjunctions and auxiliary verbs. To mention yet another block, we remove personal pronoun nodes when acting as subject (the information is passed on to the predicate) as pro-drop languages such as Spanish do not require that they appear explicitly because this is already marked in the verb.

3. **New language-specific blocks.** 3 blocks were written from scratch to deal with Spanish-specific features. These deal with attribute order, comparatives and verb tenses. Attribute order refers to the position of adjectives with respect to the unit they modify. In English, adjectives occur before the noun they modify, but this is the opposite - with some exceptions for figurative effect - in Spanish. The block addressing comparatives creates additional nodes for the Spanish structure, which is specially relevant for the cases where no separate comparative word is used in English. Finally, a block was specifically written to address the complex verb tenses in Spanish. This block uses the information about tense, perfectiveness and progressiveness of the English verb to select the appropriate verb form in Spanish.

Overall, we see that most blocks are used (i) to fill in morphological attributes that will be needed in the second step, (ii) to add function words where necessary, (iii) to remove superfluous nodes, and (iv) to add punctuation nodes.

On a second step, the lemma and morphosyntactic information on the a-tree must be turned into word forms to generate the w-tree. We used Flect (Dušek and Jurčíček, 2013) to do this, by training new models for Spanish. Flect is a statistical morphological generation tool based on Python and Scikit-Learn that learns morphological inflection patterns from corpora. We trained the system with a subset of morphologically annotated Europarl corpus (530K tokens) where the system automatically learns how to generate inflected word forms from lemmas and morphological features. Flect can inflect previously unseen words as it uses lemma suffixes as features and predicts edit scripts that describe the difference between the lemma and the form, which improves robustness.

On a third step, once we obtain the w-tree with the word forms, a number of blocks can be written to polish the final output. For example, we use a block to concatenate the prepositions *a* and *de* with the masculine singular article *el*, which should be presented as the single forms $a+el \rightarrow al$ and $de+el \rightarrow del$.

4 Evaluation

We evaluated the new English-to-Spanish and Spanish-to-English TectoMT prototypes in three different scenarios: using language-independent blocks only,[7], adding the blocks written and adapted for Spanish, and adding the domain-specific dictionary.

---

[7]This setup includes `ixa-pipes tools` and Flect models for Spanish analysis and synthesis, and bilingual transfer models.

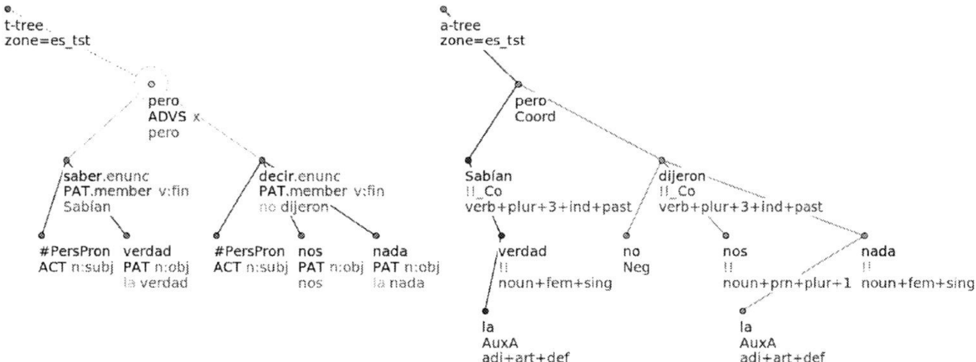

Figure 4: a-level and t-level Spanish synthesis.

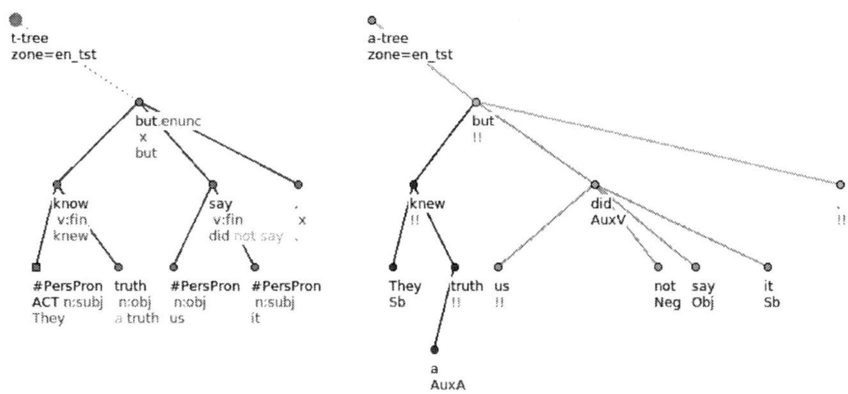

Figure 5: a-level and t-level English synthesis.

Also, we evaluated the new systems against a phrased-based statistical system. To this end, we built two SMT systems, one per language direction. We used tools available in the Moses toolkit for tokenization and truecasing, while mGiza was used for word alignment. For language modeling, we use SRILM to train a different language model (LM) for each corpus available and to combine them through LM interpolation. We trained the systems on bilingual corpora including Europarl, United Nations, News Commentary and Common Crawl (~355 million words). The monolingual corpora used to learn the LM include the target-side texts of Europarl, News Commentary and News Crawl (~60 million words). As previously mentioned, our efforts focus on a question-and-answer (Q&A) scenario in the information technology (IT) domain. Therefore, for tuning, we used a set of 1,000 in-domain interactions (question-answer pairs). The original interactions were in English and they were translated into Spanish by human translators.

We calculated BLEU scores for the systems on two different test sets. The first is another test-set of 1,000 in-domain interactions. The second is the newswire test-set used in the WMT11 campaign (Table 1) .

We can draw several conclusions from the BLEU scores obtained for each system and language pair. First, we observe that the TectoMT prototypes do not yet beat the statistical systems, although the English-to-Spanish system evaluated on the IT test-set remains very close, less than 2 BLEU points behind. Because a large portion of the TectoMT systems is based on rules, the lower scores of the baselines was to be expected given the effort put at this stage of development.

With regard to the TectoMT systems, we observe how the BLEU scores increase as we customize the system. The baseline systems with only language-independent blocks score lower than the systems

	English-Spanish		Spanish-English	
	IT	WMT11	IT	WMT11
Moses	28.12	26.91	31.92	25.24
TectoMT – language independent blocks	12.40	8.38	12.34	8.17
TectoMT – + Spanish blocks	23.62	13.92	14.67	8.50
TectoMT – + domain dictionary	26.40	13.25	15.82	8.23

Table 1: BLEU scores for the English-Spanish TectoMT prototypes

which include Spanish-specific blocks. For the English-to-Spanish system, BLEU scores almost double. For the Spanish-to-English system scores also increase although not as much. When adding the Microsoft dictionary (IT domain-specific), we observe that the BLEU scores increase almost 3 points for the English-to-Spanish direction and over 1 point for the Spanish-to-English direction. It is worth noting the small setback introduced by this specialized dictionary for the news domain with a drop of 0.67 and 0.27.

The scores also show the difference in development effort for the TectoMT systems in terms of language direction. The baseline TectoMT systems score similarly for both directions, at around 12 BLEU points for the IT test-set and 8 BLEU points for the WMT11 test-set. However, the priority given to Spanish-specific blocks for synthesis result in a better system for the English-to-Spanish direction.

Finally, it is worth mentioning the difference in scores between the test-sets, as the IT test-set scores substantially higher than the newswire test-set. This is probably because the IT domain test-set contains shorter and less convoluted sentences and most development work was based on IT-domain text analysis, even if the blocks written deal with generic linguistic features.

As a reference of the human effort required, we developed the new TectoMT systems over a period of 9 months.

5   Conclusions

In this paper we have shown the work done to develop entry-level deep-syntax systems for the English-Spanish language pair following the tectogrammatical MT approach. Thanks to previous work done for the English-Czech pair, we have reused most of the English analysis and synthesis modules, and mainly focused on the integration of tools and the development of models and blocks for Spanish. In particular, we have integrated the `ixa-pipes tools` for PoS and dependency parsing of Spanish, and adapted its output to comply with the tecto-level representation of language, which uses universal labels. For transfer, we have trained new statistical models for both English-to-Spanish and Spanish-to-English directions. For synthesis, we have trained a new morphological model to obtain Spanish word forms. Substantial effort was also put on writing sets of blocks to address differing linguistic features between the language pairs across all stages with a total of 55 reused blocks and 5 new/adapted blocks for the Spanish-to-English direction, and a total of 73 reused blocks and 19 new/adapted blocks for the English-to-Spanish direction. The system is open source and can be downloaded from `https://github.com/ufal/treex`. The evaluation has shown that the English-Spanish TectoMT prototype systems do not yet score as high as a phrase-based statistical system. However, the TectoMT architecture offers flexible customization options. We have shown that the BLEU scores can increase considerably as these are integrated and tuned to the working language pair.

Acknowledgements

The research leading to these results has received funding from FP7-ICT-2013-10-610516 (QTLeap).

References

Adam L Berger, Vincent J Della Pietra, and Stephen A Della Pietra. 1996. A maximum entropy approach to natural language processing. *Computational linguistics*, 22(1):39–71.

Michael Collins. 1999. Head-driven statistical models for natural language parsing.

Michael Collins. 2002. Discriminative training methods for hidden Markov models: Theory and experiments with perceptron algorithms. In *Proceedings of the ACL-02 conference on Empirical methods in natural language processing-Volume 10*, pages 1–8. Association for Computational Linguistics.

Matthew S Crouse, Robert D Nowak, and Richard G Baraniuk. 1998. Wavelet-based statistical signal processing using hidden markov models. *Signal Processing, IEEE Transactions on*, 46(4):886–902.

Ondrej Dušek and Filip Jurčíček. 2013. Robust multilingual statistical morphological generation models. *ACL 2013*, page 158.

Ondřej Dušek, Zdeněk Žabokrtský, Martin Popel, Martin Majliš, Michal Novák, and David Mareček. 2012. Formemes in English-Czech deep syntactic MT. In *Proceedings of the Seventh Workshop on Statistical Machine Translation*, pages 267–274. Association for Computational Linguistics.

Antske Fokkens, Aitor Soroa, Zuhaitz Beloki, Niels Ockeloen, German Rigau, Willem Robert van Hage, and Piek Vossen. 2014. NAF and GAF: Linking linguistic annotations. In *Proceedings 10th Joint ISO-ACL SIGSEM Workshop on Interoperable Semantic Annotation*, page 9, Reykjavik, Iceland.

Michael Gasser. 2012. Toward a rule-based system for English-Amharic translation. *Language Technology for Normalisation of Less-Resourced Languages*, page 41.

Jan Hajič, Jarmila Panevová, Eva Hajičová, Petr Sgall, Petr Pajas, Jan Štepánek, Jiří Havelka, Marie Mikulová, Zdenek Žabokrtský, and Magda Ševcıková Razımová. 2006. Prague dependency treebank 2.0. *CD-ROM, Linguistic Data Consortium, LDC Catalog No.: LDC2006T01, Philadelphia*, 98.

Eva Hajičová. 2000. Dependency-based underlying-structure tagging of a very large Czech corpus. *TAL. Traitement automatique des langues*, 41(1):57–78.

David Mareček, Martin Popel, and Zdeněk Žabokrtský. 2010. Maximum entropy translation model in dependency-based MT framework. In *Proceedings of the Joint Fifth Workshop on Statistical Machine Translation and MetricsMATR*, pages 201–206. Association for Computational Linguistics.

Aingeru Mayor, Iñaki Alegria, Arantza Díaz De Ilarraza, Gorka Labaka, Mikel Lersundi, and Kepa Sarasola. 2011. Matxin, an open-source rule-based machine translation system for Basque. *Machine translation*, 25(1):53–82.

Martin Popel and Zdeněk Žabokrtský. 2010. TectoMT: modular NLP framework. In *Advances in natural language processing*, pages 293–304. Springer.

Martin Popel. 2009. Ways to improve the quality of English-Czech machine translation. *Master's thesis, Institute of Formal and Applied Linguistics, Charles University, Prague, Czech Republic.*

Adwait Ratnaparkhi. 1999. Learning to parse natural language with maximum entropy models. *Machine learning*, 34(1-3):151–175.

Petr Sgall. 1967. Functional sentence perspective in a generative description. *Prague studies in mathematical linguistics*, 2(203-225).

Zdeněk Žabokrtský and Martin Popel. 2009. Hidden markov tree model in dependency-based machine translation. In *Proceedings of the ACL-IJCNLP 2009 Conference Short Papers*, pages 145–148. Association for Computational Linguistics.

Zdeněk Žabokrtský, Jan Ptáček, and Petr Pajas. 2008. TectoMT: Highly modular MT system with tectogrammatics used as transfer layer. In *Proceedings of the Third Workshop on Statistical Machine Translation*, pages 167–170. Association for Computational Linguistics.

Zdeněk Žabokrtský. 2010. From treebanking to machine translation. *Habilitation thesis, Charles University, Prague, Czech Republic.*

Daniel Zeman, Ondřej Dušek, David Mareček, Martin Popel, Loganathan Ramasamy, Jan Štěpánek, Zdeněk Žabokrtský, and Jan Hajič. 2014. HamleDT: Harmonized multi-language dependency treebank. *Language Resources and Evaluation*, 48(4):601–637.

D. Zeman. 2008. Reusable tagset conversion using tagset drivers. In *Proceedings of LREC*, pages 213–218.

First Steps in Using Word Senses as Contextual Features in Maxent Models for Machine Translation

Steven Neale, Luís Gomes and António Branco
Department of Informatics
Faculty of Sciences
University of Lisbon, Portugal
{steven.neale, luis.gomes, antonio.branco}@di.fc.ul.pt

Abstract

Despite the common assumption that word sense disambiguation (WSD) should help to improve lexical choice and improve the quality of the output of machine translation systems, how to successfully integrate word senses into such systems remains an unanswered question. While significant improvements have been reported using reformulated approaches to the disambiguation task itself – most notably in predicting translations of full phrases as opposed to the senses of single words – little improvement or encouragement has been gleaned from the incorporation of traditional WSD into machine translation.

In this paper, we present preliminary results that suggest that incorporating output from WSD as contextual features in a maxent-based translation model yields a slight improvement in the quality of machine translation and is potentially a step in the right direction, in contrast to other approaches to introducing word senses into a machine translation system which significantly impede its performance.

1 Introduction

Ambiguity is a common problem in language, caused by the phenomena of identical words having multiple, distinct meanings (Xiong and Zhang, 2014). To use a classic example, the word 'bank' could be interpreted in the sense of the financial institution or as the slope of land at the side of a river, depending on the context in which it is used. In natural language processing (NLP), word sense disambiguation (WSD) refers to the process of solving this problem by determining the 'sense' or meaning of a word when used in a particular context (Agirre and Edmonds, 2006).

In computational terms, WSD is a classification task, where the context in which a target word is used provides evidence that helps to determine which class of words – sense – it should be assigned to (Agirre and Edmonds, 2006). Most approaches to WSD in recent years have been 'knowledge-based', with those classes of words stored in lexical ontologies such as WordNet (Fellbaum, 1998), where the collective meanings of open-class words (nouns, verbs, adjectives and adverbs) are grouped together as 'synsets'. For tasks such as machine translation, ambiguous terms are a major potential source of errors, as identical words with different meanings will normally have different target translations (Xiong and Zhang, 2014). Thus, it has long been assumed that in order for a machine translation system to be optimally successful, it must incorporate some kind of WSD component (Carpuat and Wu, 2005).

Most attempts to integrate WSD components into machine translation systems have met with mixed – and usually limited – success. Early attempts at 'projecting' word senses directly into a machine translation system (Carpuat and Wu, 2005) were followed by a complete reformulation of the disambiguation process as a multi-word 'phrase sense' disambiguation approach, yeilding some improvements in translation quality (Carpuat and Wu, 2007). More recently, a 'word sense induction' approach that assigns word senses without the need for predefined sense inventories (such as WordNets) has been explored (Xiong and Zhang, 2014), but the question of whether pure word senses from traditional, knowledge-based WSD approaches can be useful for machine translation still remains.

Proceedings of the 1st Deep Machine Translation Workshop (DMTW 2015), pages 64–72,
Praha, Czech Republic, 3–4 September 2015.

In this paper, we demonstrate that by including the output from WSD as a feature in a maximum entropy (maxent)-based translation model, small gains in machine translation from English to Portuguese can be obtained. The contribution of our work, albeit preliminary in nature, is in showing these gains, however small, to be possible without having to reformulate WSD or drastically alter the way disambiguation is performed – the features added to the transfer model are direct outputs of a state-of-the-art WSD algorithm, without any kind of intermediary conversion or reformulation of either the word senses or the algorithm that delivers them.

We first explore previous efforts to integrate word senses into machine translation (Section 2), before describing our own approaches to the problem (Section 3). Next, we present our evaluation of these approaches, comparing different methods of integrating the output from a WSD process into a machine translation system (Section 4). Finally, we discuss our findings (Section 5) before making our conclusions (Section 6).

2 Related Work

Early work from Carpaut and Wu (2005) presented empirical results that cast doubt on the common assumption that the disambiguation of word senses could help to improve the quality of machine translation systems. They demonstrated that many of the contextual features important to WSD algorithms are implicit in the language models that are trained to perform machine translation, making them WSD models in their own right (Carpuat and Wu, 2005). Despite acknowledging that dedicated WSD algorithms are usually based on rich semantic data and that this should enable better predictions of lexical choice to be made, they showed a machine translation system trained on complete parallel sentences (rather than isolated target words as in WSD) to yield higher BLEU scores than a system where WSD output was forced into the translation model (Carpuat and Wu, 2005).

Based on these outcomes, a reformulated disambiguation process was proposed, with multi-word phrases the target as opposed to single words (Carpuat and Wu, 2007). Leveraging the fact that machine translation models are trained using contextual features from full sentences already, this 'phrase sense disambiguation' approach was designed to "generalize WSD to multi-word targets" and to incorporate the "crucial assumptions" that underly the sentence-based translation models into the sense disambiguation process as well (Carpuat and Wu, 2007). Across a number of evaluation metrics for machine translation, the phrase sense disambiguation approach was found to yield improved transation quality, suggesting that the sentence-based translation models used by machine translation systems can benefit from the addition of phrase-based (rather than word-based) sense disambiguation (Carpuat and Wu, 2007).

Further attempts to reformulate WSD into a more phrase-based concept followed. Chanel et al (2007) described having successfully integrated WSD into a machine translation system to obtain significantly improved results, but actually create their 'senses' by extracting English translations from full phrases in Chinese and using them as proposed translations . Inspired by traditional approaches to WSD, Giménez and Màrquez (2007) also advocated the move from 'word translation' to 'phrase translation', describing how lists of possible translations of a single source phrase can help to predict the correct translations of complete phrases in a given target language.

Recently, a renewed interest in exploring whether traditional, single word-based WSD can be useful for machine translation has emerged. Xiong and Zhang (2014) use the related technique of 'word sense induction' (WSI) to investigate whether or not pure word senses can be integrated into machine translation in such a way as to yield improvements in translation quality, being successful in their approach to predicting the senses of target words (rather than predicting their translations, as with the phrase-based approaches to disambiguation) (Xiong and Zhang, 2014). However, WSI automatically induces senses of words by clustering them together using their neighbouring words as context, *without* the need for a predefined sense inventory as in traditional WSD (Xiong and Zhang, 2014). The question still remains – how can word senses disambiguated using the rich semantic ontologies (such as WordNet) on which traditional WSD is based be successfully integrated into machine translation systems?

3 Description

This section outlines our implementation of WSD as part of a machine translation process, including descriptions of the graph-based algorithm we use to perform the WSD, the machine translation system and framework into which we implement it, and the two approaches we have taken to making use of the information output by the WSD process: 1) forcing information into the input sentences (directly affecting the alignment of words *before* the translation model is trained), and 2) including information as features in a maxent-based translation model (which does *not* affect word alignment but rather directly influences the training of the translation model).

3.1 WSD algorithm - *UKB*

To perform WSD we use *UKB*, a collection of tools and algorithms for performing graph-based WSD over a pre-existing knowledge base (Agirre and Soroa, 2009; Agirre et al., 2014). Graph-based WSD, as pioneered by a number of researchers (Navigli and Velardi, 2005; Mihalcea, 2005; Sinha and Mihalcea, 2007; Navigli and Lapata, 2007; Agirre and Soroa, 2008), allows knowledge bases such as WordNets to be represented as weighted graphs, where word senses correspond to nodes and the relationships or dependencies between pairs of senses correspond to the edges between nodes. The strength of the edge between two nodes, corresponding to the relationship or dependency between two synsets, can then be calculated using semantic similarity measures such as the Lesk algorithm (Lesk, 1986).

UKB uses graph-based representations of knowledge bases to choose the most likely sense of a word in a given context, based on the dependencies between nodes in the graph (Agirre and Soroa, 2009). Nodes (senses) 'recommend' each other based on their own importance – with the importance of any given node being higher or lower depending on the importance of other nodes which recommend it – and then follow a 'random walk' over the rest of the graph based on the importance of the nodes to whose edges they are attached (Mihalcea, 2005; Agirre and Soroa, 2009). The final probability of a random walk from the target word's node ending on any other node in the graph determines the most appropriate (probable) sense of the target word.

We choose to use UKB in our work for two reasons:

- UKB includes tools for automatically creating graph-based representations of knowledge bases in WordNet-style formats.

- The algorithm used by UKB for performing WSD over the graph itself has been consistently shown to produce results in line with or above the state-of-the-art (Agirre and Soroa, 2009; Agirre et al., 2014).

For the purpose of our work, we are thus able to perform highly-efficient WSD over an accurate graph-based representation of our chosen knowledge base (WordNet), meaning that any differences in the results of our integration of disambiguated output into the machine translation system can be confidently attributed to the integration process, rather than to the quality of the WSD output itself.

3.2 Machine Translation system - *TectoMT*

The machine translation system used in our work is *TectoMT*, a multi-purpose open source NLP framework that allows different software modules and tools to be integrated with each other (Popel and Žabokrtský, 2010)[1]. The framework is based on individual modules (known as 'blocks') that allow new or existing tools to be created or 'wrapped' in such a way that they can be easily integrated at various stages in a larger pipeline. These blocks are re-usable in different contexts and combinations (known as 'scenarios') to perform a variety of NLP tasks and are designed to be language-independent where possible, reducing the amount of repeated, expensive and time-consuming extra work usually needed to integrate tools.

For machine translation, TectoMT breaks down the source language and reconstructs the target language according to four layers of representation: the word layer (raw text), the morphological layer, the

---

[1] The TectoMT framework is now being developed under the name *Treex*: `https://github.com/ufal/treex`

analytical layer (shallow-syntax) and the tectogrammatical layer (deep-syntax). Different combinations of blocks make up each of the three scenarios needed for machine translation – one for analysis (of the source language), one for transfer (of tectogrammatical nodes from source to target language) and one for synsthesis (of the target language).

3.3 Integrating WSD output into a TectoMT-based pipeline

The first step in integrating the output produced by the WSD process into the machine translation pipeline is to wrap the WSD process as a block that can be included in user-created scenarios using the TectoMT framework. This new block converts input sentences to a format suitable for the UKB algorithm, and then performs WSD on each sentence using a graph-based representation of our chosen knowledge base, WordNet. For each word disambiguated by UKB, the returned output consists of the 8-digit synset identifier of the appropriate sense in WordNet chosen at the end of the random walk over the graph.

The TectoMT WSD block then maps this output back onto the input sentence, either as the synset identifier returned by UKB, an 'unknown' tag ('UNK', given to UKB but not able to be disambiguated) or a 'not applicable' tag ('_', not open-class and not given to UKB). This mapped WSD output is encoded into the analytical layer of each word in TectoMT as an attribute of the given word. Once words in the analytical layer have been assigned word senses as attributes, there are two ways with which we have experimented making use of this information for training actual translation models:

3.3.1 Forcing synset identifiers into input sentences prior to creating translation models

Forcing the synset identifiers produced by the WSD process onto the input sentences prior to creating translation models is achieved by taking the synset identifier from the WSD attribute stored in the analytical layer for a given word and using it in place of the original lemma. During the training of transfer models, when alignments are made between sentences from parallel corpora in the source and target languages, it should be the case that the forced synset identifiers help to create more accurate alignments between pairs of words based on their meanings, rather than solely their lexical form[2]. In this paper, we investigate two possible ways to force a synset identifier onto the lemma:

- Replacing the lemma with the synset identifier (e.g. 'word' becomes '01234567')

- Appending the synset identifier to the lemma (e.g. 'word' becomes 'word_01234567')

If we consider a link between the English word 'table' and the Portuguese word 'mesa', we may find that this alignment is made when 'table' should have been interpreted as a table of results, not in the sense of the piece of furniture which would correspond to 'mesa'. Replacing the lemma 'table' with the synset identifier for table in the sense of the piece of furniture should ensure a more accurate alignment between the appropriate sense of the word table and the Portuguese word 'mesa'. Appending the synset identifier to the lemma is an extension of this technique which we hypothesized might avoid potential problems concerning lexical choice.

For example, it might be that in some situations two words such as 'table' and 'desk' in English might belong to the same synset, but correspond to different words ('mesa' and 'secretária' respectively) in Portuguese. By replacing the English words by the synset identifier and aligning that with the Portuguese words, we are essentially assigning the main lemma of the synset (e.g. 'table') to both Portuguese words, which while being better than assigning the wrong sense of table altogether, is not quite as accurate as aligning 'desk' to 'secretária'. Hence, by appending the synset identifiers to the original lemmas (e.g. aligning 'table_01234567' to 'mesa' and 'desk_01234567' to 'secretária'), we are hopefully able to constrain alignments to the correct sense of source language words without introducing problems relating to lexical choice.

---

[2]For the work described in this paper, we make no assumption about the number of synset identifiers found in the training corpus before using them to align words. This may be an interesting caveat to explore in future work.

3.3.2 Including synset identifiers as features of a maxent-based translation model

TectoMT leverages the alignments it finds between the words in pairs of sentences from a parallel corpus to create and train maxent-based translation models, which are used later to perform machine translation tasks. Maximum entropy (maxent) classifiers, which are used when the conditional independence of a set of 'features' cannot be assumed, are common in NLP, where features such as neighbouring words usually provide context and are therefore not independent. In TectoMT, for each word in the source language that has more than one possible translation in the target language a maxent model exists to determine the probability of any of those translations being correct based on contextual features such as neighbouring words – words with only one translation have no ambiguity, and hence no need of a maxent model. For statistical machine translation systems, previous research suggests that maxent-based translation models are an effective way of leveraging the context provided by the neighbouring words of source sentences (Ittycheriah and Roukos, 2007; Bangalore et al., 2007).

In order for maxent models to be created, analysis must have been performed on both the source and target languages, in order for the models to be trained based on aligned parallel treebanks of sentences represented as tectogrammatical (deep-syntax) trees. The maxent model for each word is trained using a list of 'samples', which are themselves vectors between contextual features in the source language 'node' (the tectogrammatical representation of the given word) and an output label (e.g. the lemma of the given word). Contextual features might include information (such as lemmas) from neighbouring nodes in the tectogrammatical tree (such as parent or sibling nodes), which help to provide the context in which a particular word was used.

The maxent model learns, using this information, to output the correct label (target language lemma) given a particular vector of source language contextual features (e.g. a sentence that we want to translate). With the output from the WSD process already stored as an attribute of the analytical layer by the WSD block that we added to the TectoMT framework (and hence propagated to the tectogrammatical layer), synset identifiers can also be added as source language contextual features of words. Thus, the maxent model can in theory constrain the expected probability of a possible translation as determined by the neighbouring words in context to the particular sense in which a given word was used.

4 Evaluation

This section describes our evaluation of how the results of translation from English to Portuguese using our baseline TectoMT-based machine translation system are affected by our two approaches to including information from WSD in the process:

- Forcing synset identifiers into input sentences prior to creating translation models:

    - By replacing lemmas with synset identifiers
    - By appending synset identifiers to lemmas

- Adding synset identifers as features in a maxent-based translation model:

    - As features of single nodes (words)
    - As features of single nodes plus their parent nodes
    - As features of single nodes plus their sibling (to the left and right) nodes
    - As features of single nodes plus their parent *and* sibling nodes

4.1 Experimental System Setup

In order to run the evaluation, we introduce different combinations of interchangable blocks to the analysis scenario in TectoMT, in order that WSD is performed and that its output (synset identifiers) can be propagated from the analytical to the tectogrammatical layer, and thus included in the eventual translation model. As described in section 3.3.2, aligned parallel treebanks of sentences are needed in order for maxent models to be created for target words, and so analysis scenarios are set up for both the source language (English) and the target language (Portuguese). WSD, however, is only included on the source language side (English).

Method	BLEU
Baseline	21.67
Replacing Synsets	20.46
Appending Synsets	19.86
Synset as Feature	**21.69**

Table 1: A comparison of incorporating WSD into a machine translation system by 1) forcing synset identifiers into input sentences (replacing lemmas or appending synsets to lemmas) or 2) adding synsets identifiers to a maxent model as features

Feature Types (Synset of ...)	BLEU
None (Baseline)	21.67
Single Node	**21.69**
+ Parent	21.61
+ Siblings	**21.68**
+ Parent & Siblings	21.62

Table 2: A comparison of different types of features that can be added to a maxent model, including the synset identifiers of 1) single nodes, 2) single nodes plus parent nodes, 3) single nodes plus sibling nodes, and 4) single nodes plus parent *and* sibling nodes

For both approaches, the WSD block is used to run the graph-based UKB algorithm (desribed in section 3.1) over the source sentences in English. In order to use the algorithm, we create the required dictionary files and corresponding graph from version 3.0 of the Princeton English WordNet (Fellbaum, 1998), comprising approximately 117,000 synsets. The 8 digit identifiers of any of these synsets can be assigned by the algorithm to given words in an input text, based on the context provided by their surrounding open class words.

For the adding synset identifiers as features in a maxent-based translation model approach, the inclusion of the WSD block in the scenario is all that is needed – the synset identifiers it returns are included in the analytical layer of each word, and from there propagated to the tectogrammatical layer and, finally, the maxent model where they are called upon as features. For the forcing synset identifiers into input sentences approach, two additional (interchangable) blocks are included in the scenario: 1) a block for replacing a given lemma in the input sentence with the synset identifier returned by the WSD, and 2) a block for appending the synset identifier returned by the WSD to a given lemma in the input sentence.

4.2 Training Corpus

Transfer models are trained over a small, in-domain corpus. The corpus primarily consists of 2000 sentences of questions and answers from a chat-based technology help service (1000 questions and 1000 answers). These sentences are sourced from a real-world company who employ human technicians to provide technical assistance to their customers (technology users) through a chat interface. These 2000 sentences are supported by a number of aligned terms sourced from localized terminology data from Microsoft (13,000 terms) and LibreOffice (995 terms), making the total size of our in-domain corpus approximately 16,000 paired segments (of which 2000 are full sentences and approximately 14,000 are paired terms). No development set or tuning steps are needed in the TectoMT-based pipeline.

4.3 Results of Including WSD Output in Machine Translation

By interchanging the different blocks incorporated into the analysis scenario of TectoMT to train different translation models for evaluation, we can compare our two chosen approaches to including the output from WSD in a machine translation system: 1) forcing synset identifiers into the input sentences prior to creating translation models, and 2) adding synset identifers as features in a maxent-based translation model. For all evaluations, we analyse the different translation models using a test corpus of 1000 full answers to questions asked by people seeking assistance in resolving problems using technology, as per the domain of the training corpus described in section 4.2.

Table 1 shows that when translating these 1000 sentences from English to Portuguese using a baseline TectoMT system (without WSD), we achieve a BLEU score of 21.67. Using the first approach (forcing sysnet identifers into the input sentences prior to creating translation models), the scores we obtain are significantly lower than the baseline (at a 0.05 level of significance) – 20.46 when we replace lemmas with synset identifiers, and 19.86 when appending the sysnet identifier to the lemma. Using the second approach (adding synset identifiers as features in a maxent-based translation model) we obtain a BLEU score of 21.69, *very* slightly above the baseline.

Table 2 shows our experimentation with adding different types of features into the maxent-model for a given word: 1) synset identifiers from single nodes (the standard method, as used to obtain the score in Table 1), 2) synset identifiers from single nodes plus the parent node in the tectogrammatical tree, 3) synset identifiers from single nodes plus the sibling (left and right) nodes, and 4) synset identifiers from single nodes plus the parent *and* sibling nodes. With a baseline BLEU score of 21.67 and a slightly improved score of 21.69 when including the synset identifiers of single nodes, as before, the table demonstrates that adding the synset identifiers of sibling nodes yields a BLEU score of 21.68, slightly above the baseline but slightly below single nodes only, while adding parent nodes alone or parent *and* sibling nodes yields BLEU scores of 21.61 and 21.62 respectively, significantly and almost significantly lower than the baseline (at a 0.05 level of significance).

5   Discussion

In addition to showing that adding synset identifiers as features in a maxent-based translation model yields a BLEU score very slightly above our baseline TectoMT-based machine translation system – suggesting that with some further tweaking output from WSD *can* be useful for machine translation, without the need for any kind of intermediary reformulation or conversion – there are some interesting outcomes from our evaluation. Namely, we found it surprising that:

- Using the first approach (forcing synset identifiers into the input sentences prior to creating the tranlation models), appending synset identifiers to lemmas yielded *worse* results than replacing lemmas with synset identifers.

- Using the second approach (adding synset identifiers as features in a maxent-based translation model), adding the synset identifiers of the parent nodes as extra features in the maxent model *decreases* the BLEU score.

A possible explanation for the weaker results obtained in general using the first approach is that maxent models, as their description in section 3.3.2 demonstrates, already include lemmas from neighboring nodes as contextual features, in much the same way as graph-based WSD algorithms such as UKB rely on the open class words surrounding a given target word as context. The maxent model could be seen as repeating a very similar task, and while it may not be as wholly dedicated to it as a WSD-specific algorithm, we may find that the maxent models used in machine translation are "sufficiently accurate" so that the output from WSD is only able to improve on the lexical choice offered by the maxent model in a "relatively small proportion of cases" (Carpuat and Wu, 2005).

Taken in this context, and assuming as proposed by Carpaut and Wu (2005) that machine translation is excessively dependent on the language models it trains, it could be the case that forcing synset identifiers into the input sentences prior to creating translation models only introduces excessive data that cannot really be put to any efficient use. This might also explain how appending synset identifiers to lemmas yielded even lower results than replacing lemmas with synset identifiers – while the case made in section 3.3.1 for appending the synset identifiers in order to preserve lexical choice seems persuasive, it may in fact be that as well as introducing a redundant synset identifier that cannot be put to much use, this renders the lemma itself redundant (by way of being intrinsically tied to that identifier), thus increasing the sparsity of the input sentences.

The second surprising outcome of our evaluation was the discovery that while adding the synset identifiers of nodes as features in a maxent model yields a slight improvement over the baseline BLEU score, adding synset identifiers from parent nodes as well can have a significantly adverse effect on results (the inclusion of sibling nodes seems to 'limit the damage' to a very small degree). This seems counterintuitive – introducing the output of WSD as a feature in the maxent model seems to yield an improvement, as Xiong and Zhang (2014) also found when creating a sense-based translation model based on their re-forumulated word sense induction approach, and one would expect that providing a maxent model with more features would introduce more useful constraints.

As a possible explanation for this outcome, we consider that not all of the open class words UKB tries to disambiguate will be assigned an appropriate synset identifier – a particular word may not have had an entry in WordNet to begin with, or in a very small number of cases the synset identifier assigned by the algorithm may not have been the correct one. For parent and sibling nodes – parent nodes in particular – this inevitably means that for a given node whose synset identifier *is* included in the maxent model, it might often be the case that its parent (and to a lesser extent sibling) nodes in the tectogrammatical tree do *not* have synset identifiers of their own – we are probably not adding many synset identifiers anyway by choosing to include the extra information from these nodes. We might also consider that if multiple additional synset identifiers are all very different from each other, they might act as conflicting rather than constraining information, thus increasing the overall redundancy or sparsity of the data included in the maxent model.

6 Conclusions

We have presented preliminary findings that suggest that it *is* possible to improve machine translation results by incorporating information about word senses, making direct use of the output of WSD tools and *without* the need for any kind of intermediary reformulation or conversion of either the WSD tool itself or its output. By including the output from WSD as features in a maxent-based translation model, we obtain slightly higher BLEU scores than with a baseline version of the system running without these added features (translating from English to Portuguese), indicating that these features can increase the likelihood of pairings between words and phrases occuring in the translation model.

While the improvement we report is not statistically significant, we find any improvement at all to be in contrast to other approaches we experimented with – replacing synset identifers with lemmas, appending synset identifiers to lemmas, and including the synset identifiers of the parent nodes of words as features in the maxent-based translation model – all of which produce results significantly below our baseline machine translation system. While these results seem counterintuitive – more information should provide more constraints on the probabilities of alignments and pairings between words being made – we interpret them as showing that the extra data we introduce to the translation model with these approaches has resulted in too much sparsity, rather than constraint. It would be interesting in future work to explore whether a paraphrasing (Marton et al., 2009) or synonym-based approach as opposed to a strictly word sense-based approach might yield different outcomes.

While the work we report in this paper is in a preliminary state, the small improvement achieved by adding synset identifiers as features of single nodes in a maxent-based translation model does represent a step in the right direction, and merits further discussion and experimentation. The results reported here are based on a very controlled evaluation, trained on a small, in-domain corpus. We acknowledge that training on large, open domain corpora such as Europarl might produce different results, and aim to investigate this in the future. In addition, we also plan to explore how different types of word sense information and different approaches to WSD itself, as well as alternative machine translation evaluation metrics (possibly more semantically-oriented), might affect the gains we report using the 'senses as features' approach we describe here.

Acknowledgements

This work has been undertaken and funded as part of the EU project QTLeap (EC/FP7/610516) and the Portuguese project DP4LT (PTDC/EEI-SII/1940/2012).

References

Eneko Agirre and Philip Edmonds. 2006. *Word Sense Disambiguation: Algorithms and Applications.* Springer.

Eneko Agirre and Aitor Soroa. 2008. Using the Multilingual Central Repository for Graph-Based Word Sense Disambiguation. In *Proceedings of the Sixth International Conference on Language Resources and Evaluation (LREC'08)*, Marrakech, Morocco, may. European Language Resources Association (ELRA). http://www.lrec-conf.org/proceedings/lrec2008/.

Eneko Agirre and Aitor Soroa. 2009. Personalizing PageRank for Word Sense Disambiguation. In *Proceedings of the 12th Conference of the European Chapter of the Association for Computational Linguistics*, EACL '09, pages 33–41, Athens, Greece. Association for Computational Linguistics.

Eneko Agirre, Oier López de Lacalle, and Aitor Soroa. 2014. Random Walks for Knowledge-based Word Sense Disambiguation. *Comput. Linguist.*, 40(1):57–84, March.

Srinivas Bangalore, Patrick Haffner, and Stephan Kanthak. 2007. Statistical machine translation through global lexical selection and sentence reconstruction. In *Proceedings of the 45th Annual Meeting of the Association for Computational Linguistics*, ACL 2007.

Marine Carpuat and Dekai Wu. 2005. Word Sense Disambiguation vs. Statistical Machine Translation. In *Proceedings of the 43rd Annual Meeting on Association for Computational Linguistics (ACL-05)*, pages 387–394.

Marine Carpuat and Dekai Wu. 2007. How Phrase Sense Disambiguation Outperforms Word Sense Disambiguation for Statistical Machine Translation. In *Proceedings of the 11th International Conference on Theoretical and Methodological Issues in Machine Translation (TMI 2007)*.

Yee Seng Chan, Hwee Tou Ng, and David Chiang. 2007. Word Sense Disambiguation Improves Statistical Machine Translation. In *Proceedings of the 45th Annual Meeting of the Association for Computational Linguistics (ACL-07)*, pages 33–40, Prague, Czech Republic.

Christine Fellbaum. 1998. *WordNet: An Electronic Lexical Database*. MIT Press.

Jesús Giménez and Lluís Màrquez. 2007. Context-Aware Discriminative Phrase Selection for Statistical Machine Translation. In *Proceedings of the 2nd Workshop on Statistical Machine Translation*, pages 159–166, Prague, Czech Republic.

Abraham Ittycheriah and Salim Roukos. 2007. Direct translation model 2. In *Proceedings of NAACL Human Language Technology Conference 2008*, NAACL HLT '07, pages 57–64.

Michael Lesk. 1986. Automatic Sense Disambiguation Using Machine Readable Dictionaries: How to Tell a Pine Cone from an Ice Cream Cone. In *Proceedings of the 5th Annual International Conference on Systems Documentation*, SIGDOC '86, pages 24–26, New York, NY, USA. ACM.

Yuval Marton, Chris Callison-Burch, and Philip Resnik. 2009. Improved statistical machine translation using monolingually-derived paraphrases. In *Proceedings of the 2009 Conference on Empirical Methods in Natural Language Processing*, pages 381–390, Singapore, August. Association for Computational Linguistics.

Rada Mihalcea. 2005. Unsupervised Large-vocabulary Word Sense Disambiguation with Graph-based Algorithms for Sequence Data Labeling. In *Proceedings of the Conference on Human Language Technology and Empirical Methods in Natural Language Processing*, HLT '05, pages 411–418, Stroudsburg, PA, USA. Association for Computational Linguistics.

Roberto Navigli and Mirella Lapata. 2007. Graph Connectivity Measures for Unsupervised Word Sense Disambiguation. In *Proceedings of the 20th International Joint Conference on Artifical Intelligence*, IJCAI'07, pages 1683–1688, San Francisco, CA, USA. Morgan Kaufmann Publishers Inc.

Roberto Navigli and Paola Velardi. 2005. Structural Semantic Interconnections: A Knowledge-Based Approach to Word Sense Disambiguation. *IEEE Transactions on Pattern Analysis and Machine Intelligence*, 27(7):1075–1086, July.

Martin Popel and Zdeněk Žabokrtský. 2010. TectoMT: Modular NLP Framework. In *Proceedings of the 7th International Conference on NLP*, IceTal '10, pages 293–304. Springer Berlin Heidelberg.

Ravi Sinha and Rada Mihalcea. 2007. Unsupervised Graph-basedWord Sense Disambiguation Using Measures of Word Semantic Similarity. In *Proceedings of the International Conference on Semantic Computing*, ICSC '07, pages 363–369, Washington, DC, USA. IEEE Computer Society.

Deyi Xiong and Min Zhang. 2014. A Sense-Based Translation Model for Statistical Machine Translation. In *Proceedings of the 52nd Annual Meeting of the Association for Computational Linguistics (ACL-2014)*, pages 1459–1469, Baltimore MD, USA.

Lexical choice in Abstract Dependency Trees

Dieke Oele
Rijksuniversiteit Groningen,
Groningen,
d.oele@rug.nl

Gertjan van Noord
Rijksuniversiteit Groningen,
Groningen,
g.j.m.van.noord@rug.nl

Abstract

In this work lexical choice in generation for Machine Translation is explored using lexical semantics. We address this problem by replacing lemmas with synonyms in the abstract representations that are used as input for generation, given a WordNet synset. In order to find the correct lemma for each node we propose to map dependency trees to Hidden Markov Trees that describe the probability of a node given its parent node. A tree-modified Viterbi algorithm is then utilized to find the most probable hidden tree containing the correct lemmas given their context. The model is implemented in a Machine Translation system for English to Dutch. The output sentences, generated from the modified dependency structures, contained a lot of erroneous substituted words. This is mainly due to the fact that a large amount of synsets, used as input for the model, are incorrect. The input to the model now contains the synset that is most frequent given the lemma in general, not the optimal synset given the domain of the sentences. We therefore propose to implement a domain specific WSD-system in our pipeline in future work.

1 Introduction

This paper addresses the problem of lexical choice in the generation phase of a deep Machine Translation (MT) system using a Hidden Markov Tree Model (HMTM). In Natural Language Generation (NLG), an abstract representation is transformed into one or more linguistic utterances. Lexical choice is a subtask of this process, in which lemmas need to be chosen to adequately express the content of the intended utterance.

For the generation component of a deep MT-system, the challenge lies in the construction of sentences on the basis of deep representations. The process in this setup includes two major steps: the construction of deep structures for the sentence to be generated and the realization of the sentence on the basis of the grammar which will ensure that the created structure conforms to all the requirements for a complete structure with respect to the grammar formalism. The second step entails the selection of appropriate lexical units and the application of syntactic rules.

In a deep transfer-based MT system the problem of lexical choice also needs to be addressed. The choice of a correct lemma is a very difficult task that depends heavily on the quality of the dictionaries used. WordNet (Fellbaum, 1998) could be seen as such a dictionary, where each synset has its own definition. A WordNet is a lexical semantic database containing lemmas corresponding to their word meanings including the most general and central part of the language. Querying WordNet for a word returns a group of one or more synonyms called a synset. Those synsets contain a set of words of the same class, which are roughly synonymous in one of their

Proceedings of the 1st Deep Machine Translation Workshop (DMTW 2015), pages 73–80,
Praha, Czech Republic, 3–4 September 2015.

meanings. They are well suited for lexical choice, as they contain sets of lemmas that are synonymous in specific contexts. Unfortunately, not every lemma in a synset is a full synonym of its original word which could cause severe errors when selecting the most probable variant for each node without considering the context. We therefore claim that lexical choice should take into account both context and distributional information.

Consider for instance the English word "free" in example 1. In the current MT-system for English to Dutch, this word is always translated with "vrij". This is a satisfactory decision in example 1 where the meaning of "not occupied" is required. In the sentence in 2, however, "free" means "free of charge" which, in Dutch, should be translated with "gratis". It would therefore be useful if the input to the system would contain the meaning of a target lemma instead of a literal translation of the source lemma, for example in the form of a WordNet synset. This information could be used to find an appropriate lemma given its meaning.

(1) You can leave some **free** space in your shared folders.
→ *Je kan wat* **vrije** *ruimte overlaten in je gedeelde mappen.*

(2) This is **free** antivirus software.
→ *Dit is* ***vrije** *antivirus software.*

A similar error occurs in example 3 where the word "limiet" is translated with "grens". This translation fits in this particular context, both meaning "border", in example 4, however, the meaning of a quantitative limit is required. In both cases the chosen word by the system is the most frequent option and is therefore selected in both contexts.

(3) There have to be **limits** to all things.
→ *Overal zijn* **grenzen** *aan.*

(4) Having a large number of of shared folders can occupy your space **limit**.
→ *Als je veel gedeelde mappen hebt kan dat je ruimte* ***grens** *beperken.*

These examples indicate that a correct translation requires a lexical choice process that can determine which translation of a source word is most appropriate in its target context. In transfer-based MT the task of lexical choice can be formulated as follows: given a semantic or conceptual specification, find its best realization. We can define the process of lexical choice as the operations of deleting, modifying or adding lexical units in order to form more natural sentences with a correct meaning.

The problem of lexical choice in MT has not yet been investigated thoroughly, probably due to the fact that its output is hard to evaluate. For example, when a different lemma is returned than the one from the gold standard it might still be appropriate to the context but marked as an error by the evaluation method. Stede (1993) was the first to recognize the need to involve semantic context. A number of algorithms and models have been developed for lexical choice, for example Edmonds and Hirst (2002) developed a model for choosing between words with similar core meanings but with different connotations.

WordNet has not often been used as a dictionary for lexical choice in generation, even though work exists on the usefulness of such a resource for NLG-related tasks such as domain adaptation and paraphrasing (Jing, 1998). For instance, Basile (2014) proposed an unsupervised algorithm for lexical choice from WordNet synsets called Ksel that exploits the WordNet hierarchy of hypernyms/hyponyms to produce the most appropriate lemma for a given synset.

Also, the use of Hidden Markov Tree models for lexical choice in Wordnet synsets is novel. Crouse et al. (1996) introduced the adaptation of Hidden Markov Chains to tree models for signal processing. The corresponding adaptation of the classic Viterbi algorithm, used to restore the hidden state tree, was introduced by Durand et al. (2004). Previous applications of the tree model are: image segmentation, signal classification, denoising and image document categorization (Durand et al., 2004). The use of these models in natural language processing is fairly new and has been applied to word alignment (Kondo et al., 2013) and Machine Translation (Žabokrtský and Popel, 2009). The latter was the first to apply HMTMs to lexical choice using a variant of the Viterbi algorithm in the transfer phase of a deep-syntax based machine translation system.

To tackle the problem of lexical choice we propose the mapping of a dependency structure over synsets to a dependency structure over lemmas while taking into account both context information as the frequency of the lemma and synset combination. A dependency tree is a labeled tree in which nodes correspond to the words of a sentence. It contains edges that represent the grammatical relations between those words, such as nominal subject, direct object or determiner. We map the lemma of each content word in the tree to a WordNet synset and subsequently find a correct substitution based on a target language synset. The goal is to improve the output of a Machine Translation (MT) system built on deeper semantic engineering approaches.

The independence assumptions made by Markov Tree Models can be useful for modeling syntactic trees. They fit dependency trees well, since they assume conditional dependence (in the probabilistic sense) only along tree edges, which corresponds to intuition behind dependency relations (in the linguistic sense) in dependency trees. Moreover, analogously to applications of HMMs on sequence labeling, HMTMs can be used for labeling nodes of a dependency tree, interpreted as revealing the hidden states in the tree nodes, given another (observable) labeling of the nodes of the same tree by use of a tree-modified Viterbi algorithm.

This paper is structured as follows. In Section 2, we introduce the HMTM model for lexical choice and the modified Tree-Viterbi algorithm. Section 3 gives a brief description of experiments that test the model. Then, section 4 discusses the obtained results and possible improvements. Ultimately, this paper is concluded in Section 5.

2 Method

The first part of this section contains a brief description of Hidden Markov Tree Models. Then, the tree-viterbi algorithm for lexical choice is introduced.

2.1 Hidden Markov Tree Models

HMTMs are analogous to well known Hidden Markov Models (HMM). However, instead of a linear chain of observations and their corresponding hidden states they map over a tree of observations. They are similar to Hidden Markov chains given the fact that they both contain a sequence of observed states with corresponding hidden states. Furthermore, they both rely on transition probabilities and emission probabilities. Like HMMs, HMTMs are used with two main algorithms. Namely a smoothing algorithm that calculates the probabilities of being in state j at node n given the observed data, and a global restoration algorithm. More information about HMTMs can be found in Diligenti et al. (2003) and in Durand et al. (2004).

In the Markov process we use for the choice of lemmas, we assume that we are given a directed dependency tree. The tree is defined by an observed tree containing synsets in their nodes, $W = \{W(n_1), ..., W(n_m)\}$, and a hidden tree containing target lemmas, $T = \{T(n_1), ..., T(n_m)\}$, isomorphic to the observed tree where m is the size of the tree. The function $\pi : 1, ..., N \rightarrow 0, ..., N$, $\pi(n)$ represents the unique parent of node n with 0 corresponding to the root of the tree. Each node, except the root node, refers to a word of in the sentence. Like HMMs, HMTMs make two independence assumptions: given $T(\pi(n))$, $T(n)$ is conditionally independent of other nodes and given $T(n)$, $W(n)$ is conditionally independent of other nodes. From these assumptions, we obtain the following distribution on pairs (W, T) of observed synsets and target lemmas:

$$p(w, t) = \sum_{n=1}^{N} p\left(t_n \mid t_{\pi(n)}\right) p\left(w_n \mid t_n\right) \tag{1}$$

When using HMTM for lexical choice, the hidden states consist of actual lemmas, whereas the observations are word senses (synsets). Analogously to regular Hidden Markov Models, HTMTs are defined by the following parameters:

Transition probabilities:
- $P(hidden state | hidden state)$

Emission probabilities:
- $P(observation | hidden state)$

The transition probabilities of a lemma w given a grammatical relation rel and its parent p can be collected from large parsed corpora. For example, if we want the probability of the lemma "beer" given a parent "drink" in the dependency relation "obj":

$$p\left(beer \mid obj1, drink\right) = \frac{freq(drink, obj1, beer)}{freq(drink, obj)} \tag{2}$$

The frequency of a lemma given its parent is the count of how often its parent appears in relation rel and N is the total number of p as arguments of rel. For example, if "drink" occurs 40 times with an object, and in 20 cases that object is the lemma "beer", then we estimate the probability as 0.5.

The emission probabilities can be estimated from sense annotated corpora. We need to estimate the probability of an observed output (the sense), given the hidden state (the lemma). Consider for example the chance of the hidden state "beer" given its synset:

$$P(\{lager, beer, ale, ...\} | beer) \tag{3}$$

If the lemma "ale" is associated in the corpus with the "beer" sense in 89 out of a 100 cases, then the emission probability will be estimated as 0.89.

2.2 Tree-Viterbi

Durand et al. (2004) claim that it is not possible to involve a downward recursion starting at the root state of the tree due to the fact that this would require the results of the upward recursion. The main difference between a tree-viterbi as opposed to its original one is therefore that it starts at its leaf nodes and continues upwards. In every node of each state and each of its children, a downward pointer to the optimal hidden state of the child is stored. Downward recursion is then used along the pointers from the optimal root state in order to retrieve the most probable hidden tree.

3 Experiments

In this section, we present the data and the systems that were used for the experiments. In the experiments the tree-modified Viterbi algorithm for lexical choice is applied to the dependency structures that are used for generation in a deep MT-system. Subsequently the output, containing dependency trees, is used as input to the generator.

3.1 Data

The system for lexical choice is implemented in a machine translation system and tested on Batch 1 of the QTLeap Corpus Osenova et al. (2015). This IT help desk scenario contains translations of customer data from Portuguese into each of the project languages.

3.2 Systems

The sentences are analyzed and translated from English to Dutch with Treex, a modular framework for natural language processing (Popel and Žabokrtský, 2010). It contains a tree-to-tree machine translation system whose translation process follows the analysis-transfer-synthesis pipeline (Žabokrtský and Popel, 2009).

In the analysis phase, a source sentence is transformed into a deep syntax dependency representation which is mapped to the target language. Isomorphism of the tree representation is mostly assumed in both languages, translating the tree node-by-node. In the English to Dutch pipeline, the resulting dependency trees are transferred to Dutch abstract abstract representations that are the input for the generation of Dutch sentences.

The Alpino system for Dutch (van Noord, 2006) is a collection of tools and programs for parsing Dutch sentences into dependency structures, and for generating Dutch sentences on the basis of an abstraction of dependency structures. Since dependency structures for generation contain less information (such as word order and word inflection) than dependency trees, we refer to them as Abstract Dependency Trees (ADT's) (De Kok, 2013). ADTs model the grammatical relations between lexical items and categories built from lexical items. Similar to a normal dependency tree, it contains a syntactical representation of a sentence in the form of a tree. In the Alpino Generator (De Kok, 2013), the grammar is used in the reverse direction as for parsing. The process starts with an abstract dependency structure and then uses the grammar to construct one or more sentences.

3.3 Setup

Before passing the abstract dependency trees through the tree-viterbi algorithm, first the linguistic parent is found for each node. Then, every lemma is matched with a synset. The model takes abstract dependency structures over senses as input. The current system, however, does not provide synsets for a given node. Therefore, a first step is necessary that maps abstract dependency structures over lemmas to abstract dependency over senses.

Synonyms of frequent senses of a source lemma are more likely to provide correct substitutions than synonyms of the lemmas infrequent senses. Therefore, in order to find the input synsets for each node, the most frequent synset given a lemma in a sense tagged corpus, in this case DutchSemCor (Vossen et al., 2012), is taken. These synsets now represent the observed state of the nodes. For these synsets the probability of their hidden states is computed. For example, the most frequent synset for the English lemma "dust" in sentence 5 appears with the following lemmas in the sense tagged corpus: $substantie, materie, stof$. These lemmas can be seen as the hidden states in the model. In this context the best choice would be "stof", and is up to the The tree-viterbi algorithm to choose this option over the other lemmas, given the synset and its context.

(5) **Dust** makes the computer cooling more difficult.

To find the different variants of the lemmas for replacement, the Dutch WordNet, Cornetto (Vossen et al., 2013), is used. A transition probability matrix is created from large parsed corpora that can be queried for each lemma given its parent lemma and their relation. The tree-viterbi algorithm is then applied on the trees to find the most probable lemmas given their context and the frequency of the synsets. The lemmas in the optimal hidden tree are used to substitute the original lemma in the node. Ultimately, the trees are generated with the Alpino generator.

4 Results

From a manual evaluation of the results, it becomes clear that the system does not substitute a lot of lemmas. This is due to the fact that we only have counts for a limited amount of synsets in the sense annotated corpus. Some substitutions that are made can be considered satisfactory. For instance, the replacement of the adjective "simpel" (simple) to "eenvoudig" (simple) in sentence 6 maintains the meaning of the original sentence. However, the output mostly contains a lot of substitutions that are not considered correct, possibly changing the intended meaning of the target sentence. This happens for example when the system substitutes the noun "toets" (key) for "proef" (test) in sentence 7. Since the lemma "toets" is very common in the 1000 interactions of the corpus, it is substituted incorrectly 16 times. Other frequent words that are replaced with a wrong synonym are, for example, "controleren" (meaning "to check" in most of the contexts) is replaced with "beheersen" (to rule) 98 times while "raam" substitutes "venster" (window frame) 19 times.

(6) Je kan een **simpel [=> eenvoudig]** programma gebruiken.
*You can use a **simple** program.*

(7) Klik op de CTRL **toets [=> proef]**.
*Click the CTRL **key [=> test]**.*

One reason that a target synonym cannot substitute a source synset in some context is if the input synset appears in a different sense than the one in which it is synonymous with the target. In most cases, the algorithm chooses the same lemma. However, when the lemmas in a synset belong to the wrong sense, the system has a high chance of selection a wrong lemma.
Consider for example the lemma "menu", that appears in two Dutch synsets:

(8) a. {menukaart:noun:1', 'menu:noun:1', 'spijskaart:noun:1', 'kaart:noun:4'}
b. **{'menu:noun:3', 'keuzemenu:noun:1'}**

Since the data that was used for the experiment belongs to the IT domain, the second synset, in bold, is the preferred one. However, the first synset, with the meaning of *restaurant menu* is more frequent in the sense tagged corpus, as it was created in a general domain corpus, giving the option of substituting "menu" with "kaart" (map).
An interesting observation is that, if the target lemmas from these wrong senses are compared with other lemmas in the Viterbi-algorithm, they can cause each others to be replaced erroneously as well. This problem becomes apparent when looking at example 9.

(9) Klik op het pictogram waarop **"achtergrond beeld"** [→ **"toneel voorstelling"**] staat.
*Click on the icon that says **"background image"** [→ **"theater performance"**].*

In this sentence, both lemmas "achtergrond" (background) and "beeld" (performance) have a bigger emission probability to be replaced by their original lemma. However, the combination of "theater" (which already is a doubtful synonym for "achtergrond" in any context) and "voorstelling", has a very frequent transition probability, causing an inaccurate substitution for both lemmas in this sentence.
Domain clearly is a problem when choosing the right sense. The frequency distribution of the senses of lemmas depends on the genre and domain of the text under consideration. A possible solution to finding the right synset, without using context information, is to use Word

Sense Disambiguation (WSD) from untagged text. This method aims to obtain, for each target word, the sense which is predominant in the target, domain-specific, corpus. McCarthy et al. (2004), for example, used such a corpus to construct a distributional thesaurus of related words. Subsequently, they disambiguated each target word using pairwise similarity measures based on WordNet, taking as pairs the target word and each of the most related words according to the distributional thesaurus up to a certain threshold. This method would not only allow our system to consider more lemmas for replacement, because more frequency information on synsets would then be available, it would also have a bigger chance of starting from correct input synsets. In future work we therefore intend to integrate this method in our pipeline.

Another problem that is highly likely to cause errors in the tree-viterbi algorithm are mistakes in the analysis and/or the transfer phase. For example, errors in the assignment of part-of-speech tags or dependency relations could have negative effects on the outcome since it would not be possible to find correct transition probabilities in the transition matrix. These errors should be solved in the analysis phase of the MT-pipeline and are therefore beyond the scope of this work.

5 Conclusion

In this work we intended to tackle the problem of lexical choice in order to improve the output of a Machine Translation system. To solve this we proposed the use of HMTMs for lexical choice. A dependency structure over synsets is mapped to a dependency structure over lemmas while taking into account both information of the context and the frequency of the lemma and synset combination. Although the obtained results contain some satisfactory substitutions, the system makes a lot of unwanted ones as well. These wrong substitutions are mostly due to the choice of the incorrect (most frequent) sense for a lemma in this particular domain. We therefore proposed the use of a method that first finds the right synset for a given lemma before applying the tree-viterbi algorithm.

Acknowledgements

This work has been supported by the European Union's Seventh Framework Programme for research, technological development and demonstration (QTLeap, grant agreement no 610516).

References

Basile, V. (2014). A lesk-inspired unsupervised algorithm for lexical choice from wordnet synsets. *The First Italian Conference on Computational Linguistics CLiC-it 2014*, page 48.

Crouse, M. S., Baraniuk, R. G., and Nowak, R. D. (1996). Hidden markov models for wavelet-based signal processing. In *Signals, Systems and Computers, 1996. Conference Record of the Thirtieth Asilomar Conference on*, pages 1029–1035. IEEE.

De Kok, D. (2013). *Reversible Stochastic Attribute-value Grammars*. Groningen dissertations in linguistics.

Diligenti, M., Frasconi, P., and Gori, M. (2003). Hidden tree markov models for document image classification. *Pattern Analysis and Machine Intelligence, IEEE Transactions on*, 25(4):519–523.

Durand, J.-B., Goncalves, P., and Guédon, Y. (2004). Computational methods for hidden markov tree models-an application to wavelet trees. *Signal Processing, IEEE Transactions on*, 52(9):2551–2560.

Edmonds, P. and Hirst, G. (2002). Near-synonymy and lexical choice. *Comput. Linguist.*, 28(2):105–144.

Fellbaum, C., editor (1998). *WordNet An Electronic Lexical Database*. The MIT Press, Cambridge, MA ; London.

Jing, H. (1998). Applying wordnet to natural language generation. In *University of Montreal*. Citeseer.

Kondo, S., Duh, K., and Matsumoto, Y. (2013). Hidden markov tree model for word alignment. In *Proceedings of the Eighth Workshop on Statistical Machine Translation*, Sofia, Bulgaria. Association for Computational Linguistics.

McCarthy, D., Koeling, R., Weeds, J., and Carroll, J. (2004). Finding predominant word senses in untagged text. In *Proceedings of the 42Nd Annual Meeting on Association for Computational Linguistics*, ACL '04, Stroudsburg, PA, USA. Association for Computational Linguistics.

Osenova, P., Gaudio, R. D., Silva, J., Burchardt, A., Popel, M., van Noord, G., Oele, D., and Labaka, G. (2015). Interim report on the curation of language resources and tools for deep mt. Technical Report Deliverable D2.5, Version 2.0, QTLeap Project.

Popel, M. and Žabokrtský, Z. (2010). Tectomt: Modular nlp framework. In *Proceedings of the 7th International Conference on Advances in Natural Language Processing*, IceTAL'10, pages 293–304, Berlin, Heidelberg. Springer-Verlag.

Stede, M. (1993). Lexical choice criteria in language generation. In *Proceedings of the sixth conference on European chapter of the Association for Computational Linguistics*, pages 454–459. Association for Computational Linguistics.

van Noord, G. (2006). **At Last Parsing Is Now Operational**. In *TALN 2006 Verbum Ex Machina, Actes De La 13e Conference sur Le Traitement Automatique des Langues naturelles*, pages 20–42, Leuven.

Vossen, P., Görög, A., Izquierdo, R., and den Bosch, A. V. (2012). Dutchsemcor: Targeting the ideal sense-tagged corpus. In Chair), N. C. C., Choukri, K., Declerck, T., Doğan, M. U., Maegaard, B., Mariani, J., Moreno, A., Odijk, J., and Piperidis, S., editors, *Proceedings of the Eight International Conference on Language Resources and Evaluation (LREC'12)*, Istanbul, Turkey. European Language Resources Association (ELRA).

Vossen, P., van der Vliet, H., Maks, I., Segers, R., Moens, M.-F., Hofmann, K., Tjong Kim Sang, E., and de Rijke, M., editors (2013). *Cornetto: A Combinatorial Lexical Semantic Database for Dutch*. Springer.

Žabokrtský, Z. and Popel, M. (2009). Hidden Markov tree model in dependency-based machine translation. In *Proceedings of the ACL-IJCNLP 2009 Conference Short Papers*, ACLShort '09, pages 145–148, Stroudsburg, PA, USA. Association for Computational Linguistics.

Large Scale Translation Quality Estimation

Miguel Rios, Serge Sharoff
Centre for Translation Studies
University of Leeds
m.riosgaona,s.sharoff@leeds.ac.uk

Abstract

This study explores methods for developing a large scale Quality Estimation framework for Machine Translation. We expand existing resources for Quality Estimation across related languages by using different transfer learning methods. The transfer learning methods are: Transductive SVM, Label Propagation and Self-taught Learning. We use transfer learning methods on the available labelled datasets, e.g. en-es, to produce a range of Quality Estimation models for Romance languages, while also adapting for subtitling as a new domain. The Self-taught Learning method shows the most promising results among the used techniques.

1 Introduction

A common problem with automatic metrics for Machine Translation (MT) evaluation, such as BLEU (Papineni et al., 2002), is the need to have reference human translations. Also such metrics work best on a corpus of sentences, while they are not informative for evaluation of individual sentences (Specia et al., 2009). The aim of Quality Estimation (QE) is to predict a quality score for sentences output by MT without reference translations, for example, to judge whether they provide a suitable basis for Post-Editing by the human translator or it is better to ask the human to translate this sentence from scratch. The QE task can be framed as a classification or a regression problem, where most of the methods for QE rely on supervised Machine Learning (ML) algorithms.

The WMT evaluation campaigns (Bojar et al., 2014) goal is to create a framework to test the performance of participating systems for the QE task. The WMT organizers provide the datasets for training and testing new proposed automatic QE approaches. However, the existing training data is only available for a limited number of languages. For example, in the WTM 2014 the available pairs were en-es and en-de (throughout the paper we will be using the two-letter ISO codes to indicate the languages). Most of the final MT users and projects need a wider variety of source and target languages for evaluation.

Turchi and Negri (2014) propose an automatic approach to produce training data for QE and tackle the problem of scarce training resources. The approach is based on features across the MT output, the post edited version and the human reference translation. The method produces a classifier for binary estimation by exploiting the characteristics of good translations and their relation with the post-editing process. The produced data is labelled with a binary quality score (i.e. god or bad translation) to overcome biases on the annotation.

On the other hand, Birch et al. (2008) propose a large scale study on the performance of 110 European language pairs over Europarl. The study is based on the measuring the contribution of different features between language pairs that improve or are irrelevant to the performance of an MT system. The features consist of complexity indicators of morphology, language relatedness given word similarity, number of reordering between language pairs and number of reorderings over alignments. Overall, closely related languages showed the best potential for SMT. However, this study is mainly based on standard automatic evaluation metrics such as BLEU.

Proceedings of the 1st Deep Machine Translation Workshop (DMTW 2015), pages 81–88,
Praha, Czech Republic, 3–4 September 2015.

In this ongoing work, we propose a way to produce a number of evaluation pairs for the QE task by utilising relatedness between languages, for example, by producing a QE evaluation for the en-pt pair from an existing en-es training set. More specifically we will study the use of different transfer learning methods to transfer classifiers across related languages. Our intuition is that sentences with similar quality scores are close or share a lower-dimensional space in terms of features across related languages. In other words, good/bad quality sentences might show similar characteristics between the available training data (e.g. en-es) and unknown data (e.g en-pt). This makes possible the training of a classification algorithm to predict QE by sharing information from the available dataset into unknown datasets.

We show preliminary results on transferring training data from en-es European Parliament (Europarl) domain to en-es, en-it and en-pt in the subtitling domain. The transfer learning method that shows promising results is the one based on dimensionality reduction of the input. However, this method is sensible to the distribution of classes of the training dataset, where it tends to predict the majority of the training class. In addition, we provide further directions into transfer training data based on the similarity of related languages for source languages that are not present in the original WMT QE datasets, but also to tackle the unbalanced training dataset. We use a simple heuristic for assigning possible labels for the unlabelled data based on edit distance scores between available reference translations and MT outputs. However, this simple heuristic hurts the performance of the methods, where a more appropriate way of adding similarity information is as an indicator for domain shift.

2 Background

Methods for QE are commonly based on computing similarity scores and information supplied by the MT decoding process between source and machine translations. These sources of information are used as features to train a supervised ML algorithm to predict QE scores. Specia et al. (2013) develop the standard baseline framework for QE based on features that attempt to quantify the complexity of a segment to be translated. Other previous works extend the baseline framework by adding complex features between the source and machine translations. For example, syntax information of tree labels counts (Avramidis, 2014), information to quantify the acts of translation between any two datasets with respect to a reference in the same domain (Bicici and Way, 2014) and word alignment, word posterior probabilities and diversity scores features (Camargo de Souza et al., 2014).

Beck et al. (2014) use multi-task learning techniques to improve QE by sharing information among different domains. However, the QE task is only applied to certain language pairs. On the other hand, de Souza et al. (2015) integrate QE into a CAT tool with online learning to constantly train the quality prediction model. This method can be used to extract QE training data or prediction models for several domains and languages.

Transfer learning aims to transfer information learned in one or more source tasks (e.g. labelled dataset) and use it to improve learning in a related target task (e.g. unlabelled dataset) (Pan and Yang, 2010). In our case the labelled dataset comes from a QE training set for an existing language pair, while unlabelled datasets are either for the same pair, but in a completely different domain, or for another language pair.

2.1 Transductive Support Vector Machine

Transductive Support Vector Machine (TSVM) takes into consideration a particular test dataset and tries to minimise errors only on those particular instances (Vapnik, 1995). The particular test dataset is added into the training dataset without labels. The TSVM learns a large margin hyperplane classifier using labelled training data, but at the same time it forces that hyperplane to be far from the unlabelled data. The TSVM considers f that maps inputs x to outputs y. However, TSVM does not construct a function f where the output of the transduction algorithm is a vector of labels, and the method transfers the information from labelled instances to the unlabelled.

2.2 Label Propagation

Label propagation (Zhu and Ghahramani, 2002) is based on a graph that connects similar instances. The nodes labels (i.e. instances) propagate to neighbouring nodes given proximity. This model resembles the k-NN nearest neighbours where closer data points tend to have similar labels. The l labelled training examples $\{(x_1, y_1), (x_2, y_2)..., (x_l, y_l)\}$ and the u unlabelled training examples $\{x_1, x_2, ..., x_u\}$, where the Y classes are known. Label propagation estimates the Y_u given the training examples. The method creates a fully connected graph where the nodes are all the labelled and unlabelled instances. The edges are weighted based on the euclidean distance between the nodes where the closer nodes have a larger weight value. The nodes have soft labels that are propagated thorough all the edges modifying the unlabelled instances, and the larger the weight the easier is to propagate the label across the graph.

2.3 Self-taught Learning

Raina et al. (2007) propose a semi-supervised transfer learning method based on using labelled and unlabelled data. However, this method does not assume that the unlabelled dataset is drawn from the same distribution as the labelled. The unlabelled data is used to learn a lower dimensional feature representation of the inputs. With this representation new instances can be classified in the lower dimensional space. The unlabelled data is used for dimensionality reduction of the labelled dataset, which is commonly used with sparse high dimensional data.

The transfer learning problem algorithm is defined as:

- l training examples $\{(x_1, y_1), (x_2, y_2)..., (x_l, y_l)\}, y \in \mathcal{Y}$;
  where Y is the output.

- u unlabelled examples $\{x_1, x_2, ..., x_u\}$.

- Learn the higher-level representation by dimensionality reduction by using sparse-coding.

- Compute new labelled training dataset with new representation $\hat{x}_l$.

- Use standard classification methods with new training dataset.

3 Methodology

In this section, we describe the QE features and the transfer learning setup. We use the standard QE baseline features and available implementations of transfer learning methods making the experiments easy to reproduce. The QE task (Bojar et al., 2014) considers word-level, sentence-level and document-level estimation. The types of annotation (i.e. labels) for the predicted output scores and ranks consist in:

Post-editing effort The perceived effort of a translator to edit a sentence scored with quality labels such as:
1 = perfect translation, no post-editing needed at all;
2 = near miss translation: translation contains maximum of 2-3 errors, and possibly additional errors that can be easily fixed (capitalisation, punctuation);
3 = very low quality translation, cannot be easily fixed.

HTER The minimum edit distance score between the machine translation and its manually post-edited version in [0,1].

Post-editing time The real valued estimate of the time (in milliseconds) it takes a translator to post-edit the translation.

We focus our experiments on the sentence-level estimation with the labelling based on post-editing effort. However, the transfer learning methods can be applied on every estimation subtask. We chose the 3-way labelling in contrast to the binary classification given that post-editing is a common scenario present in our domain of interest (subtitling). We want to show to the translator sentences with good quality but also sentences that can be saved by a small post-editing effort. In addition, we belied that the 3-way labelling is a straight forward scheme for annotators. Our current experiments only cover the testing of a small number language pairs with manual evaluation.

3.1 QE feature description

The baseline features for QE are defined for the source, target (i.e. MT output) and the translations (i.e. relations between them). The QuEsT framework (Specia et al., 2013) implements different types of features. The features can be divided on different families:

Complexity Indicators Features related to the source text of how complex to translate a sentence can be, such as, number of tokens, language model and average number of translations.

Confidence Indicators Features related to the fluency of the MT output, such as, number of tokens, language model, and number of occurrences of the target word within the target sentence.

Fluency Indicators Features related to the adequacy (meaning preservation) of the translation, such as, ratios of tokens between the source and target, ratio of punctuation and syntactic similarity. The framework also introduces features related to a specific decoding process when available, such as, global score of the system and number of hypotheses in the n-best list.

We use the baseline setup of the framework that consists of 17 baseline features that are language independent.

3.2 Transfer learning setup

We aim to apply transfer learning, when texts in related languages are treated as unlabelled out-of-domain data. For example, the available en-es labelled dataset is used to transfer information into the unlabelled en-pt to predict QE scores on that unknown language pair. The methods used in this study required as input a small amount of labelled instances and large amounts of unlabelled instances for training. We define three models for transfer information from labelled QE data into unlabelled data. The models are as follows:

TSVM Model based on a Transductive Support Vector Machine.

LP Model based on Label Propagation.

STL Model based on Self-taught learning.

We use SVMlin[1] for training the TSVM, given that is optimised to work with a large number of instances. Our TSVM uses an RBF kernel with no hyper-parameter optimisation. Each instance in the unlabelled dataset is added to the training dataset. This improved training data is used to perform testing. For classification, we implement the one-against-one strategy, and the final decision is given by voting.

For the LP model, we use the implementation from the scikit-learn[2] toolkit with the RBF kernel with no hyper-parameter optimization.

We modify the STL MATALB implementation from the Stanford Deep learning course[3]. The STL model first finds the weights b from the unlabelled x_u dataset by training a sparse autoencoder. The b weights come from the optimisation of the cost function on sparse coding, where one of the components are the basis vectors. This is a technique for dimensionality representation of the input. Second, the model produces a modified training dataset by using the unlabelled b weights on an second autoencoder. The modified training dataset is a lower-dimensional representation of the input features (i.e. QE 17 baseline features). We use the softmax regression as classifier with the default parameters and the modified labelled training dataset.

---

[1] http://vikas.sindhwani.org/svmlin.html
[2] http://scikit-learn.org/dev/index.html
[3] https://github.com/amaas/stanford_dl_ex

A new test dataset can be predicted by using the weights b to represent the data points into the same lower-dimensional space. We normalize the features with the z-score. However, we do not have access to any development datasets for tuning the x_u autoencoder for our unlabelled language pairs. For the parameter selection of the unlabelled autoenconder, as suggested in (Bergstra and Bengio, 2012), we run a random search over a split of the modified training dataset (90% training, 10% validation) in order to find: the size of the hidden dimension, the sparsity parameter, the weight decay parameter and the sparsity penalty. We run the random search parameter optimisation for each unlabelled language pair, thus learning parameters on each unlabelled language pair.

In addition, we define a model based on Logistic Regression without the aid of any transfer learning as the *baseline*. The baseline is trained with an available dataset (e.g. en-es).

4   Experiments

In this section, we describe the data used to train and evaluate our transfer learning models for related languages pairs. We show results on manual evaluation for different language pairs of the en to Romance languages (es, pt and it). We also show cross validation results for the en-de pair.

4.1   Data description

The labelled data x_l for the pair en-es come from the WMT 2014 QE shared task[4], which consist of 3,816 source and target pairs. The en-es WMT data belong to the proceedings of the European Parliament (Europarl) domain. The distribution of instances for each quality label is: *1-949, 2-2010* and *3-857*. Our objective is to score sentence-level QE for related languages for the *en-target* translation direction, where we vary the target language.

The unlabelled data consist of subtitles from the **Zoo** corpus. Zoo is a proprietary corpus of subtitles produced by professional translators. We split the Zoo corpus into unlabelled training x_u and testing for each one of the pairs: en-es, en-pt and en-it. We also test the pair en-de Europarl given that labelled data is available with 600 sentences for testing, as well as, a correspondent out-of-domain data with 297 sentences. We use the Moses (Koehn et al., 2007) toolkit with a phrase-based baseline to extract the QE features for the x_l, x_u, and testing. The Zoo dataset used for the SMT baseline is: 80K training sentences, 1K sentences for tuning and 2K sentences for testing. We use the Zoo test 2K sentences for testing our proposed methods. We use fast-align[5], KenLM[6] with a 3-gram language model and Moses with the standard feature set. In addition, we run a small QE manual evaluation over a random sample of 100 sentences from the Zoo test dataset (original 2K sentences) for the pairs: en-es, en-pt and en-it. The annotation is performed by one professional translator for Post-editing effort at sentence level with 3-way labelling. The evaluation metric is the absolute classification accuracy for the 3-way labelling between the QE system prediction and the test random sample.

4.2   Results

Table 1 shows the results on the validation dataset for the parameter optimisation of the STL model.

Table 1: Accuracy results for the validation dataset with the STL model.

Model \ Pair	en-es	en-pt	en-it
STL	0.56	0.55	0.57

We run the random search for learning parameters on the modified training data $\hat{x}_l$ for each unlabelled dataset, where the number of iterations for each random search is 100. The labelled training set is en-es EuroParl and the unlabelled are: es, it and pt (subtitling domain). Each unlabelled dataset consists of

---

[4]http://www.statmt.org/wmt14/quality-estimation-task.html
[5]https://github.com/clab/fast_align
[6]https://kheafield.com/code/kenlm/

10K sentences from the Zoo training section. It is worth noticing that the learned hidden dimension for each language pair is: en-es 15, en-pt 9, en-it 13, where the original input dimension is 17 features.

Table 2 shows the accuracy results for each transfer learning method on the test samples. The TSVM shows a poor performance in comparison to the other techniques. A possible reason for this result is the lack of parameter optimisation, in specific the parameter for setting the fraction of positive instances for the unlabelled data. Our models are trained with a very unbalanced dataset. The LP results show a similar behaviour, where we manually set a low gamma parameter in order to change the strong bias of predicting all the instances into one class. However, we are able to optimize parameters for the STL given that the model operates over a transformation of the labelled training dataset.

Table 2: Accuracy results for Transfer Learning models on Romance languages pairs.

Model \ Pair	en-es	en-pt	en-it
TSVM	0.52	0.30	0.30
LP	0.49	0.26	0.31
STL	**0.53**	**0.48**	**0.49**
Baseline	0.50	0.38	0.33

The **STL** model outperforms both the baseline and other transfer techniques. The pair en-es achieves the best results given that is an instance of domain adaptation between the same translation pairs. The performance difference between the STL model and the baseline for en-es is narrow with the same language pair but with different domains (i.e. WMT and subtitling). However, the other pairs achieve lower results in comparison because they have different domains and labelled training language data.

We vary the number of training instances for the en-pt x_u to test the effect over the labelled data. Table 3 shows the 10-fold cross validation and test results on the variation of unlabelled data for the en-pt pair. The number of unlabelled data used for the variation test is as follows: 500, 1K, 10K and 20K. The variation of unlabelled instances marginally affects the cross validation, but over the test dataset the 10K dataset improves the results. However, the balance of labelled instances highly affects the space induced by the autoencoder.

The labelled dataset tends to have the majority of instances into the classes *1,2*, where the STL shows a bias on the prediction for the majority of the classes 1 and 2 from the training dataset. In order to tackle the unbalance labelled data, we use a simple heuristic of selecting the missing *3* class instances, where the Levenshtein distance between the available reference translations and MT outputs is over a certain threshold. The examples are tagged as *3* and added into the labelled training data. For the en-pt pair the number of artificial examples is *161* with a threshold of *0.5*. The accuracy result for the validation is 0.56 and the test accuracy is **0.37**. The validation score shows a marginal improvement, but the heuristic hurts the test accuracy. Yang and Eisenstein (2015) use features to characterise multi-domain shift by a binary vector of which instances share a given domain. In our case the instances can share information by computing similarity between the labelled and unlabelled datasets, as well as, the use of dimensionality reduction.

Table 4 shows the accuracy results on en-de Europarl (1400 instances) as the labelled training and

Table 3: Accuracy results 10-fold cross validation and test dataset en-pt for unlabelled data size variation.

Unlabelled data size (sentences)	10-fold cross validation Training	Test
500	0.52	0.39
1K	0.54	0.37
10K	0.54	**0.48**
20K	0.53	0.41
50K	0.53	0.40

en-de subtitling (10K instances) as the unlabelled dataset for the STL model. We use 10-fold cross validation over the modified training dataset because there is no test data available for en-de subtitling. Over the validation dataset the en-de achieves **0.61**, with a hidden dimension of 15.

Table 4: Results 10-fold cross validation for STL on the en-de pair.

Model \ Pair	en-de
STL	0.47
Baseline	**0.48**

Table 5 shows the results of the STL result for the available WMT Europarl data, WMT out-of-domain data and the baseline.

Table 5: Accuracy results for en-de WMT data.

Model \ Pair	en-de WMT Europarl	en-de WMT out-of-domain
STL	**0.51**	**0.49**
Baseline	0.44	0.41

The distribution of classes on the labelled en-de dataset is: *1-317*, *2-522* and *3-561*. This labelled dataset shows to be balanced in comparison with the en-es. The STL test results outperforms the baseline for the Europarl and out of domain, but the results are lower for the cross validation. The STL model assigns predictions to classes as follows: *1-14.14%*, *2-43.10%* and *3-42.76%*.

5 Future work

We have presented work in progress for developing QE for a large number of language pairs. We use different transfer learning mechanisms to tackle the lack of QE training data for related languages. We show results on a small sample for the English to Romance languages directions, and we test the contribution of related languages also on the en-de test dataset. The STL model shows to outperform the other transfer methods. However, this model is sensible to the balance of the labelled training data, so that a different balance in the unlabelled dataset affects the final performance. We tried to overcome the unbalanced data by adding artificial instances for the under represented class, but this heuristic was not successful.

For future work, we plan to extend the testing with various annotators in order to acquire reasonable testing datasets for the language pairs under study. We will add extra features to the QuEst baseline based on similarity scores as domain indicators to characterise differences and similarities between domains. We will also expand the available labelled resources into other language families given that the STL only requires as input a small amount of labelled data and larger amounts of unlabelled data, where we can expand QE across related languages. Finally, we would like to try converting the QE models for translation **into** related languages to a model for estimating the translation quality **between** these languages, for example, using en-es and en-pt models to estimate the quality of es-pt translations.

Acknowledgments

The research was funded by Innovate UK and ZOO Digital Group plc.
`http://www.zoodigital.com/`

References

Eleftherios Avramidis. 2014. Efforts on machine learning over human-mediated translation edit rate. In *Proceedings of the Ninth Workshop on Statistical Machine Translation*, pages 302–306, Baltimore, Maryland, USA, June.

Daniel Beck, Kashif Shah, and Lucia Specia. 2014. Shef-lite 2.0: Sparse multi-task gaussian processes for translation quality estimation. In *Proceedings of the Ninth Workshop on Statistical Machine Translation*, pages 307–312, Baltimore, Maryland, USA, June.

James Bergstra and Yoshua Bengio. 2012. Random search for hyper-parameter optimization. *J. Mach. Learn. Res.*, 13:281–305, February.

Ergun Bicici and Andy Way. 2014. Referential translation machines for predicting translation quality. In *Proceedings of the Ninth Workshop on Statistical Machine Translation*, pages 313–321, Baltimore, Maryland, USA, June.

Alexandra Birch, Miles Osborne, and Philipp Koehn. 2008. Predicting Success in Machine Translation. In *Proceedings of the 2008 Conference on Empirical Methods in Natural Language Processing*, pages 745–754, Honolulu, Hawaii.

Ondrej Bojar, Christian Buck, Christian Federmann, Barry Haddow, Philipp Koehn, Johannes Leveling, Christof Monz, Pavel Pecina, Matt Post, Herve Saint-Amand, Radu Soricut, Lucia Specia, and Aleš Tamchyna. 2014. Findings of the 2014 workshop on statistical machine translation. In *Proceedings of the Ninth Workshop on Statistical Machine Translation*, pages 12–58, Baltimore, Maryland, USA, June. Association for Computational Linguistics.

José Guilherme Camargo de Souza, Jesús González-Rubio, Christian Buck, Marco Turchi, and Matteo Negri. 2014. Fbk-upv-uedin participation in the wmt14 quality estimation shared-task. In *Proceedings of the Ninth Workshop on Statistical Machine Translation*, pages 322–328, Baltimore, Maryland, USA, June.

José Guilherme Camargo de Souza, Matteo Negri, Elisa Ricci, and Marco Turchi. 2015. Online multitask learning for machine translation quality estimation. In *Proceedings of the 53rd Annual Meeting of the Association for Computational Linguistics and the 7th International Joint Conference on Natural Language Processing of the Asian Federation of Natural Language Processing, ACL 2015, July 26-31, 2015, Beijing, China, Volume 1: Long Papers*, pages 219–228.

Philipp Koehn, Hieu Hoang, Alexandra Birch, Chris Callison-Burch, Marcello Federico, Nicola Bertoldi, Brooke Cowan, Wade Shen, Christine Moran, Richard Zens, Chris Dyer, Ondřej Bojar, Alexandra Constantin, and Evan Herbst. 2007. Moses: Open source toolkit for statistical machine translation. In *Proceedings of the 45th Annual Meeting of the ACL on Interactive Poster and Demonstration Sessions*, ACL '07, pages 177–180, Stroudsburg, PA, USA.

Sinno Jialin Pan and Qiang Yang. 2010. A survey on transfer learning. *IEEE Trans. on Knowl. and Data Eng.*, 22(10):1345–1359, October.

Kishore Papineni, Salim Roukos, Todd Ward, and Wei-Jing Zhu. 2002. Bleu: a method for automatic evaluation of machine translation. In *Proceedings of the 40th annual meeting on association for computational linguistics*, pages 311–318. Association for Computational Linguistics.

Rajat Raina, Alexis Battle, Honglak Lee, Benjamin Packer, and Andrew Y. Ng. 2007. Self-taught learning: Transfer learning from unlabeled data. In *Proceedings of the 24th International Conference on Machine Learning*, ICML '07, pages 759–766, New York, NY, USA.

Lucia Specia, Marco Turchi, Nicola Cancedda, Marc Dymetman, and Nello Cristianini. 2009. Estimating the sentence-level quality of machine translation systems. In *Proc 13th Conference of the European Association for Machine Translation*, pages 28–37.

Lucia Specia, Kashif Shah, Jose G.C. de Souza, and Trevor Cohn. 2013. Quest - a translation quality estimation framework. In *51st Annual Meeting of the Association for Computational Linguistics: System Demonstrations*, ACL, pages 79–84, Sofia, Bulgaria.

Marco Turchi and Matteo Negri. 2014. Automatic annotation of machine translation datasets with binary quality judgements. In *Proceedings of the Ninth International Conference on Language Resources and Evaluation (LREC'14)*, Reykjavik, Iceland, may.

Vladimir N. Vapnik. 1995. *The Nature of Statistical Learning Theory*. Springer-Verlag New York, Inc., New York, NY, USA.

Yi Yang and Jacob Eisenstein. 2015. Unsupervised multi-domain adaptation with feature embeddings. In *Proceedings of the 2015 Conference of the North American Chapter of the Association for Computational Linguistics: Human Language Technologies*, pages 672–682, Denver, Colorado, May–June.

Xiaojin Zhu and Zoubin Ghahramani. 2002. Learning from labeled and unlabeled data with label propagation. In *online*.

Translation Model Interpolation for Domain Adaptation in TectoMT

Rudolf Rosa, Ondřej Dušek, Michal Novák, Martin Popel
Charles University in Prague, Faculty of Mathematics and Physics
Institute of Formal and Applied Linguistics
Malostranské náměstí 25, Prague, Czech Republic
{rosa,odusek,mnovak,popel}@ufal.mff.cuni.cz

Abstract

We present an implementation of domain adaptation by translation model interpolation in the
TectoMT translation system with deep transfer. We evaluate the method on six language pairs
with a 1000-sentence in-domain parallel corpus, and obtain improvements of up to 3 BLEU
points. The interpolation weights are set uniformly, without employing any tuning.

1 Introduction

Statistical machine translation (SMT) is now a well-established field of natural language processing,
with many real-world applications. The core of an SMT system is the translation model (TM), created
from parallel data. For many language pairs, especially those where one member of the pair is English,
parallel data in several domains are often abundant; typical examples are legal texts (e.g. Europarl), film
subtitles, books, and newspapers. Thus, it is usually easy to build SMT systems for these domains with
reasonable performance.

For other domains, quite the opposite is often true – the amount of in-domain parallel data is low,
which limits the accuracy of translation systems trained on such data. Therefore, the small in-domain
data are typically combined with larger available out-of-domain data. The simplest method that can be
employed is data concatenation, where all the available parallel data are merged and used to train one
TM. However, this method is not optimal (Daumé III, 2009) because the TM is usually biased towards
translations that are more frequent in the merged data, which are often translations from the larger out-
of-domain data; the effect of the small in-domain data tends to be "washed out".

Several authors (see Section 5) have instead successfully employed the method of TM interpolation,
in which in-domain and out-of-domain TMs are created separately, and linear interpolation is then used
to obtain the final TM. As each of the TMs can be assigned a different weight, it is possible to promote
the in-domain TM, effectively biasing the decoder towards the target domain.

In our work, we successfully implement domain adaptation by TM interpolation in the TectoMT system, a hybrid SMT system based on deep language processing and deep transfer. We apply the system
to translation of user requests and helpdesk answers in the information technologies (IT) domain, with
only 1000 in-domain parallel sentences available, in addition to large out-of-domain data. For several
reasons, we use uniform interpolation weights without any tuning (see Section 3). We show our method
to be very successful, with the interpolated model achieving improvements of several BLEU points over
the individual TMs across six translation directions: EN↔CS, EN↔ES, EN↔NL (English to and from
Czech, Spanish and Dutch).

We briefly present TectoMT in Section 2. In Section 3, we describe our implementation of domain
adaptation by model interpolation. Section 4 evaluates our method using the QTLeap IT helpdesk corpus,
Section 5 reviews related work, and Section 6 concludes the paper and presents directions for future
research.

Proceedings of the 1st Deep Machine Translation Workshop (DMTW 2015), pages 89–96,
Praha, Czech Republic, 3–4 September 2015.

2 TectoMT System

TectoMT is a structural machine translation system with a tree-to-tree transfer on the deep syntax layer, first introduced by Žabokrtský et al. (2008). It is based on the Prague "tectogrammatics" theory of Sgall et al. (1986). The system uses two layers of structural description with dependency trees: surface syntax (*a-layer*, *a-trees*) and deep syntax (*t-layer*, *t-trees*).

The analysis phase is two-step and proceeds from plain text over a-layer to t-layer (see Section 2.1). The transfer phase of the system is based on maximum entropy context-sensitive translation models (Mareček et al., 2010) and Hidden Markov Tree Models (Žabokrtský and Popel, 2009) (see Section 2.2). The subsequent generation phase consists of rule-based components that gradually change the deep target language representation into a shallow one, which is then converted to text (see Section 2.3).

2.1 Analysis

The analysis phase consists of a pipeline of standard NLP tools that perform the analysis to the a-layer, followed by a rule-based conversion to t-layer.

In the analysis pipeline, the input is first segmented into sentences and tokenized using rule-based modules from the Treex toolkit[1] (Popel and Žabokrtský, 2010). A statistical part-of-speech tagger and dependency parser are applied to the tokenized sentences and conclude the a-layer analysis part.[2] The a-trees contain one node for each token of the sentence with its surface word form and the lemma (base form), its part-of-speech/morphology, and its surface dependency label.

A t-tree is a dependency tree where only content words (nouns, full verbs, adjectives, adverbs) and coordinating conjunctions have their own nodes; grammatical words such as prepositions or auxiliary verbs are hidden. Each node has the following attributes:

- *t-lemma* – deep lemma,

- *functor* – a deep-syntactic/semantic role label,

- *formeme* – a concise description of its morpho-syntactic surface form (Dušek et al., 2012), e.g., `v:fin` for a finite verb or `n:in+X` for a noun in prepositional phrase with the preposition *in*,

- *grammatemes* – a set of deep grammatical attributes, covering properties such as tense, gender, number, person, or modality.

T-trees are created from a-trees using a set of rules which collapse auxiliaries and assign all the required attributes to each t-node.

2.2 Transfer

In the transfer phase, an initial target t-tree is obtained as a copy of the source t-tree. Target t-lemmas and formemes of the t-nodes are suggested by a set of TMs, and the other attributes are transferred by a set of rules.

For both t-lemmas and formemes, we use two separate TMs:

- MaxEnt TM – a discriminative model whose prediction is based on features extracted from the source tree. The discriminative TM (Mareček et al., 2010) is in fact an ensemble of maximum entropy (MaxEnt) models (Berger et al., 1996), each trained for one specific source t-lemma/formeme. However, as the number of types observed in the parallel treebank may be too large, infrequent source t-lemmas/formemes are not covered by this type of TM.

- Static TM – this is only a dictionary of possible translations with relative frequencies (no contextual features are taken into account). This model is available for most source t-lemmas/formemes seen in training data.[3]

---

[1] `http://ufal.mff.cuni.cz/treex` and `https://github.com/ufal/treex`

[2] The modules used for the analysis in the individual languages vary, but all of them follow the same structure. For instance, the English pipeline uses the Morče tagger (Spoustová et al., 2007) and the MST parser (McDonald et al., 2005).

[3] Both the MaxEnt and the Static TM are subject to pruning during training, with a higher threshold used for MaxEnt; see Section 4.2 for more details.

When performing the transfer, the two TMs are combined via interpolation. Each of the models is assigned an interpolation weight – the translation probabilities emitted by the model are multiplied by the model's weight, and weights of both models are normalized to sum up to 1.

After the TMs are applied, each t-tree node contains a list of possible formemes and a list of possible t-lemmas, along with their estimated probabilities. There are two possible ways of combining the lists:

1. Just using the first item of both lists (the simplest way, but its performance may not be ideal since incompatible combinations are sometimes produced).

2. Using a Hidden Markov Tree Model (Žabokrtský and Popel, 2009), where a Viterbi search is used to find the best t-lemma/formeme combinations globally over the whole tree.

In the current TectoMT version, HMTM is only used in EN→CS translation. HMTM for the remaining languages will be added in the near future.

2.3 Synthesis

The synthesis is a pipeline of rule-based modules (Žabokrtský et al., 2008; Dušek et al., 2015) that gradually change the translated t-tree into an a-tree (surface dependency tree), adding auxiliary words and punctuation and resolving morphological attributes. Some basic word-order rules are also applied.

The individual a-tree nodes/words are then inflected using a morphological dictionary (Straková et al., 2014) or a statistical tool trained on an annotated corpus (Dušek and Jurčíček, 2013). The resulting tree is then simply linearized into the output sentence.

3 Domain Adaptation by Model Interpolation

The general approach of domain adaptation by model interpolation is rather simple:

1. Train a TM on out-of-domain data,

2. Train a TM on in-domain data,

3. Interpolate the TMs,

4. Translate using the interpolated TM.

As mentioned in Section 2.2, TectoMT uses four TMs by default – a Static formeme TM, a MaxEnt formeme TM, a Static t-lemma TM, and a MaxEnt t-lemma TM. Therefore, we train this set of four models on each of the datasets.

Even in the original TectoMT pipeline, TM interpolation is used to combine a Static model with a MaxEnt model; however, it only supported interpolation of one Static model with one MaxEnt model. Therefore, we extended the pipeline to allow interpolation of multiple TMs; for each model, one must specify the model file, the type of the model (Static/MaxEnt), and its interpolation weight.

In our setup, we use the default MaxEnt–Static interpolation weights as defined in TectoMT, and we use the same weights for in-domain TMs and out-of-domain TMs. This has a similar effect to training the TMs on concatenated out-of-domain and in-domain data with the in-domain data duplicated as many times as to have the same size as the out-of-domain data (modulo some hard thresholds).

The standard approach, as applied in phrase-based SMT systems, would be to use tuning on an in-domain development set to find a well-performing set of weights, by employing an optimizer such as MERT or PRO. However, we do not apply tuning in our setup our in-domain training dataset is very small (1000 sentences only) and we do not want to further divide it into training and development parts and we had not enough time to apply cross-validation. Still, we believe to be able to perform weight tuning in future, which may lead to additional performance gains.

4 Evaluation

We evaluate our implementation on a task for the QTLeap project. We first describe the datasets used for training and testing our system (in Section 4.1), then list the settings used for training (in Section 4.2), and finally discuss the results we obtained (Section 4.3).

4.1 Dataset

In-domain

Our in-domain data set comes from the QTLeap corpus,[4] which is a set of IT-related user requests ("*questions*") and helpdesk responses ("*answers*") in English, translated into Basque, Bulgarian, Czech, Dutch, German, Portuguese, and Spanish. In this paper, we only evaluate using Czech, Dutch, and Spanish.

Currently, two 1000-sentence batches are available to us, Batch1 as a development and training set, and Batch2 as a test set (this division is given by the QTLeap project setup). Moreover, the data are not divided into the batches randomly, but sequentially, so they all come from the same domain, but the topics in Batch1 and Batch2 are somewhat different (i.e., the similarity of Batch1 sentences to other Batch1 sentences is greater than the similarity of Batch1 sentences to Batch2 sentences).

For translations into English, we use Batch1q (user requests) as the in-domain training data. For translations from English, we use Batch1a (helpdesk answers) as the in-domain training data. This reflects the inteded purpose of the MT systems and the final application of translating user questions into English and helpdesk answers back to the original language (Czech, Dutch, Spanish).

Out-of-domain

We use the following corpora to train our out-of-domain models (each language contains parallel texts with English):

- Czech – CzEng 1.0 (Bojar et al., 2012), with 15.2 million parallel sentences, containing a variety of domains, including fiction books, news texts, EU legislation, and technical documentation.

- Dutch – A combination of Europarl (Koehn, 2005), Dutch Parallel Corpus (Macken et al., 2007), and KDE technical documentation; 2.2 million parallel sentences in total.

- Spanish – Europarl, containing 2 million parallel sentences.

Monolingual

For Czech as the target language, we used the WMT News Crawl monolingual training data (2007–2012, 26 million sentences in total) to train the HMTM.[5] Other target languages do not use an HMTM (see Sections 2.2 and 4.2).

4.2 Setup

We use the QTLeap TM training makefile[6] to train a Static and a MaxEnt TM on both in-domain and out-of-domain data. As discussed in Section 3, we do not use tuning on development data to set TM pruning thresholds and interpolation weights.

Two thresholds are used to prune the TMs:

- *MinInst* – the minimum number of instances required to train a model for a single source t-lemma/formeme,

- *MinPerClass* – the minimum number of instances for the same target class (translation variant of a t-lemma/formeme) so that this class is included in the classification.

The MaxEnt TM thresholds for the out-of-domain are set higher since much more data (and noise) is available. We used MinInst=100 and MinPerClass=5 for out-of-domain TMs and MinInst=2 and MinPerClass=1 for in-domain TM. The Static TM thresholds are MinInst=2 and MinPerClass=1.

For TM interpolation, we use an identical set of weights for the out-of-domain TM and for the in-domain TM; these are listed in Table 1.

TM	TM type	
for	Static	Maxent
Formemes	1.0	0.5
T-lemmas	0.5	1.0

Table 1: Weights of TMs in interpolation; the same set used both for out-of-domain TMs and in-domain TMs in all translation directions.

Translation	Out-of-domain	In-domain	Interpolation	Improvement
EN→CS	30.60	28.41	**31.27**	+0.67
CS→EN	27.11	21.51	**28.25**	+1.14
EN→ES	20.35	23.28	**26.48**	+3.20
ES→EN	18.50	18.54	**20.44**	+1.90
EN→NL	23.03	21.37	**24.29**	+1.26
NL→EN	37.03	33.68	**38.93**	+1.90

Table 2: Automatic evaluation in terms of BLEU on QTLeap corpus Batch2. Results obtained using out-of-domain TMs only, in-domain TMs only, and the interpolation of both in-domain and out-of-domain TMs. Improvement in BLEU is relative to the better of the Out-of-domain and In-domain results.

4.3 Results and Discussion

The results of our experiments on QTLeap corpus Batch2 are summarized in Table 2 (Batch2q for translations into English, Batch2a for translations from English). They show that for all translation directions, using the interpolation of out-of-domain TMs with in-domain TMs performs better than using any of the two TM types individually. The improvements range from 0.67 BLEU for EN→CS to 3.20 BLEU for EN→ES. We do not have a conclusive explanation for the variation in the amount of the improvement achieved.

In most cases, using (only) the in-domain TM leads to worse results than using (only) the out-of-domain TM. This is to be expected, as the in-domain data are extremely small. Interestingly, for EN→ES, the in-domain TM beats the large out-of-domain TM by nearly 3 BLEU points; in the other direction, the results of the two setups are comparable. We are unsure about the reason behind that.

5 Related Work

A seminal work on domain adaptation by Daumé III (2009) lists eight approaches:

- SRCONLY, TRGONLY, LININT – these correspond to our experiments (using out-of-domain model only, in-domain-model only, and a linear interpolation of both, respectively), but the linear interpolation constant is tuned on a development set.

- ALL – concatenation of training data.

- WEIGHT – as ALL, but the out-of-domain training examples are downweighted so the in-domain examples (which are typically much fewer) have bigger effect on the resulting model. The weight is chosen by cross-validation.

- PRED – the prediction of the out-of-domain model is used as an additional feature for training the final model on the in-domain data.

- PRIOR – out-of-domain weights are used as a prior (via the regularization term) when training the final model on the in-domain data (Chelba and Acero, 2004).

---

[4] http://metashare.metanet4u.eu/go2/qtleapcorpus
[5] http://www.statmt.org/wmt13/translation-task.html
[6] See cuni_train/Makefile in https://github.com/ufal/qtleap.

- EASYADAPT (called AUGMENT in the original paper, sometimes referred to as the "Frustratingly Easy Domain Adaptation") – create three variants of each feature: general, in-specific and out-specific; train on concatenation of in- and out-of-domain data, where on in-domain data, the general and in-specific features are active and on the out-of-domain data, the general and out-specific features are active.

Daumé III (2009) showed that EASYADAPT outperforms the other methods (on a variety of NLP tasks, but not including MT) in the cases when TRGONLY outperforms SRCONLY.[7] Otherwise, LININT, PRED and WEIGHT were the most successful methods. In a follow-up work (Daumé III et al., 2010), EASYADAPT was improved to exploit also additional unlabeled in-domain data.

In MT, many different approaches to domain adaptation have been attempted. Similarly to our experiments, authors combine the predictions of two separate (in-domain and general-domain) translation models (Langlais, 2002; Nakov, 2008; Sanchis-Trilles and Casacuberta, 2010; Bisazza et al., 2011) or language models (Koehn and Schroeder, 2007) in phrase-based statistical MT. Others concentrate on acquiring larger in-domain training corpora for statistical MT by selecting data from large general-domain corpora that resemble the properties of in-domain data (e.g., using cross-entropy), thus building a larger *pseudo-in-domain* training corpus. This technique has been used to adapt language models (Eck et al., 2004; Moore and Lewis, 2010) as well as translation models (Hildebrand et al., 2005; Axelrod et al., 2011) or their combination (Mansour et al., 2011; Dušek et al., 2014).

6 Conclusion and Future Work

In this paper, we presented our implementation of machine translation domain adaptation by translation model interpolation in the TectoMT system. We evaluated the method using large out-of-domain parallel data and small in-domain parallel data (1000 sentences) in the domain of computer helpdesk requests and responses, using 6 translation directions. The evaluation showed our method to perform well, achieving improvements up to 3.2 BLEU over using only a single training dataset.

In the coming year, we will obtain additional in-domain data, which will allow us to use a portion of the data for tuning the interpolation weights. We are therefore planning to implement an interpolation weights optimizer for TectoMT and try different domain-adaptation techniques (EASYADAPT, PRED and WEIGHT).

Acknowledgements

This research was supported by the grants GAUK 1572314, GAUK 338915, GAUK 2058214, SVV 260 224, and FP7-ICT-2013-10-610516 (QTLeap). This work has been using language resources developed, stored and distributed by the LINDAT/CLARIN project of the Ministry of Education, Youth and Sports of the Czech Republic (project LM2010013).

References

A. Axelrod, X. He, and J. Gao. 2011. Domain adaptation via pseudo in-domain data selection. In *Proceedings of the 2011 Conference on Empirical Methods in Natural Language Processing*, pages 355–362, Edinburgh, United Kingdom. ACL.

A. L. Berger, V. J. Della Pietra, and S. A. Della Pietra. 1996. A Maximum Entropy Approach to Natural Language Processing. *Computational Linguistics*, 22(1):39–71.

A. Bisazza, N. Ruiz, and M. Federico. 2011. Fill-up versus interpolation methods for phrase-based SMT adaptation. In *Proceedings of the International Workshop on Spoken Language Translation*, pages 136–143, San Francisco, CA, USA. International Speech Communication Association.

O. Bojar, Z. Žabokrtský, O. Dušek, P. Galuščáková, M. Majliš, D. Mareček, J. Maršík, M. Novák, M. Popel, and A. Tamchyna. 2012. The joy of parallelism with CzEng 1.0. In *LREC*, page 3921–3928, Istanbul.

---

[7]As we can see in Table 2, this is the case of ES→EN (and maybe EN→ES), so we plan to use EASYADAPT there in future.

C. Chelba and A. Acero. 2004. Adaptation of maximum entropy capitalizer: Little data can help a lot. In Dekang Lin and Dekai Wu, editors, *Proceedings of EMNLP 2004*, pages 285–292, Barcelona, Spain, July. Association for Computational Linguistics.

H. Daumé III, A. Kumar, and A. Saha. 2010. Frustratingly easy semi-supervised domain adaptation. In *Proceedings of the 2010 Workshop on Domain Adaptation for Natural Language Processing*, pages 53–59, Uppsala, Sweden, July. Association for Computational Linguistics.

H. Daumé III. 2009. Frustratingly easy domain adaptation. *CoRR*, abs/0907.1815.

O. Dušek, J. Hajič, J. Hlaváčová, M. Novák, P. Pecina, R. Rosa, A. Tamchyna, Z. Urešová, and D. Zeman. 2014. Machine translation of medical texts in the Khresmoi project. In *Proceedings of the Ninth Workshop on Statistical Machine Translation*, pages 221–228, Baltimore, MD, USA. Association for Computational Linguistics.

O. Dušek and F. Jurčíček. 2013. Robust Multilingual Statistical Morphological Generation Models. In *51st Annual Meeting of the Association for Computational Linguistics Proceedings of the Student Research Workshop*, pages 158–164, Sofia. Association for Computational Linguistics.

O. Dušek, Z. Žabokrtský, M. Popel, M. Majliš, M. Novák, and D. Mareček. 2012. Formemes in English-Czech deep syntactic MT. In *Proceedings of the Seventh Workshop on Statistical Machine Translation*, page 267–274.

O. Dušek, L. Gomes, M. Novák, M. Popel, and R. Rosa. 2015. New language pairs in TectoMT. In *Proceedings of WMT*. Under review.

M. Eck, S. Vogel, and A. Waibel. 2004. Language model adaptation for statistical machine translation based on information retrieval. In M. T. Lino, M. F. Xavier, F. Ferreira, R. Costa, and R. Silva, editors, *Proceedings of the International Conference on Language Resources and Evaluation*, pages 327–330, Lisbon, Portugal. European Language Resources Association.

A. S. Hildebrand, M. Eck, S. Vogel, and A. Waibel. 2005. Adaptation of the translation model for statistical machine translation based on information retrieval. In *Proceedings of the 10th Annual Conference of the European Association for Machine Translation*, pages 133–142, Budapest, Hungary. European Association for Machine Translation.

P. Koehn and J. Schroeder. 2007. Experiments in domain adaptation for statistical machine translation. In *Proceedings of the Second Workshop on Statistical Machine Translation*, pages 224–227, Prague, Czech Republic. ACL.

P. Koehn. 2005. Europarl: A parallel corpus for statistical machine translation. In *MT summit*, volume 5, pages 79–86.

P. Langlais. 2002. Improving a general-purpose statistical translation engine by terminological lexicons. In *COLING-02 on COMPUTERM 2002: second international workshop on computational terminology*, volume 14, pages 1–7, Taipei, Taiwan. ACL.

L. Macken, J. Trushkina, and L. Rura. 2007. Dutch parallel corpus: MT corpus and translator's aid. In *Proceedings of the Machine Translation Summit XI*, pages 313–320. European Association for Machine Translation.

S. Mansour, J. Wuebker, and H. Ney. 2011. Combining translation and language model scoring for domain-specific data filtering. In *International Workshop on Spoken Language Translation*, pages 222–229, San Francisco, CA, USA. ISCA.

D. Mareček, M. Popel, and Z. Žabokrtský. 2010. Maximum entropy translation model in dependency-based mt framework. In *Proceedings of the Joint Fifth Workshop on Statistical Machine Translation and MetricsMATR*, pages 201–206, Uppsala, Sweden, July. Association for Computational Linguistics.

R. McDonald, F. Pereira, K. Ribarov, and J. Hajič. 2005. Non-projective dependency parsing using spanning tree algorithms. In *Proceedings of the conference on Human Language Technology and Empirical Methods in Natural Language Processing*, pages 523–530.

R. C. Moore and W. Lewis. 2010. Intelligent selection of language model training data. In *Proceedings of the ACL 2010 Conference Short Papers*, pages 220–224, Uppsala, Sweden. ACL.

P. Nakov. 2008. Improving English–Spanish statistical machine translation: Experiments in domain adaptation, sentence paraphrasing, tokenization, and recasing. In *Proceedings of the Third Workshop on Statistical Machine Translation*, pages 147–150, Columbus, OH, USA. ACL.

Martin Popel and Zdeněk Žabokrtský. 2010. TectoMT: Modular NLP framework. In Hrafn Loftsson, Eirikur Rögnvaldsson, and Sigrun Helgadottir, editors, *Lecture Notes in Artificial Intelligence, Proceedings of the 7th International Conference on Advances in Natural Language Processing (IceTAL 2010)*, volume 6233 of *Lecture Notes in Computer Science*, pages 293–304, Berlin / Heidelberg. Iceland Centre for Language Technology (ICLT), Springer.

G. Sanchis-Trilles and F. Casacuberta. 2010. Log-linear weight optimisation via Bayesian adaptation in statistical machine translation. In *Proceedings of the 23rd International Conference on Computational Linguistics: Posters*, pages 1077–1085, Beijing, China. ACL.

P. Sgall, E. Hajičová, and J. Panevová. 1986. *The meaning of the sentence in its semantic and pragmatic aspects.* D. Reidel, Dordrecht.

D. J. Spoustová, J. Hajič, J. Votrubec, P. Krbec, and P. Květoň. 2007. The Best of Two Worlds: Cooperation of Statistical and Rule-based Taggers for Czech. In *Proceedings of the Workshop on Balto-Slavonic Natural Language Processing: Information Extraction and Enabling Technologies*, pages 67–74, Stroudsburg, PA, USA. Association for Computational Linguistics.

J. Straková, M. Straka, and J. Hajič. 2014. Open-Source Tools for Morphology, Lemmatization, POS Tagging and Named Entity Recognition. In *Proceedings of 52nd Annual Meeting of the Association for Computational Linguistics: System Demonstrations*, pages 13–18. Association for Computational Linguistics.

Z. Žabokrtský and M. Popel. 2009. Hidden Markov Tree Model in Dependency-based Machine Translation. In *Proceedings of the ACL-IJCNLP 2009 Conference Short Papers*, ACLShort '09, pages 145–148, Stroudsburg, PA, USA. Association for Computational Linguistics.

Z. Žabokrtský, J. Ptáček, and P. Pajas. 2008. TectoMT: highly modular MT system with tectogrammatics used as transfer layer. In *Proceedings of the Third Workshop on Statistical Machine Translation*, pages 167–170. Association for Computational Linguistics.

Factored Models for Deep Machine Translation

Kiril Simov, Iliana Simova, Velislava Todorova, Petya Osenova
Linguistic Modelling Department, IICT
Bulgarian Academy of Sciences
Sofia, Bulgaria
{kivs|iliana|slava|petya}@bultreebank.org

Abstract

In this paper, we present some preliminary results on Statistical Machine Translation from Bulgarian-to-English and English-to-Bulgarian. Linguistic knowledge has been added gradually as factors in the MOSES system. The tests were performed on the QTLeap corpus data in IT domain for Pilot 1. The training was done on news parallel data as well as on IT domain data. The BLEU scores show that the addition of linguistic knowledge improves the Machine Translation.

1 Introduction

In the recent years, machine translation (MT) has achieved significant improvement in terms of translation quality (Koehn, 2010). Both data-driven approaches (e.g., statistical MT (SMT)) and knowledge-based (e.g., rule-based MT (RBMT)) have achieved comparable results shown in the evaluation campaigns (Callison-Burch et al., 2011). However, according to the human evaluation, the final outputs of the MT systems are still far from satisfactory. For that reason, we explore an approach that incrementally incorporates linguistic knowledge into an SMT system.

There has not been much study on the language pair Bulgarian – English, mainly due to the lack of resources, including corpora, preprocessors, etc. There was a system published by Koehn et al. (2009), which was trained and tested on the European Union law data, but not on other domains like news. They reported a very high BLEU score (Papineni et al., 2002) on the Bulgarian – English translation direction (61.3). The direction from English to Bulgarian was even less explored.

In the QTLeap project[1] linguistic knowledge is gradually added to SMT systems with the aim to achieve better translation in both directions: EN-to-X language and X language-to-English. The incremental process is organized in several pilots. Pilot 0 sets the baseline, which means that no linguistic knowledge is added. Pilot 1 introduces some initial linguistic knowledge through the incorporation of some features such as part-of-speech, lemma, etc. In the setting that involved Bulgarian, we also added some general information on the ontological type of the word: referent or event. Pilots 2 and 3 will integrate further knowledge, such as lexicons, semantic annotations, etc.

In this paper, we focus on the Bulgarian-to-English and English-to-Bulgarian translation, and mainly explore the approach of building on the SMT baseline, which is already augmented with linguistic features. More precisely, we explore the impact of the bilingual morphological lexicons in the translation process.

These are the motivations behind our approach: 1) the SMT baseline trained on a decent amount of parallel corpora already proved to be a good direction to go. Thus, more knowledge has to be added

---

[1] http://qtleap.eu/

Proceedings of the 1st Deep Machine Translation Workshop (DMTW 2015), pages 97–105,
Praha, Czech Republic, 3–4 September 2015.

for further lines of improvement; 2) the MT system can profit from the incorporation of knowledge additional to the common linguistic factors. Such additions include lexicons, gazetteers, etc.

The rest of the paper is organized as follows: Section 2 mentions some related approaches. Section 3 presents information on preparation of the data and Section 4 describes the preprocessing of the data and introduces our factor-based SMT model which allows us to incorporate various linguistic features into an SMT baseline, including some semantic features. We show our experiments in Section 5 as well as some preliminary evaluation of the results. The conclusions and future work are presented in Section 6.

2   Related Work

Our work is closely connected to the transfer-based MT models. Ideally, given the availability of two deep grammars for some language pair, we would be able to translate through the transfer of the deep representations.

One such setting was developed in the framework of the Head-driven Phrase Structure Grammar (HPSG) within the DELPH-IN community[2]. The deep representation is delivered by the Minimal Recursion Semantics (MRS) analyses. They are usually delivered together with the syntactic analyses of the text. There already exist quite extensive implemented formal HPSG grammars for English (Copestake and Flickinger, 2000), Spanish (Marimon, 2010), German (Müller and Kasper, 2000), and Japanese (Siegel, 2000; Siegel and Bender, 2002). All grammars are harmonized with a Grammar Matrix (Bender et al., 2002). At the moment, precise and linguistically motivated grammars, customized on the base of the Grammar Matrix, have been or are being developed for Norwegian, French, Korean, Italian, Modern Greek, Spanish, Portuguese, Chinese, etc. There also exists a Bulgarian Resource Grammar – BURGER[3].

The transfer in this setting is usually implemented in the form of rewriting rules. For instance, in the Norwegian LOGON project (Oepen et al., 2004), the transfer rules were hand-written (Bond et al., 2005; Oepen et al., 2007), which involved a large amount of manual work. Graham and van Genabith (2008) and Graham et al. (2009) explored the automatic rule induction approach in a transfer-based MT setting two Lexical Functional Grammars (LFGs), which was still restricted by the performance of both – the parser and the generator. Lack of robustness for target side generation is one of the main issues, when various ill-formed or fragmented structures come out after transfer. Oepen et al. (2007) use their generator to generate text fragments instead of full sentences, in order to increase the robustness.

However, since a real large-scale grammar for Bulgarian is still not available, we take an SMT system as our 'backbone' which robustly delivers some translation for any given input. Then, we incrementally augment SMT with deep linguistic knowledge. In general, what we are doing is still along the lines of previous work utilizing deep grammars, but we build a more 'light-weighted' transfer model over dependency parses.

One of the MRS-related semantic formalisms is the Abstract Meaning Representation (AMR[4]), which also aims at achieving whole-sentence deep semantics instead of addressing various isolated holders of semantic information (such as NER, coreferences, temporal anchors, etc.). AMR also builds on the available syntactic trees, thus contributing to the efforts on sembanking.

Another stream of research is related to the TectoMT approach (Žabokrtský et al., 2008). The Prague Dependency Treebank (PDT)[5] is a Czech treebank, annotated in accordance to the linguistic theory of Functional Generative Description (P. Sgall and Panevova, 1986). The tectogrammatical layer[6] is the third layer of the PDT. It represents the syntactic-semantic interface, adding the functional dimension and collapsing the structural information, thus aiming at a more language-independent level of abstraction. The other two layers are the morphological and analytical ones. The morphological layer operates over tokens, assigning to them POS and lemma tags. The analytical layer reflects the surface sentence structure.

---

²http://www.delph-in.net/wiki/index.php/Home

³http://www.bultreebank.org/BURGER/index.html

⁴http://www.isi.edu/natural-language/amr/a.pdf

⁵https://ufal.mff.cuni.cz/pdt2.0/

⁶https://ufal.mff.cuni.cz/pdt2.0/doc/manuals/en/t-layer/html/ch01.html

The tectogrammatical annotation builds on the analytical level. It presents the deep semantic structure of the sentence. At the tectogrammatical level, each sentence has at least one representation unambiguously characterizing the meaning of the sentence. The tectogrammatical level representation contains all the information necessary for translating the tectogrammatical representation into the lower levels, as well as for its interpretation in the sense of intentional semantics.

In contrast to the analytical level, which follows the surface sentence structure and encodes analytical functions (in particular, grammatical relations like *Subject, Object, Predicate, Attribute*, etc.), while preserving the word order, the tectogrammatical level highlights the functional dimension (such as the semantic roles *Actor, Patient, Addressee*, etc.). Additionally, it abstracts away from the synsemantic (functional) parts-of-speech (prepositions, conjunctions, etc.) in the dependency trees, thus focusing on the autosemantic (content) words (nouns, verbs, etc.). The structural information is not lost, but just "collapsed" into the content words representations. In this way, a more abstract level of language representation is achieved, which then is used for the transfer step within the MT systems. The result on the tectogrammatical level heavily depends on the results from the processed analytical level.

In the future, we plan to have transfer architectures for Bulgarian and English in both directions in both approaches – MRS and TectoMT. However, since these endeavors require more work, for the moment we test our ideas in the already built-in setting of the factored-based MOSES system. Thus, we build on the previous language model translation experience described in (Wang et al., 2012a) and (Wang et al., 2012b). However, while in the above-mentioned publications only Bulgarian-to-English translation was explored, in this paper also the English-to-Bulgarian direction is presented.

3 Data Preparation

Two types of data are used in our experiments. The first type includes parallel news data. It is the training data. The second type includes parallel QTLeap data in the IT domain. It is the training and test data.

The parallel news data comprises the following sources:

1. SETIMES parallel corpus, which is part of the OPUS parallel corpus[7].

2. EuroParl parallel corpus[8].

3. LibreOffice Document Foundation.

The data in SETIMES corpus was aligned automatically. We first checked the consistency of the automatic alignments. It turned out that more than 25% of the sentence alignments were not correct. We corrected manually more than 25.000 sentence alignments. (The the rest of the data set includes around 135,000 sentences. The whole data set is about 160,000 sentences.) Then, two actions were taken:

1. **Improving the tokenization of the Bulgarian part**. The observations from the manual check of the set of 25,000 sentences showed systematic errors in the tokenized text. Hence, these cases have been detected and fixed semi-automatically.

2. **Correcting and removing the suspicious alignments**. Initially, the ratio of the lengths of the English and Bulgarian sentences was calculated in the set of the 25,000 manually annotated sentences. As a rule, the Bulgarian sentences are longer than the English ones. The ratio is 1.34. Then we calculated the ratio for each pair of sentences. After this, the optimal interval was manually determined, such that if the ratio for a given pair of sentences is within the interval, then we assume that the pair is a good one. The interval for these experiments is set to [0.7; 1.8]. All the pairs with ratio outside of the interval have been deleted.

The test dataset was the Bulgarian-English parallel part from the QTLeap multilingual corpus. The QTLeap corpus is composed of 4 000 pairs of questions and respective answers in the domain of ICT

---

[7]OPUS–an open source parallel corpus, http://opus.lingfil.uu.se/
[8]http://www.statmt.org/europarl/

troubleshooting for both hardware and software. This material was collected using a real-life commercial online support service via chat. The corpus is thus composed of naturally occurring utterances produced by users while interacting with that service. The support system, denominated PcWizard, aims to be the first point of contact for troubleshooting trying to offer a rapid reply and solution to not too complex questions from the users. For more information see[9].

4 Linguistic Preprocessing and Factor-based SMT Model

For the current experiments the data in the training datasets was analyzed at two levels – POS tagging and Lemmatization: **POS tagging:** POS tagging was performed by a pipe of several modules. First, we applied a morphological lexicon and a set of rules. The lexicon added all the possible tags for the known words. The rules reduced the ambiguity for some of the sure cases. The result of this step was a tagged text with some ambiguities unresolved. The next step was the application of the GTagger (see (Georgiev et al., 2012)). It was trained on ambiguous data and thus selected the most appropriate tags from the suggested ones. The accuracy of the whole pipeline is 97.83%. **Lemmatization:** The lemmatization module is based on the same morphological lexicon that was used in the tagger. From the lexicon we extracted functions which convert each word form into its lemma.

Then we built our approach on top of the factor-based SMT model proposed by Koehn and Hoang (2007a), as an extension of the traditional phrase-based SMT framework. Instead of using only the word form of the text, it allows the system to take a vector of factors to represent each token, both for the source and target languages. The vector of factors can be used for different levels of linguistic annotations, like lemma or part-of-speech. Furthermore, this extension actually allows us to incorporate various kinds of features if they can be (somehow) represented as annotations of the tokens.

The process is quite similar to supertagging (Bangalore and Joshi, 1999), which assigns "rich descriptions (supertags) that impose complex constraints in a local context". In our case, all the linguistic features (factors) associated with each token form a supertag to that token. Singh and Bandyopadhyay (2010) had a similar idea of incorporating linguistic features, while they worked on Manipuri – English bidirectional translation. Our approach is slightly different from (Birch et al., 2007) and (Hassan et al., 2007), who mainly used the supertags on the target language side, English. We experiment with both sides.

In particular, we consider the following morphosyntactic factors for both languages:

- WF - word form, which is the original text token.

- LEMMA is the lexical invariant of the original word form.

- POS - part-of-speech of the word.

- LING - other linguistic features derived from the POS tag in the BulTreeBank tagset.

In comparison to the experiments described in ((Wang et al., 2012a), (Wang et al., 2012b)) the number of the linguistic factors were reduced in comparison to the ones that contributed best to the improvement of the translation results. Thus, we have excluded all the factors based on dependency parsing of the data.

Our work on Minimal Recursion Semantic analysis of Bulgarian text is inspired by the work on MRS and RMRS (Robust Minimal Recursion Semantic) (see (Copestake, 2003) and (Copestake, 2007)) and the previous work on transfer of dependency analyses into RMRS structures described in (Spreyer and Frank, 2005) and (Jakob et al., 2010).

MRS is introduced as an underspecified semantic formalism (Copestake et al., 2005). It is used to support semantic analyses in the English HPSG grammar ERG (Copestake and Flickinger, 2000), but also in other grammar formalisms like LFG. The main idea is that it avoids spelling out the complete set of readings resulting from the interaction of scope bearing operators and quantifiers, instead providing a single underspecified representation from which the complete set of readings can be constructed. Here

---

[9]http://qtleap.eu/wp-content/uploads/2015/05/QTLEAP-2015-D2.51.pdf

we will present only basic definitions from (Copestake et al., 2005). An MRS structure is a tuple $\langle\, GT,$ $R, C\, \rangle$, where GT is the top handle, R is a bag of EPs (elementary predicates) and C is a bag of handle constraints, such that there is no handle h that outscopes GT. Each elementary predication contains exactly four components: (1) a handle which is the label of the EP; (2) a relation; (3) a list of zero or more ordinary variable arguments of the relation; and (4) a list of zero or more handles corresponding to scopal arguments of the relation (i.e., holes). RMRS is introduced as a modification of MRS which to capture the semantics resulting from the shallow analysis. Here an assumption is made that the shallow processor does not have access to a lexicon. Thus it does not have access to the arity of the relations in EPs. Therefore, the representation has to be underspecified with respect to the number of arguments of the relations. The names of relations are constructed on the basis of the lemma for each word form in the text. This main argument could be of two types: *referential index* (v) for nouns and *event* (e) for the other parts of speech. In our implementation we extend the types of the main argument of the elementary predicates. Especially for the event arguments we introduce a new type[10] "ef" for adverbs and "ec" for subordinators, because they modify other events and thus they are special type of events. In Bulgarian some parts of speech can have main attribute of both types: "v" and "e". For them we introduce a new type "e-v".

Similarly to our previous experiments, here we use only the RMRS relation and the type of the main argument as features to the translation model. We will skip here the explanation of the full structure of RMRS structures and how they are constructed. Thus, we firstly do a match between the surface tokens and the MRS elementary predicates (EPs) and then extract the following features as extra factors:

- EP – the name of the elementary predicate, which usually indicates an event or an entity from a semantic point of view.

- EoV – indicates the current EP as either an event, a reference variable or their subtypes.

Notice that we do not take all the information provided by the MRS, e.g., we throw away the scopal information and the other arguments of the relations. This kind of information is not straightforward to be represented in such 'tagging'-style models, but it will be tackled in the future.

All these factors encoded within the corpus provide us with a rich selection of factors for various experiments.

5 Experiments

For our entry level deep machine translation system (Pilot 1) we make use of the Moses open source toolkit to build a factored SMT model (Koehn and Hoang, 2007b). As it was mentioned above in the analysis stage, we create a representation of the text which encodes various levels of linguistic information as factors. These include morphological, syntactic and semantic abstractions in the source and target language.

We have experimented with several combinations of factors derived from the preprocessing with the Bulgarian and English analysis pipelines, together with semantic factors based on Minimal Recursion Semantics (see Table 1 for a subset of the results).

The following are some examples of factors for this model: word form, lemma, and morphosyntactic tags, factors modeling the parent word (lemma of the parent word, part of speech of the parent word) as well as the type of dependency relation (syntactic factors), and MRS-based factors (elementary predicate and variable type).

We contributed mainly in two directions: better analysis with an improved pipeline for Bulgarian, and different more complex types of factored models to explore successful factor combinations. We have experimented with a number of combinations of the listed factors, language model types (word and POS), translation and generation steps. The best performing model featuring a semantic factor for the direction BG→EN includes four factors: word form, lemma, POS and variable type; a word and POS-based language model. In the transfer step, two alternative approaches are used. If possible a mapping

---

[10]In fact these types are subtypes of the basic ones.

Factors	LM	Translation	Generation	Decoding	BLEU	
					BG→EN	EN→BG
WF, EP, EoV	0	0,1,2-0	–	–	31.53	24.00
WF, POS, EoV	0	0,1,2-0	–	–	32.07	24.13
WF, Lemma, EP, EoV	0	1-1+2-2+3-3	1,2,3-0	–	23.94	13.69
WF, Lemma, POS	0,2	0-0,2+1-0,2	–	t0:t1	32.59	22.86
WF, Lemma, POS, Ling	0,2	1-1+3-2+0-0,2	1-2+1,2-0	t0,g0,t1,g1:t2	32.78	22.73
WF, Lemma, POS, EoV	0,2	0,3-0,2+1,3-0,2	–	t0:t1	32.59	22.77

Table 1: A subset of the results from the factored experiments, evaluated on the second half of the QTLeap data set.

is performed between the source word form and the variable type and the target word form candidates and POS candidates. However, if the source word form has not been seen during the training phase, the source lemma together with the variable type is used instead.

For the translation direction EN→BG the model includes three factors: word form, part of speech, and variable type. In the translation step, the source word, POS, and variable type are translated into the target word form.

The automatic evaluation for both directions is described in D2.4 of the QTLeap project.

The BG-to-EN direction was evaluated on questions. Here are the numbers for Pilot 0 and Pilot 1 per metric:

1. BLEU Pilot 0 (29.7); Pilot 1 (27.7)

2. wordF Pilot 0 (22.8); Pilot 1 (22.4)

3. chartF Pilot 0 (46.7); Pilot 1 (**47.4**)

The EN-to-BG direction was evaluated on the answers:

1. BLEU Pilot 0 (25.3); Pilot 1 (24.5)

2. wordF Pilot 0 (25.6); Pilot 1 (25.0)

3. chartF Pilot 0 (46.7); Pilot 1 (46.6)

The results from the two pilots are comparable. More linguistic knowledge is needed for the translation improvement. The only small improvement was noted in BG-to-EN direction in chartF. Since up to now this translation direction was the focus, more effort is needed for improvement in the other direction as well.

5.1 Preliminary Experiments with a Parallel Morphological Lexicon

One of the main problems in the translation in both directions are the so-called out-of-training word forms. These are word form pairs of translations that do not appear in the parallel corpora used for the training. For example, in Bulgarian each adjective has 9 forms. For many adjectives many of these forms are not present in the parallel corpora. In order to solve this problem we decided to add a parallel Bulgarian-English morphological lexicon to the parallel corpora.

The lexicon was constructed by exploiting the following resources: BTB-Morphological lexicon containing all wordforms for more than 110 000 Bulgarian lemmas; BTB-bilingual Bulgarian-English lexicons (with about 8000 entries); English Wiktionary. From it the English wordforms were extracted for the English lemmas. Then we mapped the wordform lexicons for both languages to the corresponding part of the bilingual lexicon. Afterwards, the corresponding wordforms were aligned on the basis of their morphological features like *number* (singular, plural); *degree* (comparative, superlative); *definiteness* (definite, indefinite), etc.

Bulgarian	**English**
visok|visok|a	a|a|d high|high|g
visok|visok|a	high|high|g
visok|visok|a	a|a|d tall|tall|g
visok|visok|a	tall|tall|g
—	—
naj-visokata|visok|a	highest|highest|g
naj-visokata|visok|a	the|the|d highest|highest|g
naj-visokata|visok|a	tallest|tallest|g
naj-visokata|visok|a	the|the|d tallest|tallest|g

Table 2: Wordform aligned parallel lexicon. It shows the Bulgarian adjective "visok" with its two translations in English: "high" and "tall". The table represents the encoding of singular, masculine, indefinite forms and superlative, singular, feminine, definite forms. Each triple represents wf|lm|pos, where *wf* is the wordform, *lm* is the lemma and *pos* is the part-of-speech. For example, the triple a|a|d means: wordform "a"; lemma "a" and part-of-speech "determiner".

In this preliminary experiment we used only the noun and the adjective parts-of-speech from the wordform aligned bilingual lexicon. Bulgarian language encodes definiteness as an ending to the nouns and adjectives in contrast to English which encodes it as a separate determiner in front of the noun or adjective. For this reason we also encode the English definite and indefinite articles for the English wordforms. Since in some contexts the English articles are not obligatory, the English wordforms were encoded with or without them. In addition, we also represented factors for each wordform (in the example below we encode the lemma and POS). Tab. 2 shows an example from the resulting lexicon.

The lexicon represents more than 70 000 aligned wordforms. It was added to the training data. Each aligned pair of word forms is added as a pair of sentences with length one or two depending on determiners. We got the results presented in Tab. 3. They show a positive impact of the aligned wordform parallel lexicon on the translation in both directions. The table shows also that the addition of the definite forms for English does not change the result.

	without lexicon	with lexicon; with only indefinite forms	with lexicon; with all forms
BG→EN	32.59	33.02	32.88
EN→BG	22.86	23.91	22.97

Table 3: Preliminary experiments with parallel morphological lexicons.

Although the reported here experiments are only preliminary they demonstrate a possible direction of improving of the training corpus for solving the "out-of-training-wordforms" problem. There is still room for improvements which include the incorporation also of other parts-of-speech, compositional and multiword phrases, etc.

6 Conclusions and Future Work

In this paper, we reported our initial work towards building deep statistical machine translation models between Bulgarian and English in both directions. Based on previous experiments, in Pilot 1 we extended the semantic factors with new types of main arguments for MRS elementary predicates, which improved the results in English-to-Bulgarian direction and shows promising results for the Bulgarian-to-English direction. The paper also showed that the addition of a wordform aligned parallel lexicon improved the results in both translation directions.

In our future work we plan to incorporate more linguistic knowledge from the lexicon. Also we will aim at improving the incorporation of deep factors within the translation models.

Acknowledgements

This research has received support by the EC's FP7 (FP7/2007-2013) project under grant agreement number 610516: "QTLeap: Quality Translation by Deep Language Engineering Approaches."

We thank the two anonymous for their valuable comments on the initial version of the paper. All errors remain our own responsibility.

References

Srinivas Bangalore and Aravind K. Joshi. 1999. Supertagging: an approach to almost parsing supertagging: an approach to almost parsing supertagging: an approach to almost parsing. *Computational Linguistics*, 25(2), June.

Emily M. Bender, Dan Flickinger, and Stephan Oepen. 2002. The grammar Matrix. An open-source starter-kit for the rapid development of cross-linguistically consistent broad-coverage precision grammar. In *Proceedings of the Workshop on Grammar Engineering and Evaluation at the 19th International Conference on Computational Linguistics*, Taipei, Taiwan.

Alexandra Birch, Miles Osborne, and Philipp Koehn. 2007. Ccg supertags in factored statistical machine translation. In *Proceedings of the Second Workshop on Statistical Machine Translation*, pages 9–16, Prague, Czech Republic, June.

Francis Bond, Stephan Oepen, Melanie Siegel, Ann Copestake, and Dan Flickinger. 2005. Open source machine translation with DELPH-IN. In *Proceedings of the Open-Source Machine Translation Workshop at the 10th Machine Translation Summit*, pages 15 – 22, Phuket, Thailand, September.

Chris Callison-Burch, Philipp Koehn, Christof Monz, and Omar F. Zaidan. 2011. Findings of the 2011 workshop on statistical machine translation. In *Proceedings of the 6th Workshop on SMT*.

Ann Copestake and Dan Flickinger. 2000. An open source grammar development environment and broad-coverage english grammar using hpsg. In *Proceedings of the 2nd International Conference on Language Resources and Evaluation*, Athens, Greece.

Ann Copestake, Dan Flickinger, Carl Pollard, and Ivan Sag. 2005. Minimal recursion semantics: An introduction. *Research on Language & Computation*, 3(4):281–332.

Ann Copestake. 2003. Robust minimal recursion semantics (working paper).

Ann Copestake. 2007. Applying robust semantics. In *Proceedings of the 10th Conference of the Pacific Assocation for Computational Linguistics (PACLING)*, pages 1–12.

Georgi Georgiev, Valentin Zhikov, Petya Osenova, Kiril Simov, and Preslav Nakov. 2012. Feature-rich part-of-speech tagging for morphologically complex languages: Application to bulgarian. In *Proceedings of EACL 2012*. MIT Press, Cambridge, MA, USA.

Yvette Graham and Josef van Genabith. 2008. Packed rules for automatic transfer-rule induction. In *Proceedings of the European Association of Machine Translation Conference (EAMT 2008)*, pages 57–65, Hamburg, Germany, September.

Yvette Graham, Anton Bryl, and Josef van Genabith. 2009. F-structure transfer-based statistical machine translation. In *Proceedings of the Lexical Functional Grammar Conference*, pages 317–328, Cambridge, UK. CSLI Publications, Stanford University, USA.

Hany Hassan, Khalil Sima'an, and Andy Way. 2007. Supertagged phrase-based statistical machine translation. In *Proceedings of ACL*, Prague, Czech Republic, June.

Max Jakob, Markéta Lopatková, and Valia Kordoni. 2010. Mapping between dependency structures and compositional semantic representations. In *Proceedings of the 7th International Conference on Language Resources and Evaluation (LREC 2010)*, pages 2491–2497.

Philipp Koehn and Hieu Hoang. 2007a. Factored translation models. In *Proceedings of EMNLP*.

Philipp Koehn and Hieu Hoang. 2007b. Factored translation models. In *EMNLP-CoNLL 2007, Proceedings of the 2007 Joint Conference on Empirical Methods in Natural Language Processing and Computational Natural Language Learning, June 28-30, 2007, Prague, Czech Republic*, pages 868–876.

Philipp Koehn, Alexandra Birch, and Ralf Steinberger. 2009. 462 machine translation systems for europe. In *Proceedings of MT Summit XII*.

Philipp Koehn. 2010. *Statistical Machine Translation*. Cambridge University Press, January.

Montserrat Marimon. 2010. The spanish resource grammar. In *Proceedings of the International Conference on Language Resources and Evaluation, LREC 2010, 17-23 May 2010, Valletta, Malta*.

Stefan Müller and Walter Kasper. 2000. HPSG analysis of German. In Wolfgang Wahlster, editor, *Verbmobil. Foundations of Speech-to-Speech Translation*, pages 238 – 253. Springer, Berlin, Germany, artificial intelligence edition.

Stephan Oepen, Helge Dyvik, Jan Tore Lønning, Erik Velldal, Dorothee Beermann, John Carroll, Dan Flickinger, Lars Hellan, Janne Bondi Johannessen, Paul Meurer, Torbjørn Nordgård, , and Victoria Rosén. 2004. Som å kapp-ete med trollet? towards MRS-based norwegian to english machine translation. In *Proceedings of the 10th International Conference on Theoretical and Methodological Issues in Machine Translation*, Baltimore, MD.

Stephan Oepen, Erik Velldal, Jan Tore Lønning, Paul Meurer, Victoria Rosén, and Dan Flickinger. 2007. Towards hybrid quality-oriented machine translation — on linguistics and probabilities in MT. In *Proceedings of the 11th Conference on Theoretical and Methodological Issues in Machine Translation (TMI-07)*, Skovde, Sweden.

E. Hajicova P. Sgall and J. Panevova. 1986. *The Meaning of the Sentence in its Semantic and Pragmatic Aspects*. Dordrecht: Reidel Publishing Company and Prague: Academia.

Kishore Papineni, Salim Roukos, Todd Ward, and Wei-Jing Zhu. 2002. Bleu: a method for automatic evaluation of machine translation. In *Proceedings of ACL*.

Melanie Siegel and Emily M. Bender. 2002. Efficient deep processing of japanese. In *Proceedings of the 19th International Conference on Computational Linguistics*, Taipei, Taiwan.

Melanie Siegel. 2000. HPSG analysis of Japanese. In Wolfgang Wahlster, editor, *Verbmobil. Foundations of Speech-to-Speech Translation*, pages 265 – 280. Springer, Berlin, Germany, artificial intelligence edition.

Thoudam Doren Singh and Sivaji Bandyopadhyay. 2010. Manipuri-english bidirectional statistical machine translation systems using morphology and dependency relations. In *Proceedings of the Fourth Workshop on Syntax and Structure in Statistical Translation*, pages 83–91, Beijing, China, August.

Kathrin Spreyer and Anette Frank. 2005. Projecting RMRS from TIGER Dependencies. In *Proceedings of the HPSG 2005 Conference*, pages 354–363, Lisbon, Portugal.

Zdeněk Žabokrtský, Jan Ptáček, and Petr Pajas. 2008. Tectomt: Highly modular mt system with tectogrammatics used as transfer layer. In *Proceedings of the Third Workshop on Statistical Machine Translation*, StatMT '08, pages 167–170, Stroudsburg, PA, USA. Association for Computational Linguistics.

Rui Wang, Petya Osenova, and Kiril Simov. 2012a. Linguistically-augmented bulgarian-to- english statistical machine translation model. In *Proceedings of the Joint Workshop on Exploiting Synergies Between Information Retrieval and Machine Translation (ESIRMT) and Hybrid Approaches to Machine Translation (HyTra), EACL 2012*, pages 119–128.

Rui Wang, Petya Osenova, and Kiril Simov. 2012b. Linguistically-enriched models for bulgarian-to-english machine translation. In *Proceedings of the Sixth Workshop on Syntax, Semantics and Structure in Statistical Translation, SSST-6, 2012*, pages 10–19.

Machine Translation for Multilingual Troubleshooting in the IT Domain: A Comparison of Different Strategies

Sanja Štajner and **João Rodrigues** and **Luís Gomes** and **António Branco**
Department of Informatics, Faculty of Sciences
University of Lisbon, Portugal
`{sanja.stajner, joao.rodrigues, luis.gomes, antonio.branco}`
`@di.fc.ul.pt`

Abstract

In this paper, we address the problem of machine translation (MT) of domain-specific texts for which large amounts of parallel data for training are not available. We focus on the IT domain and on English to Portuguese machine translation, and compare different strategies for improving system performance over two baselines, the first using only large dataset of out-of-domain data, and the second using only a small dataset of in-domain data. Our results indicate that adding a domain-specific bilingual lexicon to the training dataset significantly improves the performance of both a hybrid MT system and a PBSMT system, while adding out-of-domain sentence pairs to the training dataset only improves the performance of a hybrid MT system. Furthermore, we perform a human evaluation of the sentences generated by the hybrid MT system and the standard PBSMT system built using the same training datasets. The results indicate some significant differences between those two MT approaches in this specific task.

1 Introduction

Although the problem of machine translation has been extensively studied in the last 30 years and is one of the main topics of the natural language processing (NLP), English to Portuguese MT is rarely addressed.

Our work aims to fill that gap by addressing the problem of English to Portuguese MT for a specialised domain (the IT domain) using two MT approaches: the standard PBSMT system and a hybrid MT system based on deep translation approach. We focus on translation from English to Portuguese of short sentences taken from real-usage scenarios, where user questions are followed by answers from an IT technician. The data was gathered in a continuous way during user interaction with a technical support team via chat. We explore three different strategies for enlarging the training dataset: (1) adding an in-domain bilingual terminology; (2) adding a certain portion of the out-of-domain corpus; and (3) adding both an in-domain bilingual terminology and a certain portion of the out-of-domain corpus. Our objective is to explore which of the three strategies leads to greater improvements in the system performance for each of the two MT approaches (PBSMT and hybrid MT). In order to gain a better insight into strengths and weaknesses of both MT systems, we also conduct a human evaluation and error analysis of their output sentences.

The remainder of the paper is organised as follows: Section 2 introduces studies that are relevant to our work; Section 3 describes the corpora, MT systems, experimental setup, goals and evaluation procedures; Section 4 presents and discusses the results of both automatic and human evaluation; and Section 5 summarises the findings of this study and gives directions for future work.

2 Related Work

The rule-based machine translation (MT) systems, such as Systran (Toma, 1977), ETAP-3 (Boguslavsky, 1995), and Lucy (Alonso and Thurmair, 2003), required linguistic expertise to operate and were difficult

Proceedings of the 1st Deep Machine Translation Workshop (DMTW 2015), pages 106–115,
Praha, Czech Republic, 3–4 September 2015.

to adapt to different languages. The emergence of the word-based IBM models (Brown et al., 1988; Brown et al., 1990; Brown et al., 1993) heralded a new approach to MT – statistical machine translation (SMT) systems. Later, the word-based SMT models were replaced by better-performing phrase-based (Koehn et al., 2007) or hierarchical phrase-based (Li et al., 2009) SMT systems. However, it was noticed that those shallow SMT approaches which do not use any deeper linguistic information or syntax are not able to capture long-distance dependences and may lead to problems with word order and grammatical and semantic cohesion (Fishel et al., 2012). Shallow syntax-based SMT systems tried to address those issues using three different approaches: a *tree-to-string* translation, where linguistic information is applied only on the source side (Huang et al., 2006); a *string-to-tree* translation, where linguistic information is applied only on the target side (Galley et al., 2004), and a *tree-to-tree* translation, where linguistic information is applied on both source and target side (Eisner, 2003). However, for the majority of language pairs, phrase-based SMT systems still produce better results.

The main limitation of SMT systems is that they require large amounts of parallel (or at least comparable) training data, which is hard to obtain for language pairs not covered by the Europarl corpora (Koehn, 2005). Even if Europarl contains data for a particular language pair, another problem arises if the SMT system is needed for a different domain, as the training data may not cover the specific vocabulary or sentence constructions present in the targeted domain. In order to address this problem, many domain-adaptation techniques for SMT have been proposed, ranging from simply adding out-of-domain data to the small amount of in-domain data for training (Foster and Kuhn, 2007) to more sophisticated techniques, such as selecting only particular sentences from the out-of-domain data which are most similar to the in-domain data (Axelrod et al., 2011) or are similar to the sentences with the lowest translation quality (Banerjee et al., 2015).

Hybrid MT systems, in turn, aim to exploit the best of both SMT and rule-based approaches, usually either by combining rule-based transfer with statistical language models in the synthesis phase (Habash and Dorr, 2002), or by combining rule-based with statistical approaches at different points of the Vauquois triangle, as the TectoMT system (Žabokrtský et al., 2008) that we use in this study.

2.1 English-Portuguese MT

The English-Portuguese translation model built using the standard PBSMT system in the Moses toolkit (Koehn et al., 2007), trained on the largest existing parallel corpora for this language pair (the JRC-Acquis corpus (Steinberger et al., 2006)) achieves a BLEU score (Papineni et al., 2002) of 55% (Koehn et al., 2009). The standard PBSMT system in the Moses toolkit trained on the Fapesp-v2 corpus of English-Brazilian Portuguese texts from the Brazilian scientific news magazine *Revista Pesquisa FAPESP*[1] (Aziz and Specia, 2011) achieves 46.28% BLEU score (Salton et al., 2014).

To the best of our knowledge, there have been no studies reporting performances of English to Portuguese MT systems for any domain-specific tasks, neither have there been any studies comparing different MT approaches for this language pair.

3 Methodology

The next four subsections describe the corpora (Section 3.1), MT systems (Section 3.2), experimental setup and the main goal of the translation experiments (Section 3.3), as well as the human evaluation procedure (Section 3.4).

3.1 Corpora

We used four corpora in this study:

1. **EP** – Europarl corpus (Koehn, 2005) with English on the source side and Portuguese on the target side (1,960,407 sentence pairs) was used as the large out-of-domain corpus.

2. **IT1** – An in-domain IT corpus with 2,000 sentence pairs (1,000 questions and 1,000 answers) compiled under the QTLeap project[2].

---

[1] http://revistapesquisa.fapesp.br/
[2] http://qtleap.eu/

Corpora	Source (EN)	Target (PT)
TERM	arrow key	tecla de seta
	gatekeeper	controlador de chamadas
	Planning System Database	Base de Dados do Sistema de Planeamento
IT1	If your disc is not recognized, try changing the USB port.	Se o disco não está a ser reconhecido, tente trocar de entrada USB.
	Which antivirus should I keep, MSE or AVG?	Qual antivrus devo manter, MSE ou AVG?
IT2	In the Insert menu, select Picture.	No menu inserir selecione Imagem.
	In the taskbar there is an icon shaped like binoculars, click and type in what you want to search.	Na barra de Tarefas há um ícone em forma de binóculos, clique e escreva o que pretende procurar.
EP	Please rise, then, for this minute's silence.	Convido-os a levantarem-se para um minuto de silêncio.
	You have requested a debate on this subject in the course of the next few days, during this part-session.	Os senhores manifestaram o desejo de se proceder a um debate sobre o assunto nos próximos dias, durante este período de sessões.

Table 1: Examples from the corpora

3. **IT2** – Another in-domain IT corpus, with 1,000 sentence pairs (answers only) compiled under the QTLeap project, and comparable with the IT1 corpus.[3]

4. **TERM** – A parallel corpus of IT terminology (unigrams or multiword expressions), which consists of the *Microsoft Terminology Collection*[4] (13,030 terms) and a small portion of LibreOffice terminology[5] (995 terms).

Examples from each corpora are presented in Table 1.

3.2 Systems

This section describes the two MT systems used for the experiments.

3.2.1 TectoMT

TectoMT (Žabokrtský et al., 2008) is a structural MT system which uses two layers of structural description, the shallow a-layer and the deep t-layer, performing the transfer on the t-layer (Figure 1). It encompasses three phases along the Vauquois triangle: analysis (which transforms the input sentence into the a-layer and t-layer in a two-step process), transfer (at the t-layer), and synthesis (which converts the translated t-layer representation to the a-layer and then to the output surface string). The analysis and synthesis phases are hybrid, while the transfer phase is mostly statistical, based on the Maximum Entropy context-sensitive translation models (Mareček et al., 2010).

In the analysis stage, all tokens from the input English sentence are first transformed into nodes in a labeled dependency tree (a-tree) to form a surface syntax layer (analytical layer or a-layer). This is achieved using various NLP tools that perform sentence splitting, tokenisation, morphological tagging, and dependency parsing. We follow the annotation pipeline used for the CzEng 1.0 parallel corpus (Bojar et al., 2012), using the Morče tagger (Spoustová et al., 2007) and the Maximum Spanning Tree parser (McDonald et al., 2005) trained on the CoNLL-2007 conversion of Penn Treebank (Nilsson et al., 2007). Dependencies are further transformed by the rule-based blocks into the a-layer which contains

---

[3]The decision to test the systems only on the answers is the result of the nature of the task in the QTLeap project.
[4]https://www.microsoft.com/Language/en-US/Terminology.aspx
[5]We would like to thank Eleftherios Avramidis and Lukas Poustka for making the LibreOffice corpus available to us.

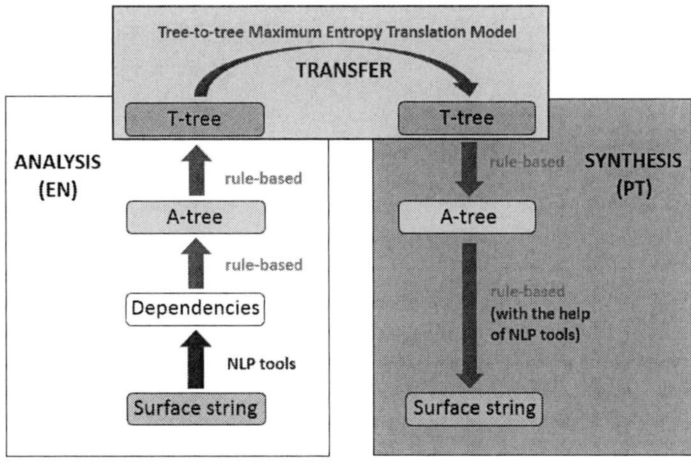

Figure 1: Schema of the TectoMT system

the corresponding *word forms*, *lemmas*, *morphological tags* and *afun* labels (which denote syntactic functions such as subject, predicate, object and attribute).

The next step in the analysis stage is performed using another rule-based block that converts a-trees into t-trees (tectogrammatical layer or t-layer). The t-layer describes the input sentence according to the Functional Generative Description (GFD), and unlike the a-layer (which contains all input tokens), the t-layer only contains content words as nodes (t-nodes). Auxiliary words, such as prepositions, subordinating conjunctions or auxiliary verbs, become attributes of the t-nodes. This is illustrated in an example of the a-layers and t-layers in Figure 2. The t-layer can also introduce new nodes (which did not exist in the a-layer), as for example, in the case of pro-dropped subject personal pronouns which do not correspond to any token in the input sentence.

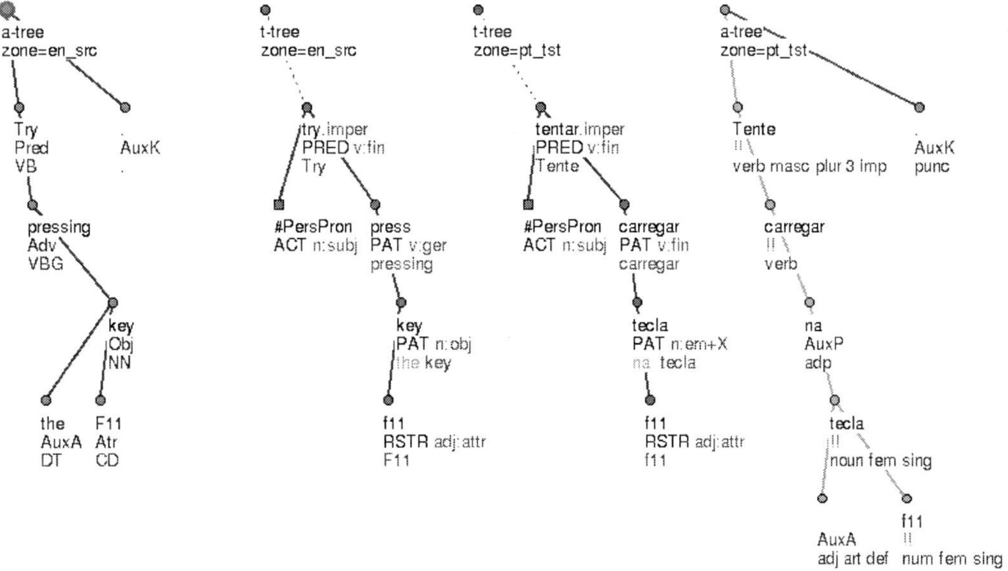

Figure 2: An example of the a-trees and t-trees in the TectoMT system (the input EN sentence: "Try pressing the F11 key." translated into the output PT sentence: "Tente carregar na tecla f11.")

After the transfer of the English t-trees into Portuguese t-trees, the synthesis phase constructs a flat surface form of the sentence from the Portuguese t-tree. This is achieved using additional rule-based blocks which take care of word reordering, insertion of negations, prepositions, conjuctions, correct agreement, compound verb forms, etc. The synthesis stage for Portuguese uses the LX-Suite (Branco and Silva, 2006) to perform such tasks.

The expected advantage of the TectoMT system over the standard PBSMT system is that the TectoMT translates t-tree nodes (and not the inflected forms) and should thus be able to generalise over the unseen morphological forms. This is particularly important for translation into morphologically rich languages (such as Portuguese) where data sparseness presents a problem for a purely statistically driven MT systems.

3.2.2   PBSMT

In all experiments, we use the same PBSMT model (Koehn et al., 2007), GIZA++ implementation of the IBM word alignment model 4 (Och and Ney, 2003), and the refinement and phrase-extraction heuristics as described by Koehn *et al.* (2003). We tune the systems using MERT (Minimum Error Rate Training (Och, 2003)) and build a 5-gram language model with Kneser-Ney smoothing trained with SRILM (Stolcke, 2002) on the whole target side (Portuguese) of the English to Portuguese Europarl corpus (Koehn, 2005), which contains 1,960,407 sentences.

3.3   Experiments

In all experiments, the PBSMT system uses the in-domain IT1 corpus for tuning, and the language model (LM) is trained on all sentences in the Portuguese side of the Europarl corpus (EP)[6]. All experiments (in both TectoMT and PBSMT systems) are evaluated on the same test dataset (IT2). In order to obtain two baselines for each MT approach (TectoMT and PBSMT) we train both systems on: (1) the full Europarl corpus (EP) as the out-of-domain large corpus (BaselineEP), and (2) the IT1 as the in-domain small corpus (BaselineIT).

In the next four experiments (IT+TERM, IT+EP1, IT+EP10, IT+EP10+TERM), we use the in-domain IT1 corpus as the basis for the training. As this corpus is very small (2,000 sentence pairs only), we explore three different strategies for enlarging the training dataset:

(S1) Adding an in-domain bilingual terminology (the TERM corpus in the IT+TERM experiment);

(S2) Adding a certain portion of the out-of-domain EP corpus (1,000 sentence pairs in the IT+EP1 experiment, and 10,000 sentence pairs in the IT+EP10 experiment);

(S3) Adding both an in-domain bilingual terminology and a certain portion of the out-of-domain EP corpus (10,000 sentence pairs from the EP corpus and the TERM corpus in the IT+EP10+TERM experiment)

3.4   Human Evaluation

In order to better assess strengths and weaknesses of both approaches (TectoMT and PBSMT), we also conduct a human evaluation of the sentences generated by both systems for 100 sentence pairs from the test set for the IT+TERM experiments (which led to the highest BLEU score for the PBSMT approach and the second highest BLEU score for the TectoMT approach).

3.4.1   Fluency and Adequacy

We ask two native speakers of Portuguese (both employed as linguists) to evaluate the fluency and adequacy of the machine translation obtained by the TectoMT and PBSMT systems trained on the IT+TERM dataset. We follow the TAUS guidelines[7], which suggest a 1–4 scale for both aspects.

---

[6]Note that TectoMT does not need a development dataset and language model.

[7]`https://www.taus.net/think-tank/best-practices/evaluate-best-practices/adequacy-fluency-guidelines`

Fluency rates "the extent to which the translation is well-formed grammatically, contains correct spellings, adheres to common use of terms, titles and names, is intuitively acceptable and can be sensibly interpreted by a native speaker":

4 – Flawless
3 – Good
2 – Disfluent
1 – Incomprehensible

Adequacy rates "how much of the meaning expressed in the source is also expressed in the target translation":

4 – Everything
3 – Most
2 – Little
1 – None

3.4.2 Error Analysis

Following the error classification proposed by Costa-jussà and Farrús (2015) for evaluation of MT from Spanish to Catalan, we asked human evaluators to classify errors of each sentence into four classes:

1. **Orthographic:** punctuation marks, accents, upper- and lowercase, letters, joined/split words, extra spaces, apostrophe;

2. **Morphologic:** gender concord, number concord, verbal morphology (tense, aspect), lexical morphology (POS);

3. **Semantic:** polysemy, homonymy, incorrect meaning, untranslated words (left in the source language), missing words;

4. **Syntactic:** prepositions, relative pronouns, verbal periphrasis, clitics, articles, reorderings.

4 Results

The next two subsections present the results of the automatic evaluation of all experiments (Section 4.1), and the human evaluation and error analysis of the selected pair of experiments (Section 4.2).

4.1 Automatic Evaluation

The experimental setup for each experiment (the type and the size of the corpora used) and the obtained BLEU scores on the whole test set are presented in Table 2.

All four experiments (IT+TERM, IT+EP1, IT+EP10, and IT+EP10+TERM) of the TectoMT system significantly outperformed both baselines indicating that in the TectoMT approach both strategies (adding different portions of the out-of-domain corpus, and adding bilingual terminology) lead to significant improvements over the BaselineIT. The combination of both strategies (IT+EP10+TERM) resulted in the highest achieved BLEU score (significantly better than all others for the TectoMT system).

For the PBSMT approach, the only two experiments which significantly outperformed the BaselineIT were those trained on the IT+TERM and on the IT+EP10+TERM corpora. This suggests that, for a PBSMT system, adding terminology has a greater impact than adding the out-of-domain corpus. In fact, adding a small portion of out-of-domain corpus (1,000 sentence pairs from EP) to the training dataset negatively influenced the system's performance, resulting in a BLEU score significantly lower than the BaselineIT. Adding a larger portion of the out-of-domain corpus (10,000 sentence pairs from EP) seems not to influence the system's performance significantly.

Experiment	Training			Dev.	Test	Results (BLEU score)	
	EP	TERM	IT1	IT1	IT2	TectoMT	PBSMT
BaselineEP	all	/	/	2,000	1,000	19.34	18.99
BaselineIT	/	/	2,000	2,000	1,000	20.77	21.55
IT+TERM	/	14,025	2,000	2,000	1,000	**21.89**	**22.73**
IT+EP1	1,000	/	2,000	2,000	1,000	**20.97**	*21.08
IT+EP10	10,000	/	2,000	2,000	1,000	**21.16**	21.66
IT+EP10+TERM	10,000	14,025	2,000	2,000	1,000	**22.20**	**22.16**

Table 2: Translation experiments setup – type and the size of the corpora used (the number of sentence pairs for the IT1, IT2, and EP corpora, and the number of unigram or multiword expression pairs in the case of the TERM corpus), and the results of the automatic evaluation (the results of the systems which significantly outperformed both baselines are shown in bold; the '*' marks the result which is significantly lower than the result for the BaselineIT; statistical significance is calculated using paired bootstrap resampling (Koehn, 2004))

4.2 Human Evaluation Results

The results of our human evaluation of the fluency and adequacy of the output are presented in Table 3. For each sentence we additionally calculate the *Total* score (for each annotator separately) as the rounded arithmetic mean of its *Fluency* and *Adequacy* scores. The TectoMT system achieved significantly higher adequacy score and total score than the PBSMT system. The mean and median value of the fluency score in the TectoMT system was higher than in the PBSMT system, but the reported difference was not statistically significant (at a 0.05 level of significance using the marginal homogeneity test).

Aspect	Mean		Median		Mode		Sign.	IAA
	TectoMT	PBSMT	TectoMT	PBSMT	TectoMT	PBSMT		
Fluency	**1.78**	1.74	**2**	1.5	2	2	0.054	0.52
Adequacy	**2.28**	2.24	2	2	2	2	**0.047**	0.55
Total	**2.27**	2.23	2	2	2	2	**0.048**	0.55

Table 3: Results of the human evaluation of the fluency and adequacy on a 1–4 scale where higher score denotes better output (IAA is calculated as the squared Cohen's κ, and the statistical significance is calculated in SPSS using the marginal homogeneity test which represent the extension of McNemar test from binary to multinominal response for two related samples)

Errors	Mean		Median		Mode		Sign.	IAA
	TectoMT	PBSMT	TectoMT	PBSMT	TectoMT	PBSMT		
Orthographic	1.15	**0.95**	1.25	**1**	1.5	**1**	**0.001**	0.50
Morphologic	0.97	**0.74**	1	**0.5**	1	**0**	**0.000**	0.54
Syntactic	1.31	**1.26**	1.5	1.5	1.5	1.5	**0.045**	0.49
Semantic	**1.37**	1.5	1.5	1.5	2	2	**0.009**	0.53

Table 4: Results of the error analysis on a 0–2 scale where 0 – no errors, 1 – one error, and 2 – two or more errors (IAA is calculated as the squared Cohen's κ, and the statistical significance is calculated in SPSS using the marginal homogeneity test which represent the extension of McNemar test from binary to multinominal response for two related samples)

The results of the error analysis of the output sentences are presented in Table 4. The number of orthographic, morphologic, and syntactic errors was found to be significantly higher in the output of the TectoMT system than in the output of the PBSMT system, while the number of semantic errors was significantly higher in the PBSMT system.

Comparison	Scores			Number of errors			
	Fluency	Adequacy	Total	Ortho.	Morpho.	Synt.	Sem.
TectoMT>PBSMT	47	55	55	69	81	58	98
TectoMT=PBSMT	117	96	96	96	77	85	102
TectoMT<PBSMT	36	49	49	35	42	57	60

Table 5: Comparison of the outputs of the TectoMT and PBSMT systems on a sentence level (TectoMT>PBSMT for *Scores* signifies better output of the TectoMT than PBSMT system, while TectoMT>PBSMT for *Number of errors* signifies worse output of the TectoMT than PBSMT system)

In order to achieve sentence-to-sentence comparison between the two systems, we calculate:

1. How many times was the output of the TectoMT system rated as better (TectoMT>PBSMT), equal (TectoMT=PBSMT), or worse (TectoMT<PBSMT) than the output of the PBSMT system; and

2. How many times did the output of the TectoMT system contain more (TectoMT>PBSMT), equal number (TectoMT=PBSMT), or less (TectoMT<PBSMT) errors of each of the four types (orthographic, morphologic, semantic, and syntactic) than the output of the PBSMT system.

In this calculation, we compare the outputs of the TectoMT and PBSMT for each original sentence and each annotator separately, a total of 200 comparisons. The results are presented in Table 5. It seems that the sentences generated by the TectoMT system tend to represent more fluent and adequate translation than those generated by the standard PBSMT system. However, the results also show that the number of cases in which the output of the TectoMT system contains more errors than the output of the PBSMT system is greater than the number of cases in which the output of the PBSMT system contains more errors than the output of the TectoMT system. These results indicate that either: (1) the fluency of a sentence cannot be well captured by counting its orthographic, morphological, and syntactic errors, and the adequacy of a sentence cannot be well captured by counting its semantic errors, or (2) the errors produced by the TectoMT system are not as severe as the errors produced by the standard PBSMT system, and thus were, not as severely penalised in terms of fluency and adequacy scores.

5 Conclusions and Future Work

The experiments presented in this paper address the problem of English to Portuguese machine translation of the domain-specific texts (text of the IT domain in this particular case), and report on results obtained using three different techniques to enlarge the training datasets for two MT approaches: the standard PBSMT approach, and the hybrid deep MT approach employed in the TectoMT system.

Our results indicate that adding in-domain bilingual terminology, as well as adding a combination of in-domain bilingual terminology and out-of-domain sentence pairs, significantly improves the performance of both systems. Adding only some portion of out-of-domain sentence pairs, however, only improves the performance of the TectoMT system, while it either impairs or does not significantly change the performance of the standard PBSMT system.

A human evaluation of the output generated by the PBSMT and TectoMT systems revealed better meaning preservation (adequacy score) in the TectoMT system. However, the error analysis showed that the TectoMT system led to a higher number of sentences that had a greater number of orthographic, morphological, syntactic and semantic errors.

We acknowledge that both systems have room for improvement, and thus this work should only be regarded as preliminary. We used only the basic domain-adaptation technique for the PBSMT system, and no domain-adaptation techniques for the TectoMT. In future, the focus will be on implementing the state-of-the-art domain-adaptation techniques for the PBSMT system, as well as on exploring the possibilities of domain adaptation in the TectoMT.

Acknowledgements

This research was funded by the EC's QTLeap project (FP7-ICT-2013-10-610516) and the Portuguese DP4LT project (PTDC/EEI-SII/1940/2012).

References

Juan A. Alonso and Gregor Thurmair. 2003. The Comprendium Translator system. In *Proceedings of the Ninth Machine Translation Summit*.

Amittai Axelrod, Xiaodong He, and Jianfeng Gao. 2011. Domain adaptation via pseudo in-domain data selection. In *Proceedings of the conference on Empirical Methods in Natural Language Processing*, pages 355–362.

Wilker Aziz and Lucia Specia. 2011. Fully automatic compilation of a Portuguese-English parallel corpus for statistical machine translation. In *Proceedings of the 8th Brazilian Symposium in Information and Human Language Technology*, Cuiabá, MT, Obtober.

Pratyush Banerjee, Raphael Rubino, Johann Roturier, and Josef van Genabith. 2015. Quality estimation-guided supplementary data selection for domain adaptation of statistical machine translation. *Machine Translation*, 29(2):77–100.

Igor Boguslavsky. 1995. A bi-directional Russian-to-English machine translation system (ETAP-3). In *Proceedings of the Fifth Machine Translation Summit*.

Ondřej Bojar, Zdeněk Žabokrtský, Ondřej Dušek, Petra Galuščáková, Martin Majliš, David Mareček, Jiří Maršík, Michal Novák, Martin Popel, and Aleš Tamchyna. 2012. The joy of parallelism with CzEng 1.0. In *Proceedings of the 8th International Conference on Language Resources and Evaluation (LREC)*, pages 3921–3928.

António Branco and João Silva. 2006. A Suite of Shallow Processing Tools for Portuguese: LX-Suite. In *Proceedings of the 11th Conference of the European Chapter of the Association for Computational Linguistics (EACL)*.

Peter F. Brown, John Cocke, Stephen A. Della-Pietra, Vincent J. Della-Pietra, Frederick Jelinek, Robert L. Mercer, and Paul Rossin. 1988. A statistical approach to language trans- lation. In *Proceedings of the International Conference on Computational Linguistics (COLING)*.

Peter F. Brown, John Cocke, Stephen A. Della-Pietra, Vincent J. Della-Pietra, Frederick Jelinek, John D. Lafferty, Robert L. Mercer, and Paul Rossin. 1990. A statistical approach to machine translation. *Computational Linguistics*, 16(2):76–85.

Peter F. Brown, Stephen A. Della-Pietra, Vincent J. Della-Pietra, and Robert L. Mercer. 1993. The mathematics of statistical machine translation. *Computational Linguistics*, 19(2):263–313.

Marta R. Costa-jussà and Mireia Farrús. 2015. Towards human linguistic machine translation evaluation. *Digital Scholarship in the Humanities*, 30(2):157–166.

Jason Eisner. 2003. Learning non-isomorphic tree mappings for machine translation. In Yuji Matsumoto, editor, *The Companion Volume to the Proceedings of 41st Annual Meeting of the Association for Computational Linguistics*, pages 205–208.

Mark Fishel, Ondrej Bojar, and Maja Popovic. 2012. Terra: a collection of translation error-annotated corpora. In *Proceedings of LREC*, pages 7–14.

George Foster and Roland Kuhn. 2007. Mixture-model adaptation for SMT. In *Proceedings of the Second Workshop on Statistical Machine Translation (StatMT)*, pages 129–135.

Michel Galley, Mark Hopkins, Kevin Knight, and Daniel Marcu. 2004. Whats in a translation rule? In *Proceedings of the Joint Conference on Human Language Technologies and the Annual Meeting of the North American Chapter of the Association of Computational Linguistics (HLT-NAACL)*.

Nizar Habash and Bonnie J. Dorr. 2002. Handling translation divergences: Combining statistical and symbolic techniques in generation-heavy machine translation. In Stephen D. Richardson, editor, *Machine Translation: From Research to Real Users, 5th Conference of the Association for Machine Translation in the Americas (AMTA)*, volume 2499 of *Lecture Notes in Computer Science*.

Liang Huang, Kevin Knight, and Aravind Joshi. 2006. A syntax-directed translator with extended domain of locality. In *Proceedings of the Workshop on Computationally Hard Problems and Joint Inference in Speech and Language Processing*, pages 1–8.

Philipp Koehn, Franz Josef Och, and Daniel Marcu. 2003. Statistical phrase-based translation. In *Proceedings of the Conference of the North American Chapter of the Association for Computational Linguistics on Human Language Technology - Volume 1*, pages 48–54. Association for Computational Linguistics.

Philipp Koehn, Hieu Hoang, Alexandra Birch, Chris Callison-Burch, Marcello Federico, Nicola Bertoldi, Brooke Cowan, Wade Shen, Christine Moran, Richard Zens, Chris Dyer, Ondrej Bojar, Alexandra Constantin, and Evan Herbst. 2007. Moses: Open source toolkit for statistical machine translation. In *Proceedings of the 45th Annual Meeting of the Association for Computational Linguistics (ACL)*. Association for Computational Linguistics.

Philipp Koehn, Alexandra Birch, and Ralf Steinberger. 2009. 462 machine translation systems for europe. In *Proceedings of the MT Summit XII*.

Philipp Koehn. 2004. Statistical significance tests for machine translation evaluation. In *Proceedings of the Empirical Methods in Natural Language Processing (EMNLP)*.

Philipp Koehn. 2005. Europarl: A parallel corpus for statistical machine translation. In *Proceedings of the Tenth Machine Translation Summit*, pages 79–86.

Zhifei Li, Chris Callison-Burch, Chris Dyer, Sanjeev Khudanpur, Lane Schwartz, Wren Thornton, Jonathan Weese, and Omar Zaidan. 2009. Joshua: An open source toolkit for parsing-based machine translation. In *Proceedings of the Fourth Workshop on Statistical Machine Translation*, pages 135–139.

David Mareček, Martin Popel, and Zdeněk Žabokrtský. 2010. Maximum entropy translation model in dependency-based MT framework. In *Proceedings of the Joint 5th Workshop on Statistical Machine Translation and MetricsMATR*, pages 201–206.

Ryan McDonald, Fernando Pereira, Kiril Ribarov, and Jan Hajič. 2005. Non-projective dependency parsing using spanning tree algorithms. In *Proceedings of the conference on Human Language Technology and Empirical Methods in Natural Language Processing (EMNLP)*, pages 523–530.

Jens Nilsson, Sebastian Riedel, and Deniz Yuret. 2007. The CoNLL 2007 shared task on dependency parsing. In *Proceedings of the CoNLL shared task session of EMNLP-CoNLL*, pages 915–932.

Franz Josef Och and Hermann Ney. 2003. A systematic comparison of various statistical alignment models. *Computational Linguistics*, 29(1):19–51.

Franz Och. 2003. Minimum Error Rate Training in Statistical Machine Translation. In *Proceedings of the 41st Annual Meeting of the Association for Computational Linguistics (ACL)*, pages 160–167. Association for Computational Linguistics.

Kishore Papineni, Salim Roukos, Todd Ward, and Wei-Jing Zhu. 2002. BLEU: a method for automatic evaluation of machine translation. In *Proceedings of ACL*.

Giancarlo D. Salton, Robert J. Ross, and John Kelleher. 2014. An Empirical Study of the Impact of Idioms on Phrase Based Statistical Machine Translation of English to Brazilian-Portuguese. In *Proceedings of the third workshop on Hybrid Approaches to Transla- tion (HyTra), EACL*.

Drahomíra Spoustová, Jan Hajič, Jan Votrubec, Pavel Krbec, and Pavel Květoň. 2007. The best of two worlds: Cooperation of statistical and rule-based taggers for czech. In *Proceedings of the Workshop on Balto-Slavonic Natural Language Processing*, pages 67–74.

Ralf Steinberger, Bruno Pouliquen, Anna Widiger, Camelia Ignat, Tomaž Erjavec, Dan Tufi s, and Dániel Varga. 2006. The JRC-Acquis: A multilingual aligned parallel corpus with 20+ languages. In *Proceedings of the international conference on Language Resources and Evaluation (LREC)*.

Andreas Stolcke. 2002. SRILM - an Extensible Language Modeling Toolkit. In *Proceedings of the International Conference on Spoken Language Processing (ICSLP)*, pages 901–904.

Peter Toma. 1977. Systran as a multilingual machine translation system. In *Proceedings of the Third European Congress on Information Systems and Networks, Overcoming the language barrier*, pages 569–581.

Zdeněk Žabokrtský, Jan Ptáček, and Petr Pajas. 2008. TectoMT: Highly modular MT system with tectogrammatics used as transfer layer. In *Proceedings of the Third Workshop on Statistical Machine Translation*, pages 167–170.

Keyword Index

Association for Computational Linguistics
209 N. Eighth Street
Stroudsburg, Pennsylvania 18360

ISBN 978-1-5108-3155-1